Women's Voices in Ireland

Women's Voices in Ireland

Women's Magazines in the 1950s and 60s

Caitriona Clear

Bloomsbury Academic
An imprint of Bloomsbury Publishing Plc

B L O O M S B U R Y
LONDON · OXFORD · NEW YORK · NEW DELHI · SYDNEY

BLOOMSBURY and the Diana logo are trademarks of Bloomsbury Publishing Plc

First published 2016
Paperback edition first published 2017

British Library Cataloguing-in-Publication Data
A catalogue record for this book is available from the British Library.

ISBN: HB: 978-1-4742-3668-3
PB: 978-1-3500-3996-4
ePDF: 978-1-4742-3670-6
ePub: 978-1-4742-3669-0

Library of Congress Cataloging-in-Publication Data
Clear, Caitríona, 1960–
Women's voices in Ireland: women's magazines in the 1950s and 60s/Caitriona Clear.
pages cm
Includes bibliographical references and index.
1. Women's periodicals, Irish–History–20th century. 2. Woman's life. 3. Woman's way.
4. Women–Ireland–Correspondence. 5. Women–Ireland–Social life and customs–
20th century. 6. Women–Ireland–Social conditions–20th century. 7. Sex role–Ireland–
History–20th century. 8. Social change–Ireland–History–20th century. 9. Ireland–Social life
and customs–20th century. 10. Ireland–Social conditions–1922-1973. I. Title.
PN5147.W6C55 2015
052.082'09415–dc23
2015017469

Typeset by Deanta Global Publishing Services, Chennai, India

Contents

List of Illustrations

Acknowledgements

My own research journey since 1981 has had many highways and byways, but ever since I started reading, I have loved comics and magazines – *Playhour*, *Bunty*, *Judy*, my mother's *Woman's Way* and *Woman's Realm*, my older sister's *Nikki* (hidden under the mattress because it was considered racy), my friend's sister's *Petticoat* and *Honey* (retrieved from under sofa cushions in that house), then *Jackie*, *Look Now*, and some years later *Cosmopolitan*, *IT*, *U*, *Image*. So in the 1990s when I started research on women's household work in twentieth-century Ireland, it never occurred to me not to use Irish-produced magazines as a source. Ongoing research into the novelist, playwright, journalist and cookery writer Maura Laverty (1907–66) also led me to magazines, not only because she wrote regularly for them, but because the Irish magazines I came across were most likely to be addressed to the people she wrote about (and for) in her novels and short stories – 'ordinary' (neither very wealthy nor very poor) Irish people in the first five decades of independence.

Another route to this research was an interest I had for a while in Irish women's changing everyday appearance (clothes and hair) between the 1940s and 1960s. I would like to thank Sean Connolly, Anne Dolan and Emmet O'Connor for enabling me to road-test some of this research at an earlier stage, in print and in research seminars, and Síle de Cléir for her scholarly insight into the interface between traditional and modern dress. While researching this particular topic I found myself straying more and more from the fashion pages to the problem, diary and letters pages and the idea for another book began to grow. Another spur to write was the invitation from two North American academics to write an article on Irish women's magazines for a book they were editing on the changing domestic space of the home. I researched and wrote and submitted the article (on the early years of *Woman's Way*) but it was not what they wanted, in the end. I'd like to thank one of them in particular, Rhona Richman Kenneally, for introducing me to some important North American sources which have proven very useful for comparative purposes and for some interesting conversations on the subject.

The National Library of Ireland was my greatest resource, recourse and refuge. The staff on the issue desk are helpful and pleasant, and the online ordering system works like a dream – the material is there ready and waiting. The Reading Room is always pleasant and tranquil. I also caught the lovely walnut-desked British Newspaper Library at Colindale in London shortly before it closed. When the British Library's magazine collection was inaccessible for a while, and I needed to look at *Woman's Own,* I wrote to the magazine and a very helpful Carolyn Truscott responded. For a week in June 2013 she brought me down to a highly secure basement of the IPC building in Southwark, London, and locked me in for a few hours at a time with *Woman's Own* volumes and a bottle of water, letting me out every few hours for a run around. She was always helpful and pleasant and I thank her from the bottom of my heart.

Norah Casey, CEO Harmonia Publishing, took time out of her busy schedule to talk to me in August 2013, and she was such a mine of information about the magazine publishing world that it occurred to me that somebody should undertake a history of women's magazines in general, on this island, and get her on record about the recent past. It was Professor John Horgan from DCU, former Press Ombudsman, who gave me the idea to talk to Norah, and he had some other very helpful suggestions too, for which I thank him.

Thanks to NUI, Galway for giving me a sabbatical for the calendar year of 2013, in which I did the bulk of the research and much of the writing for this book. Thanks to all my colleagues in the history department at NUI, Galway, for enabling this to happen, and for being such a great bunch of people to work with. These are, in alphabetical order, Gearóid Barry, Sarah-Anne Buckley, Helena Condon, Carmel Connolly, John Cunningham, Enrico Dal Lago, Steve Ellis, Tomás Finn, Alison Forrestal, Mary Harris, Róisín Healy, Pádraig Lenihan, Kimberly LoPrete, Laurence Marley, Niall Ó Ciosáin, Dáibhí Ó Cróinín, Kevin O'Sullivan and Maura Walsh.

History/academic/literary friends who have been an encouragement and help over the past few years are Marie Boran, Ciara Breathnach, Mary Clancy, Maura Cronin, Catriona Crowe, Geraldine Curtin, John Cunningham, Máire Flannery, Gerard Moran, Therese Moylan, Peter Moser, Cliona Murphy, Eunan O'Halpin, Eleanor O'Leary, Ciaran Ó Murchadha, Gearoid Ó Tuathaigh and Elizabeth Tilley. Thanks to Tadhg Ó hIfearnán for some reflections on the word 'home' *as Gaeilge.*

I also want to thank the anonymous readers of the initial manuscript for Bloomsbury for their extremely helpful, pertinent and supportive comments. Frances Arnold and Emily Drewe at Bloomsbury have been kind and straightforward from the very beginning, a real pleasure to deal with, while Emma Goode has more than lived up to her surname.

I taught a seminar course on women's magazines and household advice books as a historical source, in NUIG in 2014–15, and each and every one of the students on it contributed something to my understanding of the meaning of these sources. Thanks, therefore, to Marie Byrt, Daniel Considine, Darragh D'arcy, Eoghan Hennessy, Hannah Hughes, Kamile Jucyte, Viktoria Juhaszova, Claire Kelly, Kayleigh Murphy, Steven Nowak, Claire O'Halloran, Áine Timlin and Seán Walsh, but a special thanks to Kamile, who alerted me to the importance of *Miss* and *Young Woman*, and to Darragh, who came across some very interesting online material about Mary Grant/Angela Willans.

The biggest thanks of all go to Pádraig Lenihan.

Explanation of Titles and Glossary of Terms

Bean a'tighe or bean a'tí/woman of the house: popularly used survival from the Irish (pronounced 'bana*tee*') but often roughly translated into Hiberno-English as 'the woman of the house' meaning the woman in charge of a particular house. The term housewife did not come into popular parlance until the 1970s, and was used mainly by lobbyists (see Irish Housewives Association, below) and advertisers before this decade.

Bean Garda: a female member of the Garda Síochána, see below.

Connacht: see Provinces.

Dáil Eireann – this is the lower house of the Irish parliament, with elected members who are known as **T.D.s**. (see below).

Emigration, Report on the Commission: The Commission on Emigration and other Population Problems sat and heard evidence from 1948 to 1954, and issued its report in 1956. It represented an official recognition of the fears of government and other interested parties that Irish population was in apparently irreversible decline, and that emigration was an ineradicable part of Irish life.

Garda Síochána: (lit. the Guardians of the Peace) the unarmed police force, established after independence, often colloquially referred to as the 'guards'. See also **Bean Garda**.

Humanae Vitae: the papal encyclical written by Pope Paul VI in 1968, which set out the Catholic Church's position on birth control. It pronounced that while birth control in itself was not wrong, any 'artificial' methods (barrier, pharmaceutical) were against 'natural law', as was any interruption of the act of sexual intercourse. The only allowable method of birth control, apart from abstinence, was the safe or infertile period.

Intermediate Certificate examination: taken after three years of secondary school at around the age of fifteen, replaced by the Junior Certificate in the late 1990s. Up to the 1970s it was a milestone after which many boys and girls left school to take up apprenticeships, to do vocational courses or take up jobs in retailing and other businesses.

Irish Countrywomen's Association: set up as the United Irishwomen in 1911 and changing its title to the ICA in 1933, this organization gave evidence to government commissions in the 1940s and 1950s, and saw major growth in the 1960s. A social organization for women living in rural areas, it emphasized crafts, culture and public speaking.

Irish Housewives Association: set up in Dublin by Hilda Tweedy in 1943, this was a small but vocal lobbying organization comprising mainly urban women. It drew attention to consumer rights, health and welfare issues and other matters of interest to women in the 1940s, 1950s and 1960s.

Irish Transport and General Workers Union: commonly known as the ITGWU, this was the largest and most high-profile trade union in the country, set up as one of the 'new unions' by James Larkin in 1908. It had some female members.

Itinerants: see Travellers.

Labour Court: set up under the Industrial Relations Act 1946 to adjudicate and arbitrate in labour disputes.

Late Late Show, The: a Saturday-night talk show on RTE hosted by charismatic Dubliner Gay Byrne, this was (as well as a showcase for celebrities and music) a forum for many discussions about controversial subjects in Ireland, and is seen by historians as having been a crucial factor in social and cultural change.

Leaving Certificate: the school-leaving examination taken after five or six years of secondary school, necessary for university entry, teacher-training college, nurse training, army cadetships, the Garda Síochána, the bank, and career-track positions in the Civil Service.

Legion of Mary, the: a social-Catholic lay organization founded by Frank Duff in 1922 with an equal membership of men and women, highly active throughout these decades, with emphasis on apostolic and social work.

Leinster: see Provinces.

Leinster House – the house in Kildare St, Dublin, in which the Dáil and Seanad meet. Originally the town house of the Duke of Leinster.

Macra na Feirme: (lit. the strong young people of the farms) a rural youth organization founded by Stephen Cullinan in 1944, very popular with young men and women on the land in the 1950s and 1960s.

Medical Missionaries of Mary: founded by Marie Martin in 1931, this was a female religious congregation whose members were mainly doctors, though some were nurses. It had hospitals throughout Africa.

Mercy, Sisters of: founded by Catherine McAuley in 1828, this was the largest and most widely distributed female religious order in Ireland, which ran girls' schools, hospitals, orphanages and industrial schools.

Muintir na Tire: (lit. the people of the land) a rural development organization with a social-Catholic ethos (though with many Protestant members in Munster and Leinster), founded by Fr John Hayes in 1933. Women held equal status to men in this organization.

Munster: see Provinces.

National teacher, National schools: these are state primary schools, founded by the National Board of Education in 1831.

Northern Ireland: the six counties of north-eastern Ireland retained by the United Kingdom after the Treaty of 1922. These are Antrim, Armagh, Derry/Londonderry, Down, Fermanagh, Tyrone. Its principal cities are Belfast and Derry/Londonderry. It is often confusingly called Ulster, although the Republic retains three counties of that province.

PR: proportional representation, the electoral system imposed by the terms of the Anglo-Irish Treaty on the Irish Free State in 1922, still in use.

Presentation nuns: founded by Nano Nagle in 1776, this was the oldest and the second-biggest female religious congregation in Ireland in these decades, which mainly ran girls' primary and secondary schools.

Provinces: Although not in themselves units of local government, the provinces are a means of subdivision for the purposes of census-taking and other administrative actions, and for Irish people they serve an important socio-geographical descriptive function. Leinster comprises the south-east, east coast, the north-east that is not in Northern Ireland, and the midlands east of the River Shannon and north and east of Tipperary. Its biggest city is Dublin and it has several thriving county towns (notably Kilkenny which is traditionally a city, but also Wexford, Navan, Carlow, Athlone Mullingar, Dundalk, Portlaoise). Leinster land is good, and the farms there tend to be bigger than average in the country as a whole; there is also a large agricultural labouring class, especially in and around the tillage farms of south Leinster. Munster is made up of the south-west, and the parts west of the Shannon that are south of Galway. It has three good-sized cities – Cork, Limerick and Waterford – and several thriving towns (Clonmel, Ennis, Nenagh, Tralee). Munster in general has good-sized farms with an emphasis on dairying; the land stretching from mid-Tipperary to North Kerry and encompassing north Cork is known as the Golden Vale because of the butter, cheese and milk it produces. Coastal west Munster (Clare, Cork, Kerry) has smaller farms and rockier land, but not as small as those of Connacht. Connacht comprises the five counties south of Donegal and (more or less) west of the Shannon; despite the thriving towns of Galway and Sligo, and some big farms in the eastern part of the province, it is mostly associated with small farms and chronic rural poverty going back to the nineteenth century. In the 1950s and 1960s, the highest number of emigrants to Britain came from this province, reflecting a pattern of high emigration which went back to the late nineteenth century. The counties of Ulster which remain in the Republic are Cavan, Donegal, and Monaghan. Donegal in general is characterized by small holdings and a century-old tradition of seasonal migration to Scotland. Cavan and Monaghan, further east, have thriving towns and medium-sized farms. The Irish language was still spoken as a first language by several thousand people in west Donegal, west Mayo, west Galway, west Kerry, and west Waterford, in these decades.

Radio Eireann: set up as 2RN in 1927, the state-sponsored radio authority.

RTE: Radio Teilifis Eireann, see also Teilifís Eireann; the state-sponsored broadcasting authority, incorporating both radio and television. The television broadcasting began over the New Year 1961–2.

Seanad Eireann – the Senate or upper house of the Irish parliament, consisting of members elected and nominated by various interest groups.

T.D. – Teachta Dála, or Dáil Deputy; politician elected to the lower house of the Irish parliament or Dáil.

Tánaiste – the Deputy Prime Minister.

Taoiseach – the Prime Minister.

Teilifís Eireann – see RTE.

Thomas Davis Lectures: half-hour radio lectures inaugurated by Radio Eireann in 1953 and coming out three times a year, named for Young Irelander Thomas Davis (1814–45), one of whose sayings was 'Educate that you may be free'.

Travellers, Travelling People: nomadic Irish people who travel from place to place (although usually with some attachment to a particular part of the country), with a strong cultural identity and a traditional identification with horse-trading and tin-smithing. Their poor living conditions (tents and caravans) and lack of formal schooling made them the focus of concern in the 1960s.

Tuairim: an intellectual movement active in Ireland 1954–75, and made up of men and women mainly from professional backgrounds.

Ulster: see Provinces.

Vatican II: the popular name given to the Second Vatican Council, begun by Pope John XXIII in 1963 and continuing for most of the decade, under his successor Pope Paul VI. In Ireland, an overwhelmingly Catholic and highly devotional country, the developments of the Council were of growing interest, especially in the latter part of the 1960s.

Woman/women of the house: see Bean a'tí, above.

Introduction: 'Advice, Patterns, etc.': Women, Magazines and Ireland in the 1950s and 1960s

Magazines, memory and meaning

Caitriona: Did people read women's magazines at all?

Josephine: Not at all, *not at all*, no, no, no.

C: That's what everybody tells me, but there were women's magazines, they must have been only in the towns …

J: I forget. Possibly. And the children used to get those, the *Beano*, and those magazines. But I never saw magazines like *Woman's Own*, they were going [i.e. they existed], in those times, when I was young, I'd get the odd one, or some girl would get one and she'd lend it to half the country.

> – interview with Josephine E., referring to Co Mayo in the 1940s and early 1950s.[1]

LADY's white raincoat, trimmed tartan, 6/-; gent's felt hat, 2/6. Back-numbers *Woman's Life* and other books, 9d per dozen. Postage extra. Wexford.

> – *Woman's Life* Service Club, 1956.[2]

A coat, a length of material, a hat and magazines (or 'books' as they were often called) were all being offered for sale, via a magazine, by this woman in the southeast of Ireland in the mid-1950s. The fact that she was using a magazine to sell magazines by the dozen suggests not only that she had amassed twenty-four or more of them, but also that she was confident both of their resale value and of an interested party reading her advertisement. This woman might have been from one of Wexford's many thriving towns, or from one of its snug farms. On a small farm in Mayo a few years earlier, anything originating in 'the town' (including magazines) was fairly scarce. Josephine knew about magazines ('I'd get the odd one') and mentioned that they were lent and borrowed, but the Wexford woman who had been buying and reading magazines for several years at this stage belonged to a rather different world. Two Irish women's magazines in the 1950s and 1960s encouraged women from different Irish worlds to articulate their problems, opinions and desires in a public forum and to communicate with each other. These were *Woman's Life*, which ran throughout the decade until 1959, and *Woman's Way*, which began in 1963.

It is quite believable that somebody from rural Mayo in the late 1940s would not have bought magazines on a regular basis, but reading over the fragment of interview one can see how Josephine subsequently modifies her vigorous initial denial of ever having read, or even seen, magazines at all. When doing research on women who reared families and kept house in mid-twentieth-century Ireland, urban and rural, farming and non-farming, I found it difficult to get any of them to talk about magazines they had read. Joke Hermes and Penny Tinkler encountered a similar reluctance among Dutch and English women.[3] Periodical publications are easily read and easily forgotten, certainly, but for some women, denying having read magazines and comics in the past seems crucial to a sense of moral worth. Many women who reared families in early- to mid-twentieth-century Ireland and elsewhere have strong hardship narratives that do not admit to any luxuries.[4] It could also be that women, whether they are Irish, English or Dutch, do not like being associated with what they fear will be dismissed as trivial or silly. A recent academic work has described Irish magazine *Woman's Way* in the 1960s, somewhat inaccurately, as 'a popular weekly full of articles on fashion, make-up, romance and sex'. Janice Winship was right when she commented that women's magazines 'are perennially belittled – by many women no less than by most men'.[5]

Thankfully, academic studies of magazines over the past half-century have restored respect both to magazines and to the women who read them, laying to rest forever Betty Friedan's classic verdict on these publications as both propaganda and tranquillizer for 'the happy housewife heroine'. In 1967 Cynthia White's extensive survey of British magazines set the agenda for a fresh approach, and time has endowed her closing remarks with added historical value. Irene Dancyger's and Brian Braithwaite's surveys – some twenty years apart – stand as indispensable compendia of facts about British magazines, and Winship's lively study, while acknowledging the consumer-driven nature of many titles, argues that magazine reading gave women not only escapist leisure, but often, a forum for their opinions. Marjorie Ferguson's thorough scrutiny of the editorial content of a number of post-war British magazines shows that while these publications promoted 'a cult of femininity', they also provided women with a 'cheap and accessible source of positive evaluation'. Roz Ballaster and Margaret Beetham agree, insisting, moreover, that women's magazines did not impose definitions and standards of femaleness but offered an arena in which these can be discussed and negotiated. Jennifer Scanlan, Hermes, Nancy Walker and Valerie Korinek, looking at magazines on both sides of the Atlantic, all emphasize that magazines were consumed by women in a variety of ways and for different purposes: practicality (straightforward information, recipes and patterns, advice), fantasy (fiction, fashion, maybe also some of the food articles) and pleasure – even just the luxury of sitting down for half an hour in a busy day. And readers, they contend, were often critical of what they read, and 'resisted' much of the material.[6]

A scholarly consensus, therefore, has reinforced something regular magazine readers have always known – that women who read magazines were not stupid, passive dupes of advertisers and ideologues. But these publications were not value-free manuals of household work, or mirrors held up to women's lives, either. Novelist and veteran agony aunt Claire Rayner defended the women's magazine passionately as 'a trade journal for people doing a complex and frighteningly responsible job with remarkably little support and absolutely no training'.[7] Even the most balanced studies (including all those cited above) acknowledge that the terms of employment of this trade were established by the magazines themselves, which told women how to cook, dress, decorate their houses, engage with their boyfriends and spouses, and rear their children. And while women did not always slavishly follow consumer propaganda, advertising always influenced editorial content to some extent.

Woman's Way was greeted with rapture by several readers when it first appeared in April 1963. Typical was the following comment from a Kildare reader:

> It's good to see a really Irish magazine. ... I think it's wonderful to be able to get advice, patterns etc. without having to put up with Customs trouble or misinformation from people who have no idea of Irish tastes.[8]

This and other readers' sense of novelty would lead one to believe that *Woman's Way* was the first (or the only) Irish women's magazine. It was not. In the twentieth century alone, *Model Housekeeping* commenced monthly publication in 1927 and lasted until 1966; *Woman's Mirror*, another monthly, started in 1933 and ran, uninterrupted, till 1956; and *Woman's Life*, the other magazine that is the focus of this study, began in 1936 and kept going fortnightly until February 1959. Short-lived magazines appeared from time to time, such as a highly engaging monthly entitled *Women's Personality Parade* in the late 1940s. The early-twentieth-century *Lady of the House* was incorporated, in 1916, into the *Irish Tatler and Sketch*, which appeared monthly right up to the 1980s, when it was rebranded and renamed *IT*; in the 1950s and 1960s, although it carried articles on fashion and beauty, it concentrated heavily on the turf, male sports, motoring and the arts and was completely different to both Irish and British mass-market women's magazines of these decades.[9] *Miss*, which appeared in 1965, turned into *Young Woman* in May 1967; it ceased publication in 1968. (See Appendix 2 for a more detailed discussion of these magazines.)

Reliable circulation figures for Irish magazines are impossible to determine before the 1980s, though from the magazines themselves and from other sources, a rough picture of the geographical distribution of individual magazines can be built up. All the evidence seems to suggest, however, that reading magazines was not as common in the 1950s in Ireland as it was, for example, in Britain, or as it would become in Ireland in the 1960s. This might be why *Woman's Way* was perceived by many of its readers as the first of its kind. Another reason why it might have been welcomed so heartily was because it was the first Irish women's magazine to have a readers' letters page. Also, it was coming on the market at a time of rapid social change, attracting a new cohort of both working and home-based women who might never have read a magazine before. On the other side of the Atlantic, African-American readers hailed the new magazine *Essence*, which began in 1970, as the first of its kind, even though it was in no way the first African-American women's magazine, but like *Woman's Way*, it was the first widely distributed and widely read mass-market one.[10] Back in Ireland, *Woman's Way* had a lot in common with the most popular of the magazines that went before it, *Woman's Life*. Both magazines appeared more often (fortnightly or weekly) than other titles and were accessibly priced, both had problem pages (agony columns where emotional problems were discussed, as opposed to health and beauty queries) and both tried as best they could to throw off Britain's adumbrating influence. When *Woman's Life* ran a story entitled 'A Queen and Her Young Family' in 1953, the subject of the article was Queen Juliana of the Netherlands, not the nearer royal neighbour. On the fiftieth anniversary of the Easter Rising, *Woman's Way* published a four-page article by veteran republican Máire Comerford on the women of 1916.[11] But although enough women were buying *Woman's Life*, *Woman's Mirror* and *Model Housekeeping* to enable them to carry on until 1959, 1956 and 1966, respectively, *Woman's Way* belonged to a new consumer era with home-produced fashions and products and even home-grown media celebrities from Radio Teilifís Eireann (RTE). Aligning itself firmly with this new media, it was automatically more 'popular, relevant and lucrative' (to borrow Rooks' definition of *Essence*)[12] than its predecessors and competitors, to readers and advertisers alike.

It is customary to begin any research publication by noting how neglected the subject has been in the historiography to date. Certainly, there has been no book that deals with Irish women's magazines, and existing publications and standard texts on Irish media ignore them almost completely.[13] This book is not a comprehensive history of Irish women's magazines of the 1950s and 1960s either. It is an examination of readers' contributions to both magazines – in problems, letters, press releases and, occasionally, small advertisements – in *Woman's Life* in the 1950s and *Woman's Way* in the 1960s. Before going any further, we need to look more closely at the potential readers of these magazines: the women of Ireland.

Figure 1 Both *Woman's Life* and *Woman's Way* emphasized their Irishness. Courtesy of the National Library of Ireland.

Women and social change in Ireland in the 1950s and 60s

If Al Byrne could just picture the country lass
Who never gets out except to Mass.
Could he just see her in buttons and bows
As she sits in the cowhouse milking her cows?
Her hubby's been up all night with a pig
So he won't notice her curlers or wig ...
My lipstick is worn right down to the case
So if I get a guinea I'll treat my poor face![14]

'Weary-worn', Mallow, Co Cork, letters page *Woman's Way*, 1966.

Anyone who has experienced the drudgery of doing without piped water or electricity, even for a short period, will find baffling Ruth Schwartz Cowan's argument that the modernization of household technology over the past 200 years has created 'more work for mother'.[15] A kettle that can be filled from a tap and plugged in, instead of being filled with a jug from a bucket (that has first to be hauled in from a spring or well) and suspended over a fire (that has first to be coaxed into life); an iron that can be kept away from the smoke and grime of a fireplace; and a toilet that can be flushed after use – these are only three of the basic advantages of aquafication and electrification. In Ireland in the 1950s and 1960s, these facilities began to be provided, gradually at first, then at a faster pace, to the majority of the population. By 1970 most farmhouses had acquired taps and toilets, and nearly all the lanes, courts and tenements of the towns and cities had been abandoned for bright new three-bedroom houses or purpose-built flats supplied with electricity and running water. Life was improving in other ways, too. From the early 1950s, death in childbirth was becoming a rare occurrence, and from the early 1960s, the number of babies dying shortly after birth or in their first year fell definitively and permanently. New hospitals were built, and regular school medical inspections picked up many congenital and orthopaedic defects in children that were remedied at no cost to parents.[16] Free universal secondary education was introduced in 1966, but even before this, rising numbers of teenagers (and marginally more girls than boys), year after year, were staying on at school to sit the Intermediate or Leaving Certificate examinations. (Appendix 1 gives a more detailed account of political, economic and social changes in these decades.)

Water and electricity gradually routed squalor and grime and made housekeeping easier, and life became safer and more comfortable for many people. But one can appreciate this and still recognize that the everyday burden of coping with the rapid rise in the standard of living in these decades fell disproportionately on women. The families that were started in the late 1950s and early 1960s were smaller than before, certainly, but the oldest members of the much bigger families that were begun a decade or so earlier were still in their late teens towards the end of the 1960s; two- and three-bedroom dwellings (serviced or not) of eight, nine and ten people – and often far more – remained common in town and country well into the early 1970s. Falling infant and child mortality – obviously a good and welcome development in itself – meant that more children were reared to adulthood in houses that were not always serviced and, even if serviced, were usually without washing machines, clothes dryers, fridges and water heaters. Growing numbers of boys and girls still in school in their mid-teens or even starting work locally (instead of emigrating) as the economy improved from the late 1950s meant heavier burdens of cooking, washing and life maintenance for women of the house. (For each young adult to have done his or her own cooking and laundry in the family home would have been an unthinkable waste of resources and an unmanageable occupation of restricted household space). Therefore, even with regular employment and water and electricity, many parents, particularly mothers, were very hard-worked and hard-pressed, right into the late 1960s.

But the youngsters who generated all this extra work – those born between 1945 and 1960 – experienced pressure of a different kind. Although marriage rates began to rise in the 1960s, the bachelors and spinsters formed by the demographic patterns of the immediate post-war decade were in early middle age, vigorous and active members of society, in this decade. Far from pining away on lonely hillsides or cycling through the gloom to ballrooms on Sunday nights,[17] most of them were going out to work regularly, many were active in organizations and nearly all had at least one family of nieces and nephews close by. Single English men and women in the twentieth century, Holden tells us, were well integrated into networks of family and friends, commanding ready respect from peers and from the younger generation. This was even more true of Ireland in the 1950s and 1960s, where big families often required occasional supplementary parenting. People who grew up in Ireland in these decades had a ready supply of authoritative (if loving) elders, with high expectations of a younger generation for whom great sacrifices had been made.[18] This was also true of Britain in these years (as the Beatles lamented in 'She's Leaving Home' from *Sgt. Pepper's Lonely Hearts Club Band*),[19] but in Ireland demographic disproportion made the chorus of disappointed elders even louder.

Emigration – the outflow of over half a million people, more or less evenly divided between men and women – is the most remarked-upon feature of Irish life in the 1950s. But Irish women who did not emigrate experienced irreversible change too, in a decade often seen as a byword for stagnation. There were over 31,000 more female white-collar, industrial, professional and commercial workers in Ireland in 1961 than there had been in 1946.[20] Female trade union membership rose by 10,000 in the 1950s; the first woman (Sheila Williams) was elected onto the Irish Transport and General Workers Union Executive Council in 1956. Membership of the Irish Countrywomen's Association went from 2,500 in 1943 to 15,000 in 1960; the number of guilds (local organizations) jumped from 346 in 1950 to 498 ten years later.[21] Other community organizations also saw a rise in female membership. Only 6.5 per cent of the branch secretaries of the rural development organization Muintir na Tire were women in 1950, but by 1964, the title of a third of these officers was Miss or, occasionally, Mrs (33 per cent), and women made up 42.3 per cent of the organization's county secretaries (11 out of 27).[22] This rise in female organizational activity did not translate into higher representation in local and national politics. The number of female Teachtaí Dála (TDs) did not rise, and when Sheila Conroy (nee Williams, see above) chided the Minister for Labour in the mid-1960s for not appointing a woman to the Labour Court, he responded that he would willingly do so if she could find a woman willing to come forward. She could not.[23] The baby steps of the 1950s did not become giant steps in the 1960s. It was as if Irish women, abashed at their audacity, sat back for a little while to marvel at how far they had come.

For some women, this might not have seemed like very far at all. The accepted wisdom in all the historical surveys of the period is that the 1960s initiated a transformation of Irish society, and this is undoubtedly true. Economic growth and a rise in employment levels meant greater spending power for everybody, with more and bigger shops generating employment in retailing, transport and commerce generally. More vigorous discussion of social issues in the media at large was facilitated by a native Irish television service run by the same authority as the radio, and by four daily national newspapers, two Sunday papers, three evening papers and a vibrant provincial press. Relaxation of censorship in the mid-1960s, of course, helped.[24] Distinctive Irish national identity was given a boost by the Defence Forces' participation in United Nations peacekeeping in the early 1960s and found its fullest expression in the state's commemoration of the fiftieth anniversary of the 1916 Rising.[25] The cultural gap between urban and rural people narrowed as car ownership, better public transport and expanding numbers of shops and offices made regular, sometimes daily, urban–rural contact both necessary and feasible. Improved educational provision and a global youth culture accessible through mass media in this decade shifted public attention onto young people and reimagined them as actors and agents of social change, for better or for worse. But social and cultural transformation can be overstated, especially where women are concerned. Connolly has argued, convincingly, that it is a mistake to see the women's movement that emerged in the early 1970s as an inevitable consequence of the changes of the 1960s.[26] The number of married women in Ireland's paid workforce remained quite low into the early 1970s. The marriage bar against National School teachers had been lifted in 1958, but other public servants had to wait until 1972, and even in factory, office and shop employment where no formal marriage bars operated, married women workers were scarce. Most women had little or no access to contraception. The rites and rules of Irish Catholicism certainly relaxed in accordance with Vatican II, but the church remained embedded in every aspect and every institution of Irish life, retaining its authority virtually unchallenged until at least the 1980s. Indeed, the reforms of Vatican II, which relaxed the discipline on regular clergy and religious, allowing them far more freedom to leave their houses and speak publically, not only made ordained and professed men and women more visible, but also gave them – the men at least – a higher public profile and stronger media presence than ever before. Controversial issues were aired in the newspapers, on the radio and on television in the 1960s, but the voices of those opposed to change were as strong as those who argued for it, and women's voices were seldom heard on any side of the debate.

But Irish women and girls in the 1950s and 1960s were not completely deprived of a place where they could be heard. Ballaster and Beetham assert that women's magazines offer women a 'privileged space within which to construct and explore the female self'.[27] Year on year a growing number of Irish females expressed themselves in the letters and problem pages of *Woman's Way* in the 1960s and, before this, in the diary and problem pages of *Woman's Life* in the 1950s. For 'Weary-worn', the Cork farmer's wife whose short verse is quoted above, standard women's magazine advice about everyday appearance and spousal relationships was hilariously irrelevant. She was reacting to an article by Al Byrne, a popular broadcaster who recycled his television programme in *Woman's Way*. In this particular instance, he had described how he and his co-panellists on a programme called 'Home For Tea' had 'proven' that it was possible for housewives to be both hard-working and glamorous to greet their husbands at the end of the day. (The authoritative male offering females beauty and other advice was, sadly, a staple of magazine culture on both sides of the Irish Sea.) 'Weary-worn' from Cork begged to differ. Not only did she need to dress unattractively to do her house and farm work, but (like all farmers' wives) she could not prevent her husband seeing her throughout the working day, so there was no question of putting on a special appearance for him. Aware of the fashions of the day, she liked lipstick and probably wore it 'to Mass', to town and on special occasions. But she was not afraid or ashamed to draw readers' attention to herself and others like her. More prosaically, two readers wrote in at different times taking *Woman's Way's* service articles to task for assuming that all readers had an annual holiday; for one of them – and she was philosophical about this, wishing holidaymakers well – summer just meant 'more light to mend children's clothes by'.[28] These women were part of a growing band of confident and articulate Irish women of all classes and locations who were speaking ever louder in women's publications in these decades, and they were demanding that a magazine acknowledge and reflect their lives, too.

Structure of the book

The first chapter will look at the press releases and other items sent in by women, about their work and their activities, to *Woman's Life* from January 1951 to February 1959, when it ceased publication. The second chapter will be devoted to the problem pages in that magazine. *Woman's Way* will then be looked at – first the letters, then the problem pages – from April 1963, when it began, to December 1969. Two British magazines of around the same period will be looked at alongside, for comparison: *Woman's Realm* from 1958 to 1960, because it promised (in vain, it appears) to incorporate *Woman's Life* in 1959; and *Woman's Own*, because it was the British magazine that was most like *Woman's Way*, in 1966. Both titles were for sale in Ireland too. Irish magazines *Woman's Mirror, Model Housekeeping, Miss* and *Young Woman* will be dipped into occasionally for comparison, but for various reasons – neither the *Mirror* nor *Model Housekeeping* had a letters page or problem page, and the other two were short-lived – they will not be subjected to the same intensive scrutiny over time.

For the two magazines that form the main focus of this study, one issue after another was examined in a particular time frame. All extant *Woman's Life* issues from January 1951 to February 1959 were looked at, as were all extant *Woman's Way* issues from April 1963 to November 1969.[29] Shorter but continuous runs of the British magazines were also scrutinized. Dipping at random into the magazines and extrapolating letters and problems out of context, as some historians do, would result in a book that could prove any point this writer wanted to make, because, as Korinek points out for the Canadian magazine *Chatelaine* in the same period, contradictory and opposing viewpoints were often to be found within the covers of even one issue of a magazine. This was true of the magazines under discussion as well.[30]

It cannot be denied that the keynote in the editorial and service content of magazines on both sides of the Irish Sea, and the Atlantic, in the 1950s and 1960s was *vigilance* – about health, beauty, food, fashion, household work and, sometimes, political and occupational rights. Readers' letters, problems and other communications must therefore be read bearing this in mind. The subjects on which they wrote, the tone (exhortatory, emulatory, complaining, praising), and even the vocabulary of readers' correspondence to letters and problem pages were determined to a great extent by the content of the magazines in which they appeared. Problem pages, in their decisions as to what problems to publish, influenced – and perhaps even determined – what aspects of everyday life were seen as problematic and capable of being altered, improved or avoided. As historical evidence they must be treated, therefore, with extreme caution. But to ignore them altogether would be to neglect some of the only evidence we have of the range and complexity of women's everyday preoccupations and opinions in those times.

M. M. from Kildare, quoted above welcoming *Woman's Way* in 1963, suggested that the function of a woman's magazine was to provide 'advice, patterns etc.'. As well as being provided by the editorial content, advice was often given by readers to readers, in their communications to the magazines, while the knitting and sewing patterns provided were welcomed eagerly by women and girls who were themselves drawing new patterns for living, or adjusting and adapting old ones to the changing times.

Talking Things Over: Real Women in the Diary Pages of *Woman's Life* 1951–59

Woman's Life commenced publication in 1936 and ceased in February 1959. It was a lively and accessibly priced magazine with a rich, varied and distinctively Irish editorial content in the 1930s and 1940s. By the 1950s this content had thinned considerably, and the variety of home-grown features characteristic of the 1940s had been replaced by a greater number of service articles on cooking, fashion, knitting, health, home maintenance and, occasionally, childcare and family matters.[1] However, up to the final issue it retained, in its two or sometimes three leading 'diary' pages, the practice of showcasing Irish women's paid work, business activities and achievements in the arts, in business and in scholarship. It also highlighted girls' and women's group activities throughout the country. These diary pages were entitled 'Gossip with Finola' until April 1955, when they became 'Talking Things Over with Maxwell Sweeney'; Sweeney was a well-known radio broadcaster, and when he bowed out in August 1956, Finola took over again. In summer 1958, as part of a general makeover of the magazine, the diary page was re-titled 'What's Going On by Finola', but the content remained the same.

Readers of *Woman's Life*

Three quiet young ladies require accommodation for fortnight in Youghal in July. Three share one room if necessary, near sea and dancehall. Wexford.
                                        – *Woman's Life* Service Club, 1953.[2]

It is, as noted earlier, impossible to determine the circulation figures of any Irish magazines before the 1980s, so we cannot know how many issues of *Woman's Life* were sold throughout the country. Commercial advertisers

WOMAN'S LIFE

FEBRUARY 20, 1954   FORTNIGHTLY   VOL. 34, No. 4

MARTHA GREY'S
NEW RECIPES
*Big cookery
feature inside*

KNITTING FOR
THE FAMILY
*Three complete
patterns given*

DENISE ROBINS'
NEW SERIAL

4ᴰ NO TAX

Another article by our Doctor in this issue

Figure 2 *Woman's Life* showcased its service articles, but its diary content drew readers' attention to women's non-domestic activities throughout this decade.

certainly used the magazine, and its editor attended at least two Irish advertising conferences in the 1950s.[3] The lack of a readers' letters page in *Woman's Life* means that, in contrast to *Woman's Way* in the following decade, there is no rough guide to where opinionated and articulate readers lived. However, clues about readers' geographical distribution can be found in competition entries, in 'press releases' sent to the diary from organizations and individuals around the country and, most of all, in the buy-and-sell columns of the *Woman's Life* Service Club. To place an advertisement one had to be a member (membership cost a shilling), and the advertisement cost 1s 6d for up to twenty-four words. The usual items bought and sold through this column were clothes and shoes, but prams, machinery (sewing and knitting machines, poultry incubators, overlockers), plants and poultry also featured. Of seventy-three advertisements in one issue in 1952, forty-four (60 per cent) came from all over Leinster (eleven from Dublin, but ten from Offaly and eight from Kildare), twelve (16.4 per cent) each from Munster (six from Kerry, three each from Cork and Waterford) and Connacht (six from Sligo, three each from Galway and Mayo), and five (6.8 per cent) from Ulster (all, oddly, Cavan). Of forty classified advertisements in October 1955, fifteen, or 37.5 per cent, came from Leinster (three from Dublin), thirteen (32.5 per cent) from Munster (four each from Cork, Tipperary and Waterford and one from Limerick) and six (15 per cent) from Connacht (Roscommon three, Mayo two and Galway one) and six also came from Ulster (evenly divided between Cavan, Donegal and Tyrone).[4]

All the 'bonnie babies' featured in March 1951 came from urban addresses in Dublin, Derry, Belfast, Clonmel and Athlone. The women who sent in these pictures obviously not only read the magazine but expected neighbours, relatives and acquaintances to do so too, otherwise there would have been little point in showing off their babies or grandchildren (The cash prize might also have motivated them, of course.) Of twelve crossword competition winners in the same issue, all but two were from street addresses: in Killybegs, Co Donegal; Abbeyleix, Co Laois; Galway city; Listowel, Co Kerry; Durrow, Co Laois; Castlerea, Co Roscommon; Crinkle, Co Offaly; Clonakilty, Co Cork; and Bray, Co Wicklow. Two possibly rural entrants were from Finnan, Ballyragget, Co Kilkenny and Holycross, Co Tipperary.[5] Christmas competition winners announced in January 1955 came from Fairhill Rd, Galway; Garristown, Co Dublin; Dun Laoghaire, Co Dublin; Castle Rd, Ballina, Co Mayo; Conlon's Rd, Nenagh, Co Tipperary; and Wrexham in Wales – emigrants had a stake in the magazine too, as can be seen in the 'bonnie babies' competitions. Most babies featured came from urban addresses in Ireland or England: in January 1956, from Connell Terrace, Mullingar, Co Westmeath; Drumcondra, Dublin; Foxrock and Swords (both in Dublin); Main St, Ballyconnell, Co Longford; and St. Leonard's-on-Sea, UK and in May of the same year from Cork city; Louisburgh, Co Mayo; Sligo; Bradford; and Wakefield. [6] The number of babies with English addresses reached its height in one issue in 1957, where only five of the thirteen infants featured were domiciled in Ireland. Their details were sometimes sent in by Irish relatives, sometimes by their emigrant mothers.[7]

Cork 'Personality Girl' finalists in 1954 hailed from Ballydesmond, Mitchelstown, Newmarket, Bandon and Charleville, though it is impossible to tell whether they came from rural addresses in or near these towns and villages, or from the towns.[8] Winners of the Limerick contest hailed from quite a social mixture of neighbourhoods in the city – Janesboro and Fairgreen (both with a mixture of local authority and owner-occupied dwellings) and upper-middle-class O'Connell Avenue.[9] The Galway winners were, except for one from Loughrea, from the city itself, and they were National teachers, shop assistants, students and 'business girls'.[10]

As well as this, items were sent in to the diary pages by branches of the Irish Countrywomen's Association (ICA), Muintir na Tire and Macra na Feirme – the last two were rural organizations where women enjoyed equal standing with men.[11] Smaller Dublin-based bodies like the Irish Housewives Association sent in an occasional news item, as did the Irish Red Cross.[12] Some local organizations sought national publicity: the South Mayo Drama Festival, the Carlow Arts Council, the Colleen Bawn Cork Nurses' Social Club and the Glasnevin Lawn Tennis Club are only a few of those mentioned.[13]

Woman's Life readers, therefore, as far as we can tell, were mostly town-based women all over the country, or women who were organized in some way, with rural readers most likely to be situated in the more prosperous and modernizing farmlands of the midlands, south and southeast but occasionally in the west, as well. Were readers single or married, young or old? The 'bonnie babies' feature implies that some young mothers (and grandmothers) read the magazine, and advertisements for products to cover greying hair featured regularly, but the kind of products advertised and many of the beauty articles were aimed at women with some disposable income; and in 1950s Ireland, that meant mainly single women.[14] The advertisement at the head of this section, placed by the three 'quiet young ladies' from Wexford for holiday accommodation, gives an idea of some typical readers. The stipulation of proximity to both day and evening entertainment (in a limited word-allocation) established these women's priorities clearly. Proposing to take holidays in July, they cannot have been farmers' 'assisting relatives', because even in a tillage county like Wexford there was enough pasture farming to demand all hands on deck for the hay in July, and farmers' daughters working off-farm would have spent their holidays helping out with summertime agricultural tasks. Wealthy young ladies of leisure would have holidayed in one of the many hotels in this popular Cork resort. These three, therefore, were waged or salaried workers – perhaps secretaries, shop assistants, factory workers or even teachers – of urban, or non-farm, origin. Sharing one bedroom posed no problem; they were probably used to sharing bedrooms (and beds) at home. Whoever they were, they were confident that a potential landlady in Youghal would buy the magazine and respond to their advertisement.

The magazine, it can therefore be suggested, sold reasonably well to a mainly urban (including small-town) and limited rural readership, with more readers in Leinster and Munster than in Connacht and Ulster and possibly (though one cannot be sure about this) more single than married readers.

Gossip with Finola/Talking Things Over with Maxwell Sweeney

Both diary page titles bring to mind what Ballaster and Beetham call the 'intimate world of shared concerns' characteristic of women's magazines.[15] *Woman's Life* paid for contributions, informing readers in 1953 that 'all items of news, gossip etc ... published will be paid at our usual rates'.[16] Wedding photographs featured regularly but with simple captions of names and places; unlike in the *Irish Tatler*, there were no detailed descriptions of outfits, attendants, celebrants and guests. Other social events featured rarely; a children's party and a 'coming of age' stood out as unusual.[17] Most of the material concerned women's organizational, occupational and artistic activities.

An item in 1953 on the only Irish female harbourmaster, Kathleen Curran of Galway, was typical of the diary's range of interests. This Claddagh woman's background (she had been educated by the Sisters of Mercy) and her vision for Galway port and docks were explored over several paragraphs. The fact that this was sent in – either by her or on her behalf – suggests that familiarity with the magazine existed in one of Ireland's most traditional fishing communities.[18] But many of the women featured were already well known, and items about them were probably sent in by agents. Actresses featured included Constance Smith, Valerie Hobson, Maureen O'Sullivan ('Hollywood's happiest mother'), Siobhan McKenna, Maureen Potter, Annie Dalton, Phyllis Ryan and Maureen Cusack (sometimes alongside her small daughters Jenny and Sally, now better known as Sinéad and Sorcha). Theatrical wardrobe mistresses and costumiers Mrs Caffrey, Joan Bourke, Eileen Long and Áine Lynch, film-maker Lelia Doolin, film producer Pan Collins and Pike Theatre manager Carolyn Swift were mentioned. Musicians Mary O'Hara and Kathleen Watkins, mezzo-soprano Agnes Curtis and traditional singer Máire Ní Scolaí all featured, as did popular singers Carmel Quinn and Ruby Murray. Writers Kate O'Brien, Bridget Boland, Patricia Lynch, Maura Laverty, Una Troy, Sinead de Valera and Mary Purcell were highlighted. Scholars Nora Chadwick from Cambridge and Mairin O'Daly ('wife of the Attorney-General' – Cearbhall O Dálaigh) were noted as giving Thomas Davis Lectures in 1955.[19] The Shannon College of Hotel Management was mentioned, and the 'brides' course' (home management and housekeeping) in Ballsbridge

Technical College in Dublin claimed to have more students than ever before. When the ICA offered, in its Junior Leadership Training Week in 1957, a course in guest house management, the organization's idea of creating a genuine Irish home atmosphere in a bed and breakfast was applauded by the magazine. This is how a substantial number of rural and urban Irish women would make a living for themselves in the succeeding decades.[20]

Dress designers Sybil Connolly and Irene Gilbert featured very often, but Madeleine Keenan, Neilí Mulcahy, Ann Carroll, Kathleen Byrne, Gertrude Brady (of NYMPH clothing), Peta Swift (former games mistress, 'now Ireland's leading milliner'), Cloda Phillips and Elizabeth James designer Sheila Mullally also got a look-in. The dancing schools and modelling agencies of Betty Whelan, Peggy Carty and Miriam Woodbyrne and schools of beauty (Jill Fisher) rubbed shoulders (in print) with hairdressers Helene Griffin, Mabel Ross and Sarita Hickey, the latter only the tip of a countrywide iceberg. Mrs Gallagher of Urney Chocolates notwithstanding, one could be forgiven for thinking that all commercial and industrial endeavour in Ireland was based around female appearance. The mention of seven women at the Advertising Club Ladies' Night featured in March 1956 reminds us of women's participation in this male-dominated area of endeavour.[21]

Workers of various kinds sent in their details to the magazine, which indicates a sense of novelty and confidence about female independence and wage-earning. Saleswomen, receptionists, machinists, civil servants, telephonists, factory workers, Esso workers and even a farmer's wife featured in these pages.[22] Sometimes 'Finola' interviewed workers. Eight machinists in a Dublin lingerie factory designing for Cassidys of George's St were featured in 1953. The Cassidys, as well as running a large drapery shop, had two clothing factories in the greater Dublin area, employing 750 people.[23] Dress designer Kathleen Byrne (33) had been apprenticed at fourteen and visited London regularly; Maureen Kennedy, a number-one cutter, had also started work at fourteen. Other workers of various ages were all from Dublin city, and most had worked with the company for several years; some were supporting parents or younger brothers and sisters. The continuity of workers in both Reckitt's factory (makers of Reckitt's Blue, a detergent) in Dublin in 1954 and the Greenmount and Boyne Linen Company in Drogheda, Co Louth, in 1956 was also emphasized; some had been with the firms for twenty years, and 'many' had allegedly returned from England to work there. The Stork margarine factory, also in Drogheda, was praised in 1953 for its hygienic atmosphere and the fact that the 'white-overalled girls' had on-site medical attention. Enthusiasm about workers' welfare in Irish factories was part of the anti-emigration discourse of the era; the *Report of the Commission on Emigration* in 1956 was the culmination of years of concern about the departure of Irish people, mainly to Britain. Factory workers made up between 10 per cent and 15 per cent of Ireland's female workforce at this time, but factory employment was limited, and none of these firms was short of workers.[24] The profile of the Cassidy's workers was not a recruiting initiative, therefore, but a celebration of 'ordinary' non-glamorous working women.

Also celebrated were the 'girls on 45687', who answered the phone 364 days a year at the Coras Iompar Eireann (the Irish transport authority) information bureau in Dublin. Eileen Cullen, the supervisor, originally from Tipperary, had holidayed in Majorca, Naples, Rome and Florence, and the other employees, whose average age was nineteen, were all either amateur actresses, models or Irish-language enthusiasts in their spare time. White-collar workers like these – secretaries, clerks, receptionists and telephonists – made up a growing number (16 per cent by 1961) of all women workers in this decade and, like factory workers, they probably had disposable income to buy a magazine like *Woman's Life*. Shop workers, though fewer in number than white-collar and industrial workers, were also highly respected; the five Kelly sisters from Fairview, Dublin, all of whom worked in Dublin city-centre drapery shops, were profiled in 1952; they were going on pilgrimage to Lourdes together later in the year. Margaret Monks, Nurse of the Year from St Michael's hospital in Dun Laoghaire in 1955, was one of the few nurses featured, though earlier that year there was mention of United Nations (UN) World Health Organization nurse Eleanor Gannon from Donegal, who had trained in St Ultans, the Richmond and the Rotunda hospitals in Dublin. But apart from that, nurses hardly featured at all and teachers, never (unless as contestants in beauty contests, see above), although 'professional' women made up between 11 per cent and 14 per cent of Irish working women in this decade.[25]

But the most celebrated and coveted job of all was that of an air hostess. The magazine informed readers in March 1954 that Joan Cammon of Termonfeckin, Co Louth, a Trinity graduate who had been working as a doctor's receptionist, would become an Aer Lingus air hostess the following month. Competition for these jobs was fierce. In July 1952, the magazine announced that Elizabeth Cassidy, Dorothy Moran, Margaret Bergin, Angela McCarthy, Sally Fitzsimons and Kathleen Walsh would begin training under the hostess instructor. Starting pay would be £250 a year and £300 when they started flying, rising by yearly increment to £425 per year. The qualities expected of trainees were intelligence, 'a good manner', an attractive speaking voice, a high standard of health, tact and friendliness. A rare photograph accompanied this item – there had been no photographs of the other workforces featured.[26]

The very few Irish women in political and public life were mentioned in the magazine from time to time. It congratulated Sheila Williams, the first woman to be elected to the Irish Transport and General Workers Union (ITGWU) National Council in 1956, and the election of the sixth woman (in that particular government) to Dáil Eireann, Miss Kathleen O'Connor, was noted in the same year. A National teacher, she was filling the North Kerry vacancy left by the death of her father, John O'Connor. Labour TD Maureen O'Carroll was mentioned in 1955, and Tuairim member Miriam Hederman was warmly commended for taking part in public debate. Female delegates to the ITGWU conference in Galway in 1956 were also named – Sheila Williams, Eileen Flynn, Molly O'Neill, Una O'Sullivan and Frances Peppard.[27] Inclusion of these items reflected Maxwell Sweeney's preoccupations. Having taken over the diary pages from 'Finola' in 1955, he continually chided women for their lack of interest in politics. Why did women make up only one-third of the public gallery of the Dáil on any given day? Why, given the large number of Irish women working in factories, was there only one woman (Helen Chenevix) on the Factory Advisory Council? Why were not women consulted about house design? He also noted the suggestion by Mary Kettle (a veteran suffragist-feminist) that there should be some women district justices or peace commissioners (there was none). Why were there no women in senior positions in banks? Why was there only one woman on the Minister for Finance's committee to encourage voluntary savings (Muriel Gahan of the ICA)? And why, 'when women are found in so many occupations today', was no Irish woman sent to the United Nations Council for the Status of Women in Geneva? Sweeney also drew readers' attention to what he considered a noteworthy survey in London in 1956, which showed that secretaries and typists were more concerned with good working conditions than with salary increases; if 'a few shillings' was all the difference, 'they prefer comfort to austerity'. The previous year, he had drawn attention to successful British women's organizations, urging Irish women to emulate them. The lack of a readers' letters page means there is no way of knowing how and if readers would have responded to these exhortations. Peggy Makins of *Woman* commented in her memoir that 'bracing exhortations' of this sort were characteristic of male editors, and Johnson and Lloyd found similar comments in Australian magazines of the 1950s.[28]

Women's magazines throughout the world had an urban bias – the electrified house and evening-homecoming spouse were always envisaged as the norm.[29]

But *Woman's Life* made some effort to include farm women. The magazine reported that it attended the National Ploughing Championships in 1955, though whether this means that it actually did or that some woman sent in a press release is hard to tell.[30] In 1956, Mrs Sean Healy, wife of the general secretary of the Irish Farmers' Association, told the magazine that she had met her husband in Macra na Feirme, a detail that shows the importance of rural organizations in bringing couples together.[31] As mentioned above, the ICA often sent in items, and although it was more active in big-farming Munster and Leinster than in Connacht, this organization was far more representative of farm women in general than was the small, Dublin-based, upper-middle-class Irish Housewives Association of women of the house in general.[32] Did the rural/ agricultural magazine readership rise as farms modernized (water, electricity), and the magazine's service content became more 'relevant'? Hermes, Korinek and others remind us that women do not necessarily read magazines because of their 'relevance' and that they often enjoy them as fantasy and escapism. Infrequent visits to town, poor transport and little surplus cash on small farms, rather than 'irrelevance', could account for the magazine's apparently lower penetration in the remoter rural western areas of the country. However, the sale of small-scale agricultural machinery and livestock in the Service Club tells us that were some farming readers. Town dwellers could also keep poultry, but ducks needed the space of a farm, so it was probably a style-conscious farmer's wife (from relatively urbanized and prosperous Wicklow) who placed the following advertisement in 1952:

> AYLESBURY drakes, prize-bred, 25/-each; shoes, black patent court, 4 and a halfs, as new, 17/6; black suede laced high heel, 6's, 14/-; no appro, Wicklow.[33]

Other articles in the magazine

Service articles were the backbone of the magazine; there were at least three knitting patterns in every issue compared to one cookery article, something on health, plenty on 'beauty' and occasional articles on childcare. There was always a serial and at least one short story; fiction was more often than not by well-known non-Irish writers like Monica Dickens, Norah Lofts, Barbara Cartland, Pamela Hinkson, Denise Robins, Faith Baldwin, A. A. Milne and Marghanita Laski. Maura Laverty (who may or may not have also been agony aunt Mrs Wyse at this stage) contributed some characteristically well-written stories with an Irish setting, which stand out as unusual.[34]

Opinion columns and other features were very scanty, and some had the air of being syndicated. The short series in 1956, 'A Man Looks at You', was definitely home-grown, however. In this, a pipe-smoking silhouette called 'Brian' gave his opinion on various aspects of women's lives. He insisted on the importance of educating girls as well as boys and urged women to be more active in political life and to vote for women. He used the example of women in the religious life to prove that the Catholic Church (which he called simply 'the Church') wanted women in positions of authority and pointed out that even in 'Mahommedan' countries women had become leaders; 'but you wouldn't even trust a woman to be mayor of Ballybough'. 'Brian' also believed women could smoke in public as long as they used a cigarette case and a lighter. The advice about smoking was given with no-less authority than the exhortation to improve educational achievement and political representation.[35]

The question of whether or not married women should earn was addressed in 1951 in an unusually long article, which commented that it was 'sad to think' that a man would resent a wife who earned more than he did. The author – who remained anonymous – believed that women, by law, would soon be fully equal partners in marriage. Married with four children, she had earned 'sums up to and beyond my husband's', but this did not affect their marriage. In 1955, an unsigned article called 'Should Wives Work?' commented that while nobody objected to women who were compelled 'by sheer economic necessity' to work, the wife who continued to work when there was no need for it was 'making a rod for her own back'; her husband's sense of responsibility would shrink.[36] On this, as on many other issues, there was room for a variety of opinions.

Single, working women and married women who did all their own housework were the target audience of *Woman's Life*. Strikingly unusual was the mention of the setting up of Aunts Unlimited by Mrs Maud Pearson ('a widow with time on her hands') in the diary pages in 1953. An Irish version of Universal Aunts, which had been set up in Britain in 1921, was an agency that matched 'ladies' in reduced circumstances with employers who wanted somebody less permanent and more 'ladylike' than a traditional servant. Aunts Unlimited, the Irish version, claimed to be for people who urgently needed services like 'a child to be met at the airport and escorted to school'.[37] This employment agency would have been more suited to the aristocratic/upper-middle-class/diplomatic readership of the *Irish Tatler* than the lower-middle/skilled working-class readership of *Woman's Life*. It was never mentioned again.

The magazine's position regarding religion was fairly complex. Strict censorship laws meant that an Irish women's magazine had to play it very safe indeed, and this might partly explain the scarcity of articles on pregnancy and childbirth, and the fact that sex and unmarried pregnancy never featured on the problem pages, except perhaps as 'reply only'. (British women's magazines that mentioned such topics were sometimes censored in Ireland.[38]) Correspondents who wrote to the problem page looking for information on 'the facts of life' were recommended a booklet by an 'expert'. The booklets promoted in 1953 were *Growing Up* by A Catholic Doctor, *Happiness in the Home* by Very Rev D. Barry, *The Irish Mother* by a Medical Missionary of Mary, *Matrimony* by Rev M. Quinlan and *The Expectant Mother Looks at Life* by Mrs Blundell. Mrs Blundell, who also wrote under the title M. E. Francis, had died in 1930.[39] The religious culture of the decade is also evident in the embroidery motifs available from the transfers department. These were all religious legends like 'My Jesus Mercy', 'Sacred Heart of Jesus' and 'Legio Mariae'.[40] The Legion of Mary was a several-thousand-strong lay Catholic organization at this time and an important forum for female public activity.[41] But this was the only mention (however oblique) of the Legion in *Woman's Life*, because although the magazine stayed within the limits of what was acceptable to Catholics, it never promoted Catholicism as such. Certainly there were references to Catholic cultural organizations, such as the Catholic Stage Guild and the Catholic Film Office, and items about the occasional convent Past Pupils Union.[42] But the Marian year of 1954 (when, Fuller tells us, trade unions, workplaces and other publications went into a near-frenzy of competitive pietism) went completely unremarked.[43] Nuns hardly featured at all. The Medical Missionaries of Mary were featured in 1952 and again in 1958,[44] but the teaching and nursing congregations (Presentation, Mercy and others) who made up the largest group of professional women in the country featured only through their pupils, present and past. And, unlike some of its British counterparts, the magazine did not have a regular letter from a priest or clergyman. In the following decade, *Woman's Way* would carry a regular letter from a priest, but Catholic teaching, especially on matters to do with women, would also be questioned and challenged vigorously by its journalists and readers in a way unthinkable in *Woman's Life*.

Conclusion

Four times as many 'girls' as 'boys' were getting work in junior grades in the Civil Service, the magazine noted happily in 1956,[45] and it continued to encourage women in work and education right up to its final issue. In August

1958 it got a smart new cover design, and there were a number of editorial changes also: a new record review section called 'Going Round in Circles' and an occasional Topical Teen Page.[46] The Service Club still had thirty-three classified notices in an October issue – not a disastrous number by any means, though the cost of twenty-five words had been reduced from 1/6 to a shilling, and the fact that over a fifth of all advertisements originated in Britain was itself ominous.[47] The number of commercial advertisements in the magazine had been falling for some years. There were forty-five advertisements in one July issue in 1956; exactly two years later this had fallen to thirty-three, and a low point of twenty was reached some weeks after that. The bumper Christmas number in December 1958 carried eighty-six advertisements, but over half of these had a seasonal theme or were for once-off toys and gifts.[48]

The magazine, however, ceased publication on an optimistic note: 'We have great news for you.' It would thenceforth be known as *'Woman's Realm and Woman's Life'*; readers were given a list of the *Woman's Realm* editorial staff taken from that magazine's masthead – those who dealt with beauty, health, fashion, home decoration and so on. The final chapters of the serial 'Meet Me in Istanbul' would be available in the new publication the following week.[49] This magazine title cannot be found in the catalogues of either the National Library of Ireland or the British Library. There was no mention of it in *Woman's Realm* in February 1959 or at any other time before or after.[50] If it ever materialized, it must have survived only a short while. *Woman's Realm* was first published by Odhams in London in 1958 and outsold all its rivals, including the long-established *Woman*, *Woman's Own* and *Woman's Weekly*, until 1963. It concentrated mainly on house and home, with cookery, knitting, beauty, medical and family advice and a page for children. There was a religious column, 'Our Padre writes', and occasional questions and answers on holidays, fashion and beauty. Two short stories and a serial comprised the fiction in every issue. It was attractively designed and intelligently written, letters to the editor were solicited and eagerly supplied and problems were answered by Clare Shepherd, the nom de plume of Georgette Floyd.[51] Its service articles were slicker and its concentration on the domestic sphere was more intense than that of the Irish magazine it bought out. Some of its reader-supplied content (letters and problems) will be discussed in greater detail in Chapters 2 and 3.

Woman's Life diary pages quite explicitly set out to encourage Irish women to tell each other about what they were doing. Like most magazines, it featured workers whose occupations needed publicity (actors, authors, dress designers and makers of cosmetics and sweets and other luxuries), and those whose occupational identity was by definition glamorous – air hostess, for example. But the magazine's openness to factory workers, shop workers and receptionists suggests that the editors saw even 'ordinary' working life for women as something to be admired and applauded. Women's community and leisure organizations also used *Woman's Life* to struggle their way into the light. The scarcity of nurses and complete absence of teachers and other professionals in the diary pages suggests that these professionals were entrenched enough in their occupational identity not to need affirmation – or simply, perhaps, that they were not *Woman's Life* readers in the first place.

Woman's Life did not have a readers' letters page. However, its problem page gives us a glimpse (albeit an oblique one) of some readers' lives and opinions, and it is to these pages we now turn.

'Wasting Time Feeling Sorry For Yourself': *Woman's Life* Problem Page, 1951–59

Introduction

Problem pages in women's magazines in the past are most emphatically *not* straight historical evidence of the troubles and difficulties people had at any given time. In the first place, for a problem to be defined as such, it must be given a name by contemporary commentators – in sermons and psychiatry, in newspapers and novels – and a vocabulary must be made available to describe it. In every age (including our own, no doubt), people have troubles that cannot be articulated, either because there are no words for them or because they are seen as inevitable and unchangeable aspects of everyday life. In 1950s Ireland, for example, everyday conflict between husband and wife might have been seen as normal and not as something to complain about to an outside authority; and people with traumatic, life-destroying problems (physical abuse, incarceration) might not have believed that what was happening to them was either 'wrong' or that it could be changed. More pragmatically, many problems could not have been published in the heavily censored media of the 1950s or, perhaps, the 1960s. Furthermore, not all women read magazines, and not all women who did so would have written to a magazine with a problem. The problems written into *Woman's Life*, therefore, are a *kind* of evidence (which must be treated with extreme caution) of *some* of the problems *some* Irish girls and women (and occasionally, men and boys – but it is the females who concern us here) were *able to articulate* in these years and Irish magazines were *able to print*. The responses of the problem answerer or agony aunt give us an idea of the norms laid down by somebody in authority.

However, the problems were not 'all made-up'. Agony aunts everywhere have defended vociferously the integrity of their correspondence. Both 'Mrs Wyse' (the *Woman's Life* agony aunt) and Angela Macnamara (who responded to problems in *Woman's Way* in the following decade) usually had at least one obliquely

worded 'answer only' problem per page, a detail that alone would seem to testify
to the page's authenticity. Peggy Makins (*Evelyn Home*) tells us that *Woman* tried,
in the 1950s and 1960s, to select and present, in each issue, a balance of different
kinds of problems in order to appeal to different readers, but her magazine was
so inundated with problems that it was in a position to make such a selection.
More recently, Angela Willans (formerly agony aunt Mary Grant on *Woman's
Own*) attested to the authenticity of such pages and their genuine desire to help
readers; and Claire Rayner, for her part, took her magazine agony-aunting, in
the 1960s and 1970s, very seriously indeed. *Woman's Life* does not seem to have
been flooded with correspondence of this kind, as will become apparent below,
but the surest guarantee that the problems featured were genuine is the fact that
in issue after issue they were too repetitive, banal and occasionally bizarre for
anybody with a shred of imagination to have made them up. In the 1960s and
1970s, Irish people became more accustomed to writing to strangers about their
problems; Angela Macnamara in both the *Sunday Press* and *Woman's Way*, and
Valerie McGrath or Linda James who answered problems in the *Sunday World* in
the early 1970s, found it hard to keep up with their correspondence.[1]

Given all these caveats, attempting to arrive at a rough numerical analysis of
the problems written in to Mrs Wyse[2] in *Woman's Life* might seem like a waste of
time. But these published problems are the only evidence we have of what some
Irish girls and women[3] believed to be 'problematic' in their lives, and they are
virtually the only evidence we have of advice given to women by a woman in a
position of authority that was secular – insofar as anything could be secular in
Ireland in this decade.

Problem pages in women's magazines have, since their origins, been mainly
identified with 'advice to the lovelorn', so it is hardly surprising that those in
romantic difficulty made up by far the largest category of problem, 41.5 per cent
of the 477 problems written in between 1951 and 1959 (Table 2.1).

'Courtship' covers 'romantic' difficulties experienced by every unmarried
person from the insecure teenager to the impatient forty-year-old. 'Extended
Family' includes tensions with in-laws and disagreements with parents about
choice of spouse, and these accounted for 12.7 per cent of the entire lot. The
'adult daughter as carer' problem made up 4.8 per cent of all the problems
written in – not a huge proportion, but significant nonetheless. Those looking
for information on work/education/training made up over 11 per cent of all
problems. 'Marital', 10.4 per cent of all problems, covers any disagreement
between spouses, young or old. The miscellaneous category takes in every
problem that does not come into the other categories. This category, at

Table 2.1 Readers' problems published in *Woman's Life*, January 1951–February 1959

Subject	Number	Percentage of all problems
Courtship	198	41.6
Miscellaneous	89	18.7
Extended Family	61	12.8
Work/Education	55	11.6
Marital	51	10.5
Adult Daughter/Carer	23	4.8
Total Problems	477	100

18.6 per cent, is the second biggest. Correspondents with gynaecological and obstetrical problems in *Woman's Life* were answered privately by 'Our Medical Adviser' or addressed in print with response only, as in the following, poignant advice to 'Rosemary': 'If he were sufficiently fond of you, and knew beforehand that there would be no children, he would not be disappointed.'[4] They were not printed on the page.

Courtship

The tone of this letter from 1952 was typical, not only of *Woman's Life*, but of problem pages everywhere in those decades:

> I am 22 and friendly with a man 8 years older than myself. Last year he asked me to go out with him but I didn't, I couldn't make up my mind whether I wanted him or not. I see him almost every day on my way to work: he is always very nice but I think perhaps he feels he has not much money and does not like to ask me again. Do you think I am in love with him or not?

Mrs Wyse's response was brisk:

> It is impossible for me to say whether you are in love with this man. ... By all means stop and have a chat and get to know him better. If you are thinking of the difference in age ... eight years is nothing when it is on the man's side. As to the money, you should know yourself whether this is important to you or not.

Mrs Wyse also dealt rather impatiently with the 'torn-between-two-lovers' dilemma: 'Here's another lucky girl with two grand boys in love with her!' she commented in 1951 (third-person commentary on the problems was fairly common in 1950s problem pages in both Britain and Ireland, less so in the 1960s). Girls aged fifteen to seventeen were told firmly that they were too young to go out exclusively with boys, and women and men of all ages were counselled to accept the ups and downs of love philosophically. A woman who had gone out with a man in her office for two years and was now hurt that he was going out with somebody else was told that as they had not been engaged, he had every right to do as he pleased. Sometimes a firm stand was taken, as in the case (the only one) of a reader who while on holiday had met a married man who wanted her to correspond with him as a friend.[5] An Irish problem that was drawing a lot of negative comment generally (both concerned and amused) in the 1950s was that of the long courtship. There were only a few of these problems in *Woman's Life* over this eight-year period, maybe because those who were in long relationships either did not see them as problematic or did not think anything could be done about them. However, those who wrote in about boyfriends of some years' standing who had not mentioned marriage were told to confront them firmly; the woman 'doing a line' for fifteen years with a 'boy' who had not proposed was advised to 'ask him straight out' what his intentions were. But if a man changed his mind, little could be done, as in the case of the 29-year-old woman who had helped her boyfriend (presumably financially) set up two businesses, only to be told he was no longer in love with her. Mrs Wyse helpfully told her she had been a doormat but assured her that her 'chances' were by no means gone. In Britain, Clare Shepherd in *Woman's Realm* a few years later was baffled by a woman who resented the amount of time her boyfriend was spending in the business she had helped him build up, but maybe he, like his Irish counterpart, had also fallen out of love. Getting back to the Irish magazine, women at the courtship stage were told not to tolerate jealousy, bossiness, drunkenness and in-public as opposed to in-private nastiness (a fairly common male problem that crops up again and again on both sides of the Irish Sea in these decades). In Ireland, the woman who was a bad dancer, and whose fiancé therefore danced with other women all the time when they were out, was told not to tolerate it; the 26-year-old whose boyfriend took her for granted and never called to the house for her was told he needed 'shaking up'.[6] The *Woman's Realm* agony aunt showed a similar intolerance towards lukewarm, jealous and moody boyfriends.[7]

In the first problem cited above, Mrs Wyse did not believe an age difference of eight years 'on the man's side' worthy of comment. An eighteen-year-old 'keeping company' with a 'very keen' man ten years older, 'but some people think he's too old', was advised not to listen to others' opinions. Similarly, a nineteen-year-old, worried because a 36-year-old wanted to make a date with her, was advised to give him a chance. A 22-year-old was not dissuaded from going out with a man of thirty-five, and a woman was also advised to give a man of forty-three, seventeen years her senior, a try. However, a seventeen-year-old vacillating between a boy two years older than her and a teacher of twenty-nine ('I feel sorry for him because he has no home and his people are dead') was advised that the teacher was 'much too old for you', probably because of the note of sympathy.[8] The woman older than the man was not always a problem. Four years' seniority on the woman's side was nothing, and never mind what friends said, two different readers were told at different times. Parents who worried because their 25-year-old daughter's 'perfectly nice' boyfriend was several years younger than her were advised to relax. However, a woman of thirty-five was warned to think very carefully before she married a man ten years younger, and a woman of forty-seven (with a 'youthful appearance and good teeth') in love with a man of twenty-eight was told firmly that he was too young. A 36-year-old woman, 'fairly tall and attractive', who was thinking of marrying a man nine years younger because her brother, with whom she was living, was getting married was advised not to get married just for the sake of it; '9 years is a lot of difference, especially for a woman.'[9] The bride four or five years older than the groom was not uncommon in Ireland in the 1950s, when having to surrender jobs on marriage was an incentive for some women to stay in the workforce into their late twenties and early thirties. They often came into contact, through their work, with younger men who had no reason to postpone marriage and might have been attracted by the air of independence and authority that these women radiated.

Religious differences featured hardly at all. A seventeen-year-old Catholic girl in love with a Protestant boy, neither of whose parents approved, was advised to listen to the parents. Class differences were not taken as seriously. A woman worried about her son marrying a girl 'who is not of our class' because 'she works and her mother worked' was told she was snobbish. A woman who broke off her son's relationship (sic) with an 'unsuitable' neighbouring girl and was now annoyed because the girl's family was unwilling to do a favour she needed, was given very short shrift. However, the girl (only one) who was going out with a boy of a 'higher social standing' and whose parents (both the girl's and the boy's) were against the relationship was advised not to rush things.[10] Clare Shepherd, in the British *Woman's Realm,* like Mrs Wyse, usually underplayed class differences as well.[11]

Going back to the Irish magazine, there were some insoluble problems, like the 23-year-old city woman, in love with a farmer, who didn't want to go and live in the country. The man had offered to give up the farm and come and live in the city, but Mrs Wyse advised against this (in the British magazine, Clare Shepherd gave identical advice to an English woman in a similar situation). Mrs Wyse had little understanding of rural Ireland. A 21-year-old farmer's daughter going out with 'a very nice young boy' of eighteen who was a 'servant boy' – an in-house agricultural labourer – faced the obstacle of her parents' objections. In an era when cross-class rural marriages were notoriously frowned upon, Mrs Wyse's response was either naïve or disingenuous: 'You do not say on what grounds your parents object to your boyfriend.' (The three years' seniority on the woman's side was not seen as an obstacle by either the correspondent, the agony aunt or, presumably, the family.) Poor understanding of small-town/rural life is also evident in her response to the following problem:

> I am a nurse and have been going out with a farmer's son for the past two years. I hear from my patients in the hospital that he goes out with other girls on week nights. He meets me every Sunday night and takes me to dances. It is very hard for me to meet other men but if I met another boy I would give up this one, as he must think very little of me if he goes out with other girls.

Mrs Wyse, attempting to reassure her, scoffed at the notion that bed-bound patients would know what was going on in the outside world.[12] But of course they would! Bored patients had only visitors' talk to keep them entertained, and other people's social lives were intensely interesting. The patients might have been genuinely concerned that a 'nice girl' they respected was being taken advantage of by a farmer's son, or they might have been laughing at her, but whatever they were doing, they were talking.

Parent–child/adult–child

The mother of three very 'disobedient and defiant' little boys was advised that the slacker the rein the more developed the personality, and a mother worried about sending her boy, an only child of ten, to boarding school because he was not used to other children, was reassured.[13] But these problems were very unusual, and if Irish mothers agonized about child-rearing, they did not confide in *Woman's Life* about it. Similarly, the problem of the troublesome teenager featured hardly at all; parents in 1950s Ireland probably did not suffer in silence – they laid down the law. But this law was beginning to be resisted by the younger generation. A seventeen-year-old factory worker whose mother would not let her go out in the evening was advised that her mother was unreasonable. A fifteen-year-old, an only child, who had started working and whose mother was always 'giving out' to her was advised that her mother must not be well, though Mrs Wyse believed that somebody her age should be in by 10.00 pm at the latest.[14] There was a perceptible rise in the number of young, single women – some hardly more than girls – working in shops, offices and factories in Ireland in this decade, so some tentative challenges to parental authority were to be expected.

Parents objecting to boyfriends was 'a problem that faces a lot of young people today', Mrs Wyse commented in 1951, before admitting that she had no solution to it. She advised a 26-year-old going with a boy for four years, whose parents (the woman's) were against him because of his poor job and low salary, that she was old enough to make her own decision, and she gave similar advice to another woman in her mid-twenties engaged to a boy (sic) 'suitable in every way', whose mother (the woman's) became hysterical every time she mentioned her impending nuptials.[15]

But another woman who wrote in that her family was consistently rude to her fiancé was told by Mrs Wyse that she was imagining it, and she was equally dismissive of a reader's complaint that her future mother-in-law 'seizes every opportunity to pick a quarrel with me'. A woman with a very critical and unpleasant mother-in-law was told (on no grounds whatsoever!): 'If you did ask her to join your household I am sure all her complaints would stop.' And a wife whose husband's sister interfered all the time was told she was taking it 'far too seriously'.[16] These problems were few, however; Woman's Realm, the British magazine, carried far more problems of this kind in 1958–60, as chronic housing shortages and rapid social change accentuated cross-generational tensions. The British agony aunt had no solutions to offer either, except patience and mutual tolerance.[17] In Britain and to a lesser extent in Ireland, young married couples were normally expected to live independently of other relatives – that was the ideal at any rate – but young unmarried people, if they were working locally, still lived in their families of origin. A reader asked the Irish agony aunt in 1954 why it was considered 'selfish' for young single women to move out of home and to live alone. Mrs Wyse's response was that the extended family (she used that term, which would not have been in common usage) was 'a strong support in society'.[18]

The adult-daughter-as-carer problem cropped up regularly enough to be noticeable. These were daughters solely responsible for ageing parents, or eldest daughters rearing brothers and sisters (because a mother was dead, sick or working) and finding themselves without work, training or marriage prospects.

According to Mrs Wyse, the first duty of unmarried adult daughters was to their ageing parent or parents, even if this clashed with the prospect of work. One reader had been working away from home for five years and at the time of writing had the chance to take up a new and important post; she was the only daughter, her brothers were unmarried and her family wanted her home to care for her sick mother. The reader insisted that she could pay a nurse, but Mrs Wyse was firm: 'Don't you think it's time you made an effort to be really part of your family and not just in name only?' She was even harsher with another correspondent who had graduated from college three years before but had given up her job to care for her sick mother. The mother had since died, and the daughter had the chance of another job, but her father didn't want her to go until she had trained a housekeeper for him. Mrs Wyse admonished her severely and assured her that if she sacrificed this job, something equally good would come up for her again. She had a little more sympathy for a woman who wanted to train as a nurse but had to look after a very sick mother; things would pick up, the reader was assured, 'in a few years the picture will change and she will be happily married with a home of her own'. This was an odd comment, because it was training for a career, not marriage, that this correspondent yearned for.[19]

There was more sympathy, but hardly much hope, for a motherless daughter rearing six brothers and three sisters, whose father would not give her any allowance or any freedom. She wanted to leave home, but Mrs Wyse reminded her that 'two wrongs don't make a right' and advised her to try to make her father see that she needed some time off and money. A twenty-year-old woman, the oldest of five children, who had given up the chance of college to rear the two youngest while her mother went out to work, had no job, no money and no freedom and was miserable. Mrs Wyse was brutal:

> Certainly you have had hard luck my dear … but instead of wasting time feeling sorry for yourself you should have used your spare time to study something.

Another woman in her twenties had worked and saved for some years and now wanted to go to university, but her parents still needed her financial help to rear the younger children. Mrs Wyse: 'You are not being victimized if you have to make this sacrifice, remember that; they helped you.' Although this problem did not crop up as frequently in the British magazine, when it did, Clare Shepherd usually gave similar advice.[20]

Mrs Wyse had some sympathy, however, for the motherless nineteen-year-old who had kept house since she was fourteen for her father and seven brothers:

> Please do not think me silly. My aunts just say, 'Oh we'll get a man for you.' Of course I hope to meet someone nice and quiet … (but) I would also like to be able to do something.

Mrs Wyse applauded this woman's reluctance to go straight from one domestic setting to another and promised to send her addresses with information about jobs and training. She was also sympathetic to a woman who had kept house for her very controlling adult brothers since her mother died, advising her to demand an allowance and time off – 'They'll probably marry, and where will you be then?'[21]

Having to stay at home because of the claims of the very young or very old was one thing, but an 'ugly duckling' among four sisters who felt her parents were grooming her to stay at home 'as if my future is an accepted fact' was advised to get as far and as quickly away as she could. But sometimes the parent–child bond threw up problems to which Mrs Wyse could offer no solution. One letter in 1951 was from a reader who had no brothers and sisters, only a recently deceased mother 'to whom I was greatly attached, [who] never liked me to have friends'. Now in middle age, and slightly deaf, she was completely alone. Mrs Wyse asked the reader to send in more details so that she could make her aware of local resources, but she used the response mainly to warn mothers about selfishness. In the same spirit, she took very seriously the worries of a widow who feared she had made her 27-year-old son (with an 'excellent job') too comfortable at home to look for a wife.[22]

One kind of parent–child relationship that was simply not recognized by agony aunts on either side of the Irish Sea was that between the unmarried mother and her child. 'Mary', a convent-reared 'orphan', wrote in to Mrs Wyse that she had been told by a friend that her mother was still alive. She wanted to go back to the convent to get more information. Mrs Wyse told her that the nuns had told her the truth, that her parents were dead:

> Even if her [the friend's] story (which I do not believe for one moment) were true, you have no reason to be broken-hearted. Rather you should be proud, since you have become the nice upright girl you are without the help of parents and family.[23]

In Britain, Clare Shepherd gave similar advice both to adopted children wanting to contact their mothers and to women who wanted to contact the babies they had given up.[24] Anonymous adoption was predicated on the belief that upbringing and environment trumped nature, or blood or genes. However, the correspondent who wrote to the Irish agony aunt did not even have adoptive parents and was still discouraged from finding the only mother she had ever had or ever would have. Her mother might not have been dead at all, and Mrs Wyse would have been aware of this possibility.

Work and education/training

More girls than ever before were attending secondary school in the 1950s. Most of the schools were fee-paying until 1966, and keeping a child at second-level education still demanded considerable sacrifices on the part of parents. Mrs Wyse, therefore, had no sympathy for the sixteen-year-old school girl who felt she was missing out on life, and to a few others who had similar complaints, she responded, 'no-one ever has the gay time one is supposed to have, at sweet 16'.

The category of work-related problems was greater than that of marital conflict, which gives a clue to the age profile of the readers. A steady trickle of vocational queries was sent in to Mrs Wyse – just two of those featured were a reader who wanted to be a 'mannequin' (model) and a seventeen-year-old correspondent who wanted a change from her drapery apprenticeship. A reader nervous about her first day as a shorthand typist was told that she should always have sharpened pencils, dress suitably in neat and unobtrusive clothes and avoid 'jangling bracelets'. Above all, she should 'learn to fit in with the other girls'. One 25-year-old working woman was tired of a cheeky eighteen-year-old male colleague's personal remarks. She was advised to ignore him – advice also given by British agony aunts in an era before sexual harassment was identified as such.[25]

Women workers sometimes felt vulnerable at a time of advancing age, as in the case of a reader whose problem Mrs Wyse described in the third person: a 'business woman holding a responsible position', who was afraid her greying hair would give the impression that she was slowing down. Mrs Wyse counselled her to dye the hair and not to worry. Two issues later, a sixty-year-old woman wrote in to assure the previous correspondent that 'as the years go by, the firm seems to appreciate me more and more, and at no time have I been made to feel unwanted'.[26]

Marital conflict

Marital conflict made up 10.4 per cent of the problems sent in over the entire period. It should not be inferred from this that Irish marriages were blissfully happy. Perhaps a certain amount of marital conflict was taken for granted; maybe those with very serious marital problems would have been ashamed even to articulate them. We can only go on what we can see in front of us.

Mrs Wyse was gentle with newly disillusioned brides, married for a short time and bored already, but after a few years' grace, some level of maturity was expected, and a 26-year-old woman with one child in a modern serviced house, so overwhelmed with housework she was neglecting her appearance and provoking complaints from her husband, was told firmly to get organized.[27]

Uncommunicative, undemonstrative husbands were normal, if regrettable, and Mrs Wyse acknowledged this as a problem in one of her third-person comments, quoting a reader: 'I'm simply here, like the tables and chairs, and he is content.' A woman whose husband never talked to her at mealtimes and engrossed himself in his paper was advised to read the paper more herself so that she could avoid 'the domestic slant' in conversations. A woman with five children aged under eight and another on the way complained that her husband, although a good provider, would not help her at all with the children; Mrs Wyse had 'no cure whatever to offer! Personally, I think you'll just have to be thankful for a good man's love'. A wife whose husband preferred his men friends and never wanted to go anywhere with his wife, to the extent that even the (adult) children had noticed, was told she had probably neglected him when the children were growing up and was advised (somewhat grotesquely) to pretty herself up and invite his men friends around to the house. A woman who described herself as 'happily married for 7 years' with four children explained that her husband had been seen around town with another woman. Mrs Wyse urged her not to let the children (four under the age of six, if she was married seven years) monopolize her attention.[28] Laying the blame for a husband's neglect of the wife or extra-marital affair on the wife's overconcentration on children was common in the problem-answering of the 1950s everywhere; Clare Shepherd in the British magazine was even more uncompromising on this point, advising a 'heartbroken' correspondent, expecting her third child, whose husband wanted to leave her for another woman to do all she could to save the marriage and never, ever, to blame him or to nag him about the other woman.[29]

But the nastier the husband, the more unsympathetic Mrs Wyse was. One wife complained about a difficult husband, 'seething with rage', who filled the house with his friends but was nice only to them, never to her. He never thanked her for anything, her sons were grown-up and gone, and she felt very isolated. Mrs Wyse:

> Imagine (though this may surprise you) that your husband finds you just about as aggravating as you find him. … There is obviously nothing wrong with your marriage that a little give and take won't put right, and I suggest that you try to adapt yourself as much as possible to your husband's way of life. Above all, don't

expect gratitude for doing things that are simply a wife's job, and remember that
you have security.

She was slightly kinder, but no more helpful, to a woman whose husband was
bad-tempered to her and the children, jealous of even her contacts with her
family and so frightening at times that she was thinking of leaving him:

> No husband – or wife for that matter – is perfect. You may even have some big
> fault yourself which he finds irritating. I am sure your husband has many good
> points that go far towards making up for his jealousy. … In any case, put such
> drastic thoughts as running away out of your head. Could you support yourself
> and your children if you did? And don't you think you should make the best of
> your bargain even if it sometimes seems a bad one?[30]

Across the water, Clare Shepherd could only counsel examination of wifely
conscience and patience to women with moody, even violent, husbands.[31]
But violent or not, the husband's wishes came first, and back in Ireland Mrs
Wyse told a shy woman who found it 'torture' to attend functions because of
her husband's 'position' to snap out of 'this feeling of self-pity' and to be proud
that he wanted her at his side. The mother of two very young children (aged
four and two) whose husband wanted her to accompany him on work trips was
told not to make the mistake of putting her children before her husband – 'and
when you've found a kind and competent nanny, try not to interfere with her
decisions!' The 'needs' of the young husband even trumped those of older men,
as a grandmother found out when she told Mrs Wyse that her daughter had
asked her (the grandmother) to look after the three grandchildren for a month
because she wanted to accompany her husband on business and had been very
upset when the older woman had refused. The older woman's husband (the
children's grandfather) was chronically ill and in need of constant attention, but
Mrs Wyse advised her to take the children just the same.[32]

Mrs Wyse gave no comfort at all to women with husbands who told them
nothing about money or whose spending or speculation was running out of
control. 'He hasn't ruined you yet!' was her blithely irresponsible answer to a
woman whose husband's extravagance threatened the family's security.[33] Nor
had she much sympathy for women who believed they had married 'beneath'
them. A woman who dreaded rearing her son in the 'atmosphere of vulgarity'
created by her husband's 'lack of education and boorishness', a teacher married
to a manual labourer and a woman whose husband had no 'intellectual tastes'
wrote in to complain.[34] Few in number though they were, these problems
could be an indication of one of the social phenomena of the period, the higher

level of educational attainment of females from lower-middle-class, skilled working-class and farming backgrounds. It was common from the mid-1940s for such girls to be kept on at school so that they could get office jobs or train as nurses or teachers, while their brothers and the boys in their social circle were taken out of school early and put to trades or inherited farms or businesses.[35]

Miscellaneous problems

The next largest category after boy–girl, man–woman was the miscellaneous one. Being single came into this category.

Mrs Wyse respected, even applauded, the single life. A woman in her thirties who had no interest in marriage was warmly reassured about her preference; a mother worried that her 25-year-old daughter showed no signs of settling down was briskly told to give her time; a happily single woman of forty who loved her job but was suddenly and unaccountably depressed was not encouraged to think that her marital status was responsible for her state but was advised to make some changes in her routine. One mother wrote in, worried about her daughter of forty-eight who had no time for men; she was intelligent, she painted and wrote poetry and was a 'good girl' (*sic*) who went to Mass, but she was very much 'taken up with' older women. Mrs Wyse addressed the mother's unspecified fears of lesbianism directly: 'There is nothing wrong with the fact that she prefers women friends to men friends.' With marriage bars in most good jobs, staying single was a logical choice for many women in Ireland in the 1950s.[36] In the British magazine, Clare Shepherd assured a happily single 'loner' woman that there was nothing wrong with her, but a single woman in her twenties, for example, who had a job, friends and a life she enjoyed and wondered if there was anything wrong because she didn't have a boyfriend was told that her self-sufficiency was scaring off the men.[37]

But in the Irish magazine there were also letters from women who could not meet potential husbands. Girls and younger women were given practical advice – get involved in clubs and organizations or 'make girlfriends who have male cousins and brothers'. A woman in her late twenties, worried about her marital prospects, was told: '27 is young!' – as indeed it was, when the average age at marriage for women in Ireland was twenty-nine. But even the ever-optimistic Mrs Wyse acknowledged the difficulty of the ageing woman when she cited, in the third person, a letter from a woman of thirty-five who saw the future ahead of her as a 'long grey trail'. Mrs Wyse recommended a new job, perhaps, and a

Figure 3 Although it was given a smart new makeover in the middle of 1958, as can be seen from this cover design, *Woman's Life* did not survive to the end of the decade, and this was its last issue.

Courtesy of the National Library of Ireland.

change of scene that might bring the reader into contact with the opposite sex – there was an abundance of single men in Ireland, after all – but advised this woman, and all such correspondents, not to seek out marriage for its own sake.[38]

Widows and widowers were almost always advised to remarry if they had the chance. Objections from adult children, the first spouse's family and neighbours were to be ignored. Worries about imposing small children on a new spouse (or vice versa) were firmly dismissed.[39]

Regular queries on wedding and twenty-first birthday party etiquette and on how to behave in restaurants indicate the formalization of family ritual and the rise of a dining-out culture among a minority of the population at this time.

Inquiries about books explaining the facts of life were regular.[40] Letters about blushing, shyness, spots and superfluous hair – the four horsemen of the female teenage apocalypse – were common, but periods and how to manage them were never mentioned at all, and related problems, if they were sent in at all, were probably addressed in 'reply only'.

Conclusion

Peggy Makins's reminder that *Woman*, at least, often selected a balance of problems should make us think twice before attempting a statistical breakdown of any British magazine. With this borne firmly in mind, it is still useful to attempt such an analysis, if only as an indication of what those categories were. *Woman's Realm* problems were looked at for four discrete periods: July–December 1958, January–October 1959 and, in 1960, January–April and September–December (Table 2.2).

Courtship, at 32 per cent, constituted the biggest single category of problem, as in the Irish magazine, but there were far more extended family problems in the British magazine – 28.7 per cent of the total (even if selection was being made, there were more to select from); and, while the marriage category was a little bigger than it was in Ireland (15.4 per cent), that concerning work and training was smaller, at 5.9 per cent, than in the Irish magazine.

The desperately lonely, however, were no rarer on one side of the Irish Sea than the other. A single woman of forty scorned the Irish agony aunt's regular recommendations of club-like activities:

> The suggestions are that classes, societies etc. are a remedy for that deep longing for a home and loved ones which grows with the years. How can these things help to fill the lack of that sense of belonging to anyone, which no spinster can ever acquire?

Table 2.2 Breakdown of problems published in *Woman's Realm* July–December 1958, January–October 1959, January–April 1960, September–December 1960

Subject	Number	Percentage of all problems
'Courtship'	183	32
Extended Family	164	28.7
Miscellaneous	105	18
Marriage	88	15.4
Work	34	5.9
Total Problems	574	100

Mrs Wyse responded that clubs and classes were filled with people and that only people can fill the gaps caused by loneliness.[41] The fact that this *cri de coeur* was published, however, is an indication of the authenticity of the problems. In British magazines, similar advice was given to the unhappily single and the lonely.[42] It is difficult to imagine what other advice could have been given.

There were a number of problems written in to the British magazine between 1958 and 1960 from young women torn between husbands wanting to emigrate to Australia or Canada or even just wanting their wives to accompany them on two-year postings to Malta, Canada or Germany, and parents threatening heartbreak if the daughters went.[43] On the readers' letters page of the same magazine, readers wrote in with an air of defiant contentment, not just from Australia, South Africa and Canada, but from Tanganyika, Nyasaland, Bechuanaland, Rhodesia, East Pakistan and many other places, the very names of which betray to the modern reader a political instability that went unremarked by correspondents.[44] Ireland in this decade was experiencing levels of emigration of around 40,000 a year, but going away rarely, if ever, featured as a problem or a contentious subject between parents and offspring. There were constant reminders of the realities of emigration in some readers' communications to *Woman's Life* (competition entrants with English addresses, and buy-and-sell Service Club addresses in Leeds, London and Huddersfield), but apart from these hints, a researcher who read this magazine knowing nothing of Irish history could come away with the idea that emigration from 1950s Ireland was an idea entertained by (very few) bored young women in comfortable circumstances rather than an economic imperative for hundreds of thousands of women, as well as men, at this time.

A problem which was inadvertently published twice in *Woman's* Life gives the clearest indication of Mrs Wyse's own values. (It also shows that the magazine, especially in the early 1950s, was sometimes short of problems to put on the page!) A 'well-educated' woman of twenty-five kept going from one job to another:

> My friends say I am becoming a 'rolling stone', and you know what happens to rolling stones. Do you think I am wrong in refusing to settle down in a job I don't like for the sake of security?

Mrs Wyse's rousing advice, in 1952 and again in 1954,[45] was that that the correspondent should keep moving as long as she wanted to, in order to fulfil her dreams (the two responses were not identically worded, but they were similar in content and tone). There was no mention of marriage or family in either the problem or the response to it; no suggestion was made that chances to attain them might be missed. The fact that this problem was repeated shows that the agony aunt believed it to be an authentic and relevant one. Married women were a lost cause, who could and should expect nothing from their menfolk, not even financial security, but single women should grab independence and adventure with both hands.

In the following decade Irish women – and their agony aunts – developed somewhat higher expectations both of working life and of marriage, and they expressed these both in letters to the editor of *Woman's Way* and in the problems they sent in.

'No Regrets For The Days That Are Gone': *Woman's Way* Letters 1963–69, 1: Young People and Miscellaneous

Readership and distribution

Woman's Way, from its very first issue, presented itself as a manual for a new age – an optimistic, self-consciously Irish one – and judging by their letters to the editor, this was how many readers saw it too. The changes in living standards and consumption that had been happening slowly in Ireland in the previous decade accelerated in the economic upswing of the 1960s (see Appendix 1). Women's magazines' immense popularity in post-war Britain was, Ferguson tells us, because they showed housewives what refrigerators (for example) were for, how to decorate serviced modern houses and how to cook new and unfamiliar foods. Also in Britain at that time, a rising standard of living for working-class people and a necessary simplification of household routines for the wealthier classes in the absence of domestic servants brought about greater homogeneity in everyday life-maintenance – clothing, cooking, housing, fashion and beauty – and broadened magazines' appeal across social classes. This change happened in Ireland in the late 1950s and throughout the 1960s, and letters to *Woman's Way* show that its readers came from a variety of social backgrounds. This was probably why it seems to have outsold all its predecessors, and its main rival, to the extent that presidential candidate T. F. O'Higgins thought it worthwhile to take out a full-page advertisement in the magazine in 1966.[1]

Irish television was just over a year and a half old when *Woman's Way* started, and Radio Eireann was, of necessity, changing too in response to this new media challenge. *Woman's Way* presented itself quite self-consciously as part of this new world. Thus, Kitty Barrett's welcoming letter in 1963:

Hurrah! *Woman's Way* arrived today,
Complete with glossy cover

I dropped my work, I eagerly flipped
Its pages over,
Oh! Charles Mitchel and Frank Hall,
Maura Laverty – you've got them all!

Mitchel was a newsreader, Frank Hall was a popular broadcaster and Maura Laverty (a popular playwright, novelist and cookery book writer referred to in Chapter 2) was a regular voice on Radio Eireann. Many other radio and TV personalities, such as cookery expert Monica Sheridan, billed as 'Ireland's most popular broadcaster', and TV personality Al Byrne regularly contributed opinion pieces in the 1960s.[2] And the readers who took the trouble to write to *Woman's Way* expressed a variety of opinions in this challenging decade, with some resisting change and some welcoming it heartily. The magazine's coverage of current affairs in its editorial content presupposed an intelligent and active readership.

Editorial content of the magazine

Woman's Way appeared every fortnight up to August 1966, when it began to appear weekly. It was competitively priced at between 8d and 10d throughout the decade. Sean O'Sullivan edited the magazine in its early years, and then it was taken over by Caroline Mitchell in 1965. O'Sullivan, a husband and father who had served in the US Army and then attended University College Galway on the GI bill, got the magazine on its feet. He proactively solicited letters from readers and delivered himself of many judgements on family life, consumer affairs and politics in his regular 'Gossopinion' column.

The magazine's editorial content was rich and varied. Opinion columns by home-grown radio and television personalities and other celebrities such as Limerick city's former mayor, Mrs Frances Condell, sat alongside discursive articles on women in prison, women's legal rights, women in jobs without pensions, prostitution, bedsitter life, children in institutions, the Mormons in Ireland, educational reforms, unmarried mothers, interracial marriage, wives who go out to work and the female religious life. Journalists included Monica McEnroy, Mary Leland, Heather Lukes and Maeve Binchy. Máire Comerford's article on the women of 1916 has already been mentioned. Mary Leland drew attention to the fact that there were only five women TDs out of 144 in the Dáil in 1965, all of them widows or daughters of former TDs. Irish female achievement in all fields was celebrated; ballad singer Dolly MacMahon, comedians Rosaleen Linehan and Maureen Potter and sculptor Imogen Stuart were among those featured. The only female engineer in the country, Katherine Walsh, was profiled in 1967.[3]

Woman's Way urged its readers to take more of an interest in politics. Seán O'Sullivan upbraided them in 1963:

> The trouble is that females are still, after 40 years of self-rule in this part of the country, not taken seriously. Oh women become famous, and some newspapers are always filled with the doings of famous and infamous women ... [but] once a mere 78 women got into Leinster House, things would really simmer.

Figure 4 An early *Woman's Way* cover.

Courtesy of the National Library of Ireland.

Less than a year later, he returned to the same theme, sounding very like Maxwell Sweeney (and 'Brian') in *Woman's Life* in the previous decade. Caroline Mitchell, who took over as editor in 1965, was equally forceful:

> Assuming that housekeeping is the be-all and the end-all of a woman's existence (which manifestly isn't so – thousands of perfectly 'feminine' women [are] keeping house competently and taking an interest in the world beyond the backyard) whey then don't those dedicated domestic types carry their obsession a step further and see that the country is being run as they think fit? Politics, you see, is the national housekeeping.[4]

Woman's Way's service articles were bright and attractive; cookery articles glorified the traditional (soda bread) and promoted the new (moussaka – though without aubergines), and in 1966–7 Audrey O'Farrell and Una Lehane's food columns mixed philosophy, social comment and recipes, in good, vivid writing that has not turned stale over the years. In the medical advice columns – from 1964 split into Sister (as in Nurse) Eileen SRN's Young Motherhood Bureau and the Patients' Postbox – women were advised on pregnancy, birth and infant and child care and on such diverse topics as slimming, varicose veins, vaccinations, menstrual problems, plastic surgery and fibroids. These were not the only information columns, however, and there were, from 1967, regular question-and-answer forums on food and cookery (Checkpot), on etiquette (Social Know-how) and on legal issues (Counsel's Advice).

The magazine was aimed at girls and women of all ages; married, single or widowed; working outside the home and inside it. 'Teen styles' were often featured in the fashion pages, the career guidance section (with questions and answers) was a staple, a pop music column (by Eanna Brophy) in the early years was entitled 'Hits for Misses' and, as we shall see, many of the problems were sent in by young, unmarried women and teenage girls – an increasing number as time went on. Monica McEnroy's trenchant articles on women's legal position, women and the Catholic Church, birth control and unmarried mothers provoked plenty of reader reaction. Controversies of the day were discussed. Readers' letters expressed opinions on all of these matters, but sometimes letters were spontaneously generated by readers' own thoughts and opinions.

Letters to *Woman's Way*

There were around 1,826 letters to *Woman's Way* between April 1963 and December 1969. The letters page was initially entitled 'Pen to Paper', but in 1965 it changed to 'Over to You', a phrase borrowed from broadcasting handovers, which may have amplified the sense of addressing a broad public for both writers and readers of the column. Every letter published won a guinea for its writer, and from early 1967 the writer of one letter every week won a guinea and a prize bond worth £5. The letters can be broken down into five categories – women's social, legal, occupational and marital status; husband–wife relationships; children and young people's work, education and leisure; miscellaneous; and the fifth category, which had three sub-categories rolled into one and was a staple of British magazine letters' pages – 'Handy Hints' (in *Woman's Way* these were called 'Hints That Help'), 'Things They Say' and 'Why Don't They'. These were two- or three-sentence short letters (Table 3.1).

Hints That Help/Things They Say/Why Don't They made up by far the largest percentage – 42.8 per cent – of all letters between April 1963 and December 1969, inclusive. Next came the miscellaneous category at 25.5 per cent, which covered a multitude of topics, usually current affairs. Letters specifically about children/ young people/education, work and training made up 13.3 per cent of all the letters; women's status (everything from paid work to contraception) comprised 12.3 per cent; and husband–wife relations were the subject of 5.8 per cent of all the letters written in.

The editor commented in 1964 that the magazine could only publish one-fiftieth of all the letters received. It is a mystery, therefore, why the same correspondents featured over and over again. The rather cranky Noel P. Collins of Midleton, Co Cork, was featured four times in the early years; other regular correspondents (with more than two letters, spread out over a period) were Margaret O'Donoghue of Buttevant, Co Cork; Sheila O'Farrell from Cork (the city,

Table 3.1 Letters (i.e. Letters to the editor, not problems) to *Woman's Way* 1963–9

Subject	Number	Percentage of all letters
Hints/Things They Say/ Why Don't They	783	42.8
Miscellaneous	467	25.5
Work/Ed/Youth	244	13.4
Women's Status	225	12.5
Marital Relationships	107	5.8
Total Letters*	1,826	100

*A total of three issues were missing over these years; this number refers to the letters looked at for all the extant issues.

presumably); Jean Bunyan from Listowel, Co Kerry; P. D., Tullamore, Co Offaly; and John Hutton, Co Kildare, a stay-at-home father, who expressed his opinion on a number of topics between 1966 and 1969. A regular *Woman's Way* correspondent, Mrs Eileen Quinn of Westport, Co Mayo, also had letters published in *Young Woman*, in 1967, and Patricia Burke of Portlaoise, Co Laois, featured as correspondent in both *Miss* and *Woman's Way* – both times on the topic of appearance, which makes it likely that she was the same person.[5] Maybe some letters were too badly written to publish, and maybe some had to be censored, even in the comparatively liberal regime of the 1960s. Unlike *Chatelaine* in Canada, *Woman's Way* did not archive these letters, so we will never know on what basis letters were selected for publication or rejected. It would not be useful, therefore, to quantify the letters that were for or against, for example, rights for 'itinerants' (the respectful 1960s term for Travellers) or contraception and to infer some kind of public opinion from that. First and most obviously, not all people wrote letters to magazines, but even taking into account the letters written, the editor might have wanted to publish a balance of letters on a particular topic or might have had a bias against one or another point of view. The letters are important, therefore, for what they tell us about a variety and range of opinions on various topics over time. They also tell us that more and more Irish women, every year, valued their opinions enough to write them down and send them off to a magazine, an important finding in itself.

Hints That Help/Things They Say/Why Don't They

Dismissed as trivial by some magazine historians,[6] this category of letter enabled enterprising wives and mothers to make money (a guinea was no small amount, when a starting-out civil servant earned £9 a week or a tradesman £14) selling their expertise, describing their families' idiosyncrasies and suggesting how goods and services could be improved. These letters were useful, worthwhile and occasionally funny. Slow-to-set apricot jam could be retrieved by two sticks of pineapple jelly, which gave it a firm set and a delicious flavour. Irish-made goods should have a distinctive mark, ran a suggestion in 1967, predating the 'guaranteed Irish' symbol by a decade. A little girl was delighted to hear on the radio that President John F. Kennedy was 'dressing the doll' (addressing the Dáil), and a boy who was asked what he wanted to be when he grew up responded that first he wanted to be a priest, then a bishop, then the Pope, and then a Clancy Brother.[7] (The Clancy Brothers were an internationally acclaimed Irish folk music group in this decade.)

The same correspondents' names appear more often in this section than in any others. Mrs M. Stakem, Co Westmeath, and Mrs B. Landers, Co Kilkenny, seem to have made this a cottage industry between 1967 and 1969 – Mrs Stakem had thirteen letters published and Mrs Landers at least twelve.[8] Hints and Why Don't They were prompted by the magazine's service articles and consumer information; Things They Say/Do, also common in British women's magazines, extracted humour from correspondents' relatives. Husbands and children were always good for a laugh, of course, but the longer, more serious letters (not in the Things They Say/Do category) praising the kindness, loyalty and overall goodness of individual family members, which were a regular feature of *Woman's Realm* and *Woman's Own* in these years, were markedly absent from *Woman's Way*.[9]

Miscellaneous

The letters in this category changed with every passing media preoccupation, which suggests that some readers of *WW* read newspapers and other publications avidly, listened to the radio and, as time went on, watched current affairs on television.

Concern with the plight of Irish nomadic people was inevitable in a decade so preoccupied with the two things that Travellers were seen to lack: housing and education. It was a sign of the times that Ewan McColl's ballad 'The Travelling People', recorded in Ireland by The Johnstons, reached number one in the Irish charts in August 1966. In *Woman's Way*, 'Fair-minded', Portlaoise, was being old-fashioned rather than offensive in her terminology when she commented in 1964 that 'in God's eyes the tinkers are as important as any other group of human beings'. Two years later the word itinerant – a transitional term between the newly offensive 'tinker' and the new, more neutral 'Traveller' – had entered the vocabulary, when Mrs K. Crotty, Waterford, referred to 'the grave injustices the itinerants have suffered at our hands'. An article about 'itinerants' that had appeared some weeks previously sparked four letters early in 1967, all of them supportive, though M. F., Mallow, Co Cork, recommended that any help given should be conditional on the children being sent to school. Later, Mrs B. N., Nenagh, Co Tipperary, referred to a 'dashing young tinker' who came to her door with a twelve-month-old baby: 'I thought it was well for her to be travelling round the country with neither rent nor rates to pay.' Travellers, or itinerants, were mentioned again a number of times – why weren't 'itinerant men' taught how to do a day's work, and why were not the women taught 'household duties', Mrs J. K., Tullamore, Co Offaly, wanted to know early in 1969, but Mrs M. M., Limerick, praised the honesty of those who came begging to her door: 'The call of the open road and rain-drenched tents seem preferable to our so-called civilized, hypocritical, "I'm all right Jack" way of life.' Mrs B. C., Co Tipperary, believed that if settled in houses, 'itinerants' as a distinct group would die out in three generations. She did not think they should be put into industrial schools – 'why should our religious hold every problem baby of society?' – but suggested that the children be integrated into settled families.[10]

Social inequality in general was rarely commented on in these letters, though anger was directed at familiar targets, sometimes in a scattergun kind of way. Was it any wonder there was industrial unrest when politicians were paid so much, M. M. F., Co Offaly, won a prize for pointing out in 1968, while M. C., Manorhamilton, Co Leitrim, got the prize letter two months later for pointing out that rich people were throwing out food while poor people were malnourished. In November of the same year, attention was drawn to the Biafran war and the civil rights movement in Derry by Mrs Kay McSweeney, Cork, who somehow connected these injustices to the 10 per cent extra given to students who sat their state examinations through Irish and the fact that Ireland had embassies all over the world. A more focused letter earlier that year from Mrs M. McD., Co Donegal, drew attention to ongoing housing problems; married thirteen months in 1968, she and her husband had no hope of a council house until they had children and were paying £3 a week for a damp, poorly furnished living room/bedroom and kitchen.[11] This level of personal detail about housing was unusual in the letters page, but it indicates that the magazine's readership was not confined to comfortable homeowners.

Much of the criticism of the Catholic Church in the letters page concerned contraception and will be discussed in the section on women's status. All the letters took a sort of universal Catholicity for granted, no doubt encouraged in this by an assertion of Sean O'Sullivan: 'We'll have to assume that the average housewife is a Catholic since there are only some 60,000 housewives and mothers in the Republic who are not of the papist persuasion.' (Sixty thousand in such a small country was not a negligible number!) The editor who succeeded him from 1965, Caroline Mitchell, was a Protestant, as were several of the regular contributors from the very beginning – Charles Mitchel, the newsreader, and Frances Condell, the former mayor of Limerick, to name but two. But while there was trenchant criticism of the church in the magazine's editorial content and letters, there was never any criticism of priests, brothers or nuns as such. A very positive article on 'The Cloistered Life' by Monica McEnroy (who, it will be seen, vigorously challenged the church on birth control) deplored authors Polly Devlin, Edna O'Brien and Honor Tracy for their negative portrayals of nuns. In 1961, vocations to the religious life in Ireland reached their highest point, and over the succeeding decade the relaxation of regulations brought about by Vatican II meant that priests, nuns and brothers were more publicly visible than ever before. Therefore it was not at all outlandish for 'No Nonsense', Mallow, Co Cork, to advise parents whose daughters might be tending towards the religious life:

> If your girl wants to be a nun, teach her to get a kick out of life, to laugh at herself, to cook, to housekeep ... but don't force her to go to Mass every morning ... nuns, you see, are made of whole-hearted girls who firmly grasp the nettle of life.[12]

In the same practical vein, Mrs Maura Hann, Wicklow, called for more sermons from the pulpit about ordinary life:

> Landlords, are you overcharging your tenants? In-laws, do you interfere in your childrens' marriages? Are you a snob?

Mrs E. Donaghy, Belfast, commented that theologians could find no reason why women should not be ordained and urged women to play more of a role in the church 'apart from flowers and cleaning'. Matters of practice were also discussed. The magazine was taken to task in 1969 by Mrs L. Morris, Co Fermanagh, for its assertion some months previously that women no longer needed to cover their heads in the church. Miss C. L. commented that it was a 'disgrace' to see women going up to Holy Communion with their heads uncovered, but Nora Curran, Co Dublin, disagreed quite strongly, adding that her great-grandmother in Connemara as a mark of respect in church used to pull her shawl to the back of her head, 'a custom that can be seen in Galway even today'. Other comments on matters religious were too mixed to be categorized, but change was in the air. It was unfair that mixed-religion marriage couples could not adopt, M. P. L., Dublin 1, commented in 1968; this injustice was highlighted in RTE's popular weekly drama, *The Riordans*. Mrs J. Andrews, Castlecomer, Co Kilkenny, praised popular Dublin priest Fr Michael Cleary in March of the same year for 'coming down to the level of the people', but his populism was deplored by H. B., Mallow, Co Cork, some weeks later. Sheila Kerr, Belfast, commenting in 1969 on David Frost's television interview with the new English cardinal, John Heenan, hoped that the latter's 'human kindness and charity' would be noticed by Irish bishops: 'It is time that the Irish hierarchy stopped hiding behind a veil of awe.'[13]

Possibly because the preservation of the Irish language was seen as a struggle with as much moral weight as church teaching, Cáit Ní Mhuinineacáin, An Muilleann Chearr, was not afraid to take issue with Fr Michael Cleary's widely publicized claim that teaching children Irish did not prepare them for decent employment in English cities. The regulation that Leaving Certificate students had to pass Irish in order to pass the entire examination was much discussed throughout this decade. Eibhlín Bean Uí Chochláin opined in 1965 that this regulation did not do the language revival any good, and in November 1966 the magazine published two letters from opposing sides of the debate, from P. Midhearch, Blackrock, Co Dublin, and Eibhlín Ní Mhuineacháin, Dublin 8. 'A Parent', Tuam, Co Galway, the following January called for less compulsory Irish and more health and hygiene education, generally, which was typical of the tone of many of the letters. It was brave of M. K., Dublin 6, to state in 1969 that one of the advantages of learning Irish would be the ability of Irish people to learn new languages when Ireland joined the Common Market – the usual argument was that learning Irish wasted time that could be spent learning continental languages. The magazine's own editorial opinion – favourable towards Irish as a language but against compulsion – sparked the following exasperated comment from Damhnait Ní Néill, Port Láirge: 'The learning of a language does not require intelligence as such, only good will. Every normal human being can talk.'[14]

The transfer of civil servants in certain government departments from Dublin to Mayo provoked the first of a number of letters in March 1968. Mrs M. J. L., Cork, drew attention to the hardship this caused civil servants' wives, in particular, and suggested that an organization of some sort be formed for them. Two letters, one from Miss M. McC., Co Sligo, another from Miss A. C., Castlebar, flatly contradicted a letter from 'Eileen' some weeks previously, which had implied that it was almost impossible to buy nylons west of the Shannon. Mrs T. M. R., Dublin 4, saw life in the west as 'dire poverty' and dreaded moving her five children there; her concluding comment reveals the depth of some middle-class Dubliners' ignorance about life outside the capital:

I have read about Castlebar Chamber of Commerce having published a booklet to enlighten civil servants in the Department of Lands. Why did they not do something similar long ago to encourage *their own people* to stay in the west? [italics not in original].

But Mrs M. H. D., Dublin, (in a prize letter) told readers that she had lived in both Athlone and Castlebar and that in each place her problem was choosing between at least a dozen 'charitable and recreational societies'. The shops, and the fashion, compared favourably with those of Dublin, and she had a parting shot:

> It would be interesting to know how many of those who complain of being forced to leave their city friends have ever held out a friendly hand to a neighbour who has left her country friends and come to live in the city.

The following year John MacDonald, Dublin 9, advised those relocating from the capital to think of how proud they would be 'when the West was won', that it was 'not as a case of "To Hell or to Connaught"', a Cromwellian reference which would have struck a chord with many readers. Some months later A. O'R., Dublin, pointed out how beautiful the 'West' was, and reminded civil servants how lucky they were to have permanent and pensionable jobs.[15]

Some world affairs provoked comment. Mrs M. L., Waterford, was upset about the Kennedy–Onassis marriage, wondering why 'Jackie' had put herself outside the church: 'We all loved her'; but Mrs M. T. D., Galway, argued that 'he could be the gentlest of creatures', and reminded readers that beauty was 'only skin-deep' – no doubt comparing Aristotle Onassis's looks with those of Mrs Kennedy's first husband. The alliance drove Mrs K. O'S., Killarney, however, to comment on the inequalities of wealth in the world, while Mrs R. S., Kilmallock, Co Limerick, robustly asserted Mrs Kennedy's right to do what she liked.[16]

Old ways of cooking and housekeeping were very occasionally praised in a ritualistic way (without too much personal detail) but not by Mrs K., Carlow, who wrote in praise of 'plastics, cookers and heaters' in 1963:

> I am almost 50 years of age and I remember no good days but the present ones. I remember cooking on an open fire; I remember wash-day, the house filled with steam from the big pot boiling the whites. I remember the dark, dismal homes of the countryside, lit by candles and oil-lamps, the dark, drab paint chosen to hide the dirt. I still have visions of heavy kitchen tables being carried out to the yard for the weekly scrubbing. I have no regrets for the days that are gone.

For Mrs D. G., Limerick city, the challenge four years later was to create an 'old conservative kitchen' in a modern house; she described proudly how she installed a solid fuel range to heat water, but she saw no incongruity in using that most modern window covering, the Venetian blind. These letters were unusual, and in contrast with the British magazines, housing in either old or new surroundings was not a regularly featured topic. When Mary Dee, Liselton, Co Kerry, deplored her parents' modern, serviced house and yearned for the old thatch, it was in a nostalgic, non-specific way, and no other readers wrote in sympathy.[17]

Other letters supported interracial marriage, extolled the importance of scientific knowledge and celebrated or excoriated the practice of Sunday 'dropping-in' (Mrs P. F., Thurles, Co Tipperary, welcomed it, but Mrs M. K., Sligo, advised that the hat and coat be put on whenever there was a knock on the door, and you could tell unwelcome callers you were just going out, or welcome ones that you had just come in). Miss C. Fahy, Co Dublin, wondered why men, like women, did not remove body hair. Mrs J. F., Co Limerick, objected to being called 'love' and 'dear' by shop assistants: 'Don't waste these endearments on old ladies.' There were some philosophical musings, though not as many as in the British magazines that were examined. M. O., Strokestown, Co Roscommon, offered readers the benefit of her seventy years of wisdom in 1964 – optimism and trust in God tide you over difficulties and sorrows, never meet trouble half way, sharing another's burden brings as much if not more solace to the giver as to the recipient. Miss I. R., Athy, Co Kildare, in 1968 had learnt over 'half a life span' that you can get over anything, you will not die of a broken heart and, if unhappy, a change of scene is the greatest cure.[18] She was addressing herself to young people, who were also the focus of many letters around this time.

Young people: Education, work, training

In 1965, 'Sweet Sixteen', Clonmel, Co Tipperary, urged readers to maintain friendships made on holiday 'when we return to our humdrum existence in office or factory'. Her remark reminds us that the normal teenage experience in this decade was not necessarily that of a school-goer.

There was a brief flurry of concern on the letters page throughout 1966–7 about teenage emigration (far less common than it had been in the previous decade). Perhaps it was prompted by John Healy's impassioned autobiographical memoir of 1940s and 1950s youth emigration, which appeared in 1966. Offaly Student, Tullamore, asked why young people emigrated when there were jobs to be had in Ireland. Mrs Sheila Lynskey, Co Mayo and R. O'T., Tipperary, deplored the sadness of emigration in general, and Mrs J. Andrews, Castlecomer, Co Kilkenny, praised Fr Michael Cleary for stating that nobody under seventeen should go to England unless they were going to relatives. Mrs Brigid O'Donnell, Donegal, blamed parents, priests and teachers for both youth emigration and 'falling by the wayside' – putting both on the same level. Many parents, however, still needed their children's earnings, abroad or at home, and M. G., Lifford, Co Donegal, pragmatically defended emigration: 'Without [emigration] what would many a poor woman with a large family do?' There certainly were jobs to be had in Ireland, but pay and conditions in some sectors were very bad. Sixteen-year-old hotel worker H. C., Sligo, told readers in 1968 of how she was housed in a hotel dormitory with twenty-five girls upstairs and twenty-five boys downstairs, in stuffy rooms, with no supervisor, bad food, poor wages and no trade union: 'There are many girls like me all over rural Ireland, members of large families and we need the money to help out at home.' According to Jean Bunyan, Co Kerry, young hotel workers in her locality in 1969 often earned only £3 10s per week for sixteen-hour days, six days a week.[19]

Some of the comment on young people concerned the reforms of 1966–7, when Minister for Education Donogh O'Malley introduced free universal secondary education. This would result in a lowering of standards, argued J. Carr, Dublin 14, but John Jacobs, Rathnew, Co Wicklow, retorted that this was not so and argued that plenty of young people would still go into trades. Trades aside, the fear that there would be nobody left to do unskilled jobs was expressed by M. S., Mallow, Co Cork: there was 'far too much talk' about education, s/he opined, and this would lead to the uneducated and unskilled being 'despised', and who would make roads and sweep streets? P. G., Abbeyfeale, Co Limerick, wondered if, and indeed how, the equality of educational provision would carry over into later life, and Mrs Flynn, Killarney, said free education was 'all very well' but where would the jobs come from? Would it be 'pull [influence] all over again'? Miss E. K., Co Mayo, won a prize early in 1969 for suggesting that free education broke part of the bond between parents and teenagers, as the latter did not see their parents making sacrifices to keep them at school. Mrs M. M., Co Wexford, pointed out that even with free education, it was still a struggle to feed and clothe non-earning teenagers on a low income. What good was free education without transport, asked Mrs M. F. C., Carlow; what good was free secondary education to the daughter or son who had to stay at home to mind a sick parent, Miss M. G., Cork, asked. Still, even Sheila O'Farrell, who wondered who, if everybody was educated, would do the 'unskilled, unprofitable jobs', conceded that it was good to see 'that all our children are being cherished equally'.[20]

There were also the letters about young people's apparently problematic behaviour. The cranky Noel P. Collins in 1964 believed that parents were to blame for 'this Beatlemania and stupid carry on of their children'. D. MacCabe, Bray, Co Wicklow, in 1965, was 'utterly disgusted' at the 'current trend of broadmindedness in Ireland. ... I'm a teenager and write this letter to the youth and the grown-ups.' 'Contested', Clonmel, Co Tipperary, in 1966 took issue with

Mrs W., Co Westmeath, who had written in complaining that young people cared for nothing but 'pop and transistors'; s/he wrote that young people were not all long-haired and mad for pop music (though they liked it) and if 'Contested' won a guinea for the letter, s/he would use it to buy Sean O Riada's *Mise Eire*. (In the 1960s, traditional music exemplified in its purest form by O Riada and popularized by the Clancy Brothers and other groups was seen as somehow inimical to modern pop and rock music; by the early 1970s it was possible to enjoy both.) 'I'm Not', Terenure, Dublin, wondered some weeks later why parents were always complaining, and this was a constant lament in the letters column, showing that teenagers read the magazine. No wonder R. F., Fermoy, Co Cork, suggested jokingly early in 1969 that a Teenagers' Defence Council (TDC) be set up.

Complaints about young people found a focus in the student protests of 1968, which, however minimally they affected Ireland, frightened enough people to cause them to write to magazines and papers. M. O., Galway, in 1968 believed that rioting students should pay for the damage they caused. Criticism of student behaviour was encouraged by editorial comment on the 'international anarchy of student revolt'. Alison Hanton, Dublin 7, the following spring was 'weary' of students' taking up the cudgels on behalf of other disadvantaged groups. Students should first become 'valuable members of the community' and only then address themselves to the problems of the less fortunate. This might have been a response to a letter in January of the same year from Cassian Sweeney, Dublin 6, who argued that 'we teenagers' should care more about issues like the rising cost of living 'and the class distinctions of every capitalist society'. A prize-winning letter in May 1969 from M. S. Ní S., Co Westmeath, recommended that students' grants be taken away from them if disturbances continued. The previous month, however, E. Nealon, Gormanston, Co Meath, had won the prize letter for pointing out that adults, not teenagers, were 'ruining the country financially and politically' with 'strikes and political disputes'. Another prize-winning letter, in May 1969, from Sheila Fox, Co Longford, insisted that it was unfair to criticize the youth for violence: 'We are not wild aimless creatures but human beings who are willing, if allowed, to work ... for peace and harmony in the world.' Mrs N. C., Waterford, however, recommended that students who liked to march should be sent to the west to work on drainage and the preservation of ancient monuments.[21] This disproportionate reaction to what was by any standards a low level of student protest shows the embattled authoritarianism of many middle-aged and older people in this decade.

But not all young people were students, and E. S., Co Donegal, was tired of hearing young people criticized: 'My husband and I are barely out of our teens and he works a 7-day week and I work a 6-day week.' Some readers would have considered such youthful marriage to be problematic in itself. In Ireland in the 1960s, people began to get married at a younger age after nearly a century and a half of above-average ages at marriage. Siobhan Murphy, Galway, opined in 1968 that the trend towards early marriage 'is generally recognised and encouraged everywhere, yet in this country there are those who condemn teenage marriage for a variety of frivolous reasons'. But Mrs M. H., Dublin 9, asked why parents allowed teenage girls to go steady, when the inevitable result was early marriage (taking for granted that this was not a good thing). Miss P. O'C., Wexford, agreed, in 1969: 'Who wants to be tied down?'[22]

Corporal punishment in schools was controversial, and in 1967–9, campaigns calling for its abolition provoked reader reaction. M. O., Galway, was ahead of the others in 1966 when she urged that parents 'insist that they [children] are humanely and decently treated at school'. She criticized the five female TDs for not having expressed any opinions on this. Three letters published in August 1969 reacted to an article on the subject by Tom McSweeney the previous June. Thirteen-year-old C. K., Dublin 5, agreed that corporal punishment was bad, but asked what the alternative was; one teacher in her school just ignored (in the sense of freezing out) the miscreant, and she believed that this was just as bad. Daniel O'Riordan, Co Cork, totally agreed with McSweeney, and young National teacher M. D. L., Kilkenny, won a prize for her letter against corporal punishment some months later.[23]

Readers who praised the young, like Betsy, Sligo, in 1965 – 'Long may the teenager reign! Mine has given her old mother much joy and amusement' – were extremely rare. Not in the letters page as such, but quoted by columnist Charles Mitchel as having been sent to him personally, was a mother's praise in 1967 of her daughter:

> Jacqueline cycles to school three and a half miles every day to be there at 9 a.m. She ... has never been lower than fourth in her class. She arrives home about 4.30 and after some lunch ... milks 18 cows by machine, gives various meals to about 14 calves, bucket feeds 6 calves with milk, sees to the horses and sundry other jobs. She then has her tea, does her homework, and sees a little bit of television before going to bed. On Saturday and Sunday she does the milking morning and evening. She gets 6s a week.

This kind of letter praising a daughter was a staple of the British magazines looked at, but almost non-existent in the Irish one. One wonders, indeed, if Mitchel made it up – Jacqueline would have been a very unusual name for an Irish rural *teenage* girl in 1967, the name not becoming popular for Irish baby girls until Jacqueline Kennedy came into the public eye with the election of her husband in 1960. There must have been thousands of other daughters throughout the country who did the same, if not more, work than the probably mythical 'Jacqueline', but open pride in one's offspring was frowned upon in Ireland in this decade, and in any case, perhaps such hard work on the part of daughters was taken completely for granted.[24]

'Jacqueline' was attending secondary school and therefore would have been typical of farmers' daughters from the mid-1950s onwards. Girls' education was also the subject of debate, and although it could fit in more with issues of women's status, it directly concerned education so it will be dealt with here. 'Mod Mad', Mount Merrion, who sat her Leaving Certificate in 1966, wanted to know how 'preposition 16 and "ode 14" and lines 300–400 from *Paradise Lost* prepare young girls for entry into the world'. Miss B. N., Co Clare, in 1968 believed girls should be taught housekeeping and nursing as most girls 'waste' academic education, but a letter the following month from Mrs Margaret O'Donoghue, Buttevant, Co Cork, made the familiar argument that educating a girl even to university standard was never a waste, because educating mothers meant educating a family. Mrs K. O'N., Glanmire, Co Cork, agreed with her, as did other readers. Mrs Moira McDowell, Dublin 6, gave pragmatic, if somewhat outdated, reasons for educating girls: first, 25 per cent of Irish women never married (that figure was changing but she might not have been aware of that); second, there was always a possibility of widowhood; and third, the better a job the woman had, the more likely she was to meet 'a man of a higher income group and make a good match'. Mrs A. C., Cobh, Co Cork, agreed in 1968 on the importance of educating and training girls – she herself had typing skills and could earn money at home, after marriage. However, M. S., Dublin 4, the previous year had criticized parents who sent girls into 'boring badly-paid' office work instead of helping them to train for a career, and M. T. B., Cork, agreed – she was an office worker earning £9 a week after eight years, while two of her former school friends, one a nurse, the other a hairdresser, were each earning around £20 a week. And if one correspondent, Miss P. E., Cork, argued in 1968 that the curriculum of all girls' schools should include compulsory home economics, Mrs K. Kennedy, Co Mayo, the following year believed that boys as well as girls should be taught cookery. Nobody disagreed with M. F., Mallow, Co Cork, who declared in 1967 that girls should have the courage to 'kick for what they want'.[25]

There was a very small number of letters (apart from Things They Say) about the care of young children; those that featured concerned management rather than philosophy. A Mrs N. L., Togher, Co Cork, won a prize for a letter in 1968 complaining about children playing on the road on long summer evenings and then getting up late in the mornings, and M. W., Dublin 5, who wrote to support her two months later, affirmed that she had her two girls in bed before 6.00 pm (!) every summer evening and up before 8.30 am – mothers only kept children up late, she argued, so that they (the mothers) could have a sleep-in in the morning. A mother of ten, Mrs Eilis Ryan, Co Wexford, told of how she loved the free and easy atmosphere of the school holidays – getting the small ones to help and not watching the clock. Children's Allowance was also discussed; it should, M. Dineen, Cork, argued in 1967, be saved as a nest egg for when the child reached twenty-one. Readers reacted to this, some weeks later. F. W., Co Laois, was 'always waiting for it', (i.e. she could not afford to save it); Mrs P. K., Thurles, Co Tipperary, shod and dressed her children out of it; Statia Herlihy, Greystones, Co Wicklow, spent hers immediately, but E. T. P., Newbridge, Co Kildare, saved hers to give her children 'a good education'. This idea had been scorned some months earlier by Carmel Hallissey, Dublin 6: 'The money is children's allowance, not a scholarship for young ladies and gentlemen.' Children's Allowance was not paid directly to mothers until 1974 (Appendix 1) but husbands could sign for their wives to collect it, and this is why some women at least had a say in how it was spent.[26]

This brings us on to the whole area of women's status, work and legal position, which will be explored in the next chapter.

'Have You Been Reading *Woman's Way* Too?' *Woman's Way* Letters 2: Women's Status

Introduction

Immediately, *Woman's Way* was seen as a champion of women's rights by some of its readers, like Mrs M. E. Bentley, Dublin 4:

> My daughter has several girls working under her in her job, and the other day one of them was moaning that she would have to go home and make her brother's tea. When my daughter expressed surprise, the girls said, 'Oh, have you been reading *Woman's Way* too?'

The concern about women's rights inside and outside the home that animated the columnists in the magazine was reflected in – and no doubt stimulated – the letters page of *Woman's Way* throughout the decade. Subjects that generated the most debate were married women working outside the home (or not), birth control/family size and farm women's lives. There were also short bursts of discussion on women and politics, home versus hospital birth, marital relationships and unmarried mothers.

Married women earning

Former National teacher Mrs John Cunnane, Castlerea, Co Roscommon, opened the debate on married women working in 1963:

> I have a full-time job now as a housewife with care of child and home, since I retired as an NT when I married. I find I have lots of work to occupy my time and I have no time to contemplate. I decided when I married that no career should encroach upon the time that should be spent in the home. I can get out

and about whenever I like and I always have friends and relatives calling. And as
I know I can take a job whenever I like, I feel I have nothing to regret.

Female National teachers had been allowed to keep on their jobs after marriage
since 1958, so Mrs Cunnane had chosen to give up her job and would be able
to take it up again. Skilled self-employed women such as Mrs Anne Molloy, a
hairdresser from Dublin 9, who wrote two years later that she did not regret giving
up her hairdressing business when her children were born, would also be able to
do this. Working unsupervised was the chief advantage of her way of life for stay-
at-home mother Thurles, who might have had an unhappy workplace experience:

> Give me these simple joys in preference to being in the limelight with every
> action watched and every word you say contradicted and criticized.

'Co Leitrim Granny' believed that if married women earned money, a couple's over-
dependence on two incomes might delay the starting of a family. This common
fear that affluence might be chosen over family life was addressed by Muriel
Redmond, Dublin 9, some years later when she said that she intended working
after marriage until she 'felt like giving up', but so as not to become too dependent
on two salaries, her wages were going into a special fund. Mrs M. O'S., Bandon,
Co Cork, believed that mothers should not go out to work when children were
small; Mrs J. M. O'F., Sligo, agreed with her, but insisted that women needed some
activity outside the house all the same. Mrs Nóirín Doyle, Cobh, Co Cork, claimed
to have more time and energy for her baby when she came home from a day's
work, and 'Delighted', Shantalla, Galway, was a 'better wife' for working because
she was not 'fed up' when her husband came home; besides, they had more money
and she met more people. John Hutton, Sallins, Co Kildare, the father of a family,
had been obliged to give up work for health reasons, so his wife got a job and was
'happier and years younger'. Mrs Bríd Vernon, Dublin 5, believed it was a shame
to waste a highly trained secretary by retiring on marriage, and work, moreover,
was a 'marvellous stimulant'; she worked part-time and was 'more alert to the
needs of my family when I come back to the kitchen sink'. Mrs Mary Conway,
Wicklow, supported women working after marriage – and argued that they should
receive equal pay – provided they did not neglect the house. Earning inside the
home, or taking in work, did not feature very often. Were women ashamed of
admitting that they did it? None of the women who wrote in about it gave their
full names. In 1968, M. M. G., Cavan, complained that home knitters were only
paid 1s 7d an ounce, explicitly linking this to 'the women's rights campaign, long
overdue'. Mrs M. H., Drumcondra, Dublin, agreed with her some weeks later, and
Mrs T. D., Kilkenny, drew readers' attention to the health hazards of this poorly

paid occupation – raging headache, sore eyes. Home knitting of traditional garments might have been an important source of income for women but it was also a very cheap and convenient labour force for a nation developing its tourism. These home-working women saw the *Woman's Way* letters page as an appropriate forum for their grievances, but their complaints did not fit into any of the issues of the time as explored by the magazine, so nothing came of them.[1]

Birth control

Readers' letters on the subject of family planning began in 1966, in anticipation of the forthcoming papal encyclical, but the issue had come up in the magazine before. Founding editor Sean O'Sullivan was against it but in favour of some kind of family planning and sex education. The editorial line of the magazine under Caroline Mitchell was broadly in favour of birth control, while Angela Macnamara's problem page was firmly opposed to contraception, although it supported sex education.

An article by Monica McEnroy in 1966 on the Pope and the Pill sparked so many responses that a special page was given over to them. A. M. objected to this 'untimely, aggressive and irresponsible article' and condemned McEnroy's 'censorious and ill-timed pontificating'. 'Prospective Wife', however, invoked God's relationship with the couple as a private one and repeated the old saying, 'If men were to have every second child, there would never be more than three in a family'. John Murphy, Dublin 14, believed that this was an issue not just for women but for couples; he hoped the church would listen to husbands and wives, not only doctors, because doctors could only judge physical health but 'what about mental health? Who can judge that except the wife?' Other letters to this particular page from Mayo, Limerick, Kildare and Cork supported some form of artificial birth control. The debate continued for the rest of the decade in fits and starts. Mrs G., Mayo, pointed out early in 1967 that 'our Dutch, Belgian and American [Catholic] sisters have spoken out' and wondered how long Irish (Catholic) women were going to 'suffer in silence'. However, Elizabeth Dalton, a mother of five (who had been practising the safe period since after her first child was born), who awaited the Pope's decision 'as anxiously as anyone else', expressed the uneasiness many intelligent and articulate Catholics felt about disobeying the church:

> For Monica McEnroy to imply that the women of Ireland have only to stand together and have a little moral courage to change one of the oldest rules in the Church is, I think, going too far.[2]

Those letters that were against contraception were not all negative; some were quite positive in their support of the unplanned family. Mrs E. R. Kirwan in 1966 explained her position:

> As the mother of four young children I'm sure that I speak for many other mothers when I say that I would not be without any of my children, even though we may resent another pregnancy in its early stages.

This point was made by several other mothers of big families in the letters page. Mrs Paddy Casey, Gort, Co Galway, had dreamt of a big house and two children but had ended up with seven children in 1967 in a small house and professed herself happy. Mrs A. J., Rathangan, Co Kildare, wondering how people managed big families in the past without any modern conveniences, believed it was 'a shame to hear Irish Catholic mothers talk of family planning'. Many couples who had started their large families in the poor housing and material shortages of the 1940s and early 1950s found the very idea of family planning difficult to reconcile with their own life narrative of triumphant struggle against the odds. Mrs A. Roberts, Ferns, Co Wexford, was married twenty-five years (in 1967) with eleven children and three grandchildren, one of whom was older than her youngest child; her husband was twenty-seven years older than her 'and all the neighbours admire us for being so happy'. In 1968 Mrs Eilis Ryan, also Co Wexford (who liked the long school holidays; see Chapter 3) wondered how different her life would have been had she had the chance to plan her family, but with ten children under eighteen on 'a small wet farm', the house was full of song and laughter and 'I sincerely thank God that we left the planning of our family to Him'. The belief that God/ fate, and not human beings, should 'decide' who came into the world, and when, was not peculiar to Ireland or to Catholics. Kate Fisher's oral history of English working-class attitudes to sex in the first half of the twentieth century discovered that couples (regardless of religious affiliation) were most comfortable with birth control methods in which a certain openness to pregnancy, even uncertainty, was built in; there was a similar ambivalence about using contraception in Lincolnshire and in Scotland (among Protestants as well as Catholics) in the same period.[3] In overwhelmingly Catholic Ireland, attitudes like this were reinforced by an all-pervasive and authoritative religious culture.

Few, however, were as blithe as 'Happy Kilkenny', Ballyragget, who acknowledged that big families were hard work but quoted the saying 'every baby comes with a loaf under his arm'. Indeed, demographic changes coupled with rising living standards caused some writers to express qualified, even reluctant, support for family planning. Mrs B. D., Boyle, Co Roscommon, noted that the earlier marriages that were becoming the norm would mean twenty-five childbearing years, unless couples took some steps to limit their families. (Her implicit suggestion that the later marriage prevalent among rural and middle-class people generally for over a century had placed certain limits on family size was accurate.) Mrs A. G., also from Roscommon, went further: children were a blessing, but big families often entailed 'hardship and squalor'. Mrs N. W., Dublin 12, referred to the 'mental anguish of ill-timed pregnancy'. Mrs A. F., Wicklow, was perhaps an extreme exemplar of this anguish; she had nine children, four of whom were dead, and 'every second child was seriously handicapped'. The priest had told her that the laws of the church could not be changed: 'Every mother will understand the heartbreak I have suffered.'[4]

Family size did get smaller from the early 1960s, which implies that family planning, whether by 'natural' or artificial means, was practised by many young couples throughout the country. Although Mrs M. E. D., Co Laois, was disgusted when in hospital to hear the other mothers on the ward talking openly about it, and did not want to practise it herself (she had '5 and wouldn't mind another 5'), she conceded that family planning was right. Mrs P. C., a mother of seven from Monkstown, Co Dublin, believed that children were a blessing but that couples should be given the knowledge to plan. The letters of 6 September 1968 were all reactions to the Pope Paul VI's encyclical Humanae Vitae. Mrs M. B. D., Tullamore, was shocked at the pronouncement that 'we are to be kept in slavery'. Mrs R. H., Cork, aged almost thirty, who had married at nineteen and had borne six children in eight years (five living,), asked if it was any wonder that so many women were suffering from mental breakdown. Mrs N. G., Mayo, linked Ireland's historically low marriage rate directly to lack of birth control and quoted theologian Karl Rahner to the effect that it should be left to the conscience of the individual. Mrs Maura Hann, Co Wicklow (who had called, earlier, for sermons on everyday subjects), objected to the encyclical as

> a thoroughly male thesis, written and conceived by a man who will never know the strain of pregnancy, nor suffer the pangs of morning sickness, nor have his sleep interrupted.

But Mrs M. D., Liselton, Co Kerry, objected to the too-frank discussion of birth control in the media, and M. F., Tullamore, who professed herself disappointed with Humanae Vitae, reflected that marriage was for bringing children into the

world, and selfish people made bad parents.[5] Eileen Quinn, Co Mayo, believed
the Holy Father should be obeyed as he always has been in past, 'when families
were bigger, happier and healthier'. Mrs F. O'Sullivan, Dublin 8, believed that
people whose health was endangered by pregnancy should be special cases
but that others should practise self-control. Mrs Sadie Leonard, Kilcormac, Co
Offaly, deplored criticism of the encyclical; people wanted pleasure without
responsibility, she wrote. (Young and fashionable, her photograph appeared as a
finalist for CalorGas Housewife of the Year the following week.) Monica McEnroy
continued to write articles on birth control, prompting Mrs N. Linehan, Cork,
to ask 'Would you please ask Monica to stop talking about the Pill as if it was
the panacea for all women?' And a prize-winning letter from Mrs M. D. T. F.,
Co Louth, in 1969 took vigorous issue with Monica McEnroy's championing of
English Catholic contraception campaigner Dr Anne Biezanek. Ann Murnaghan
of Dundalk objected to McEnroy taking so lightly 'learned theologians and
the Holy Father himself', while M. O'S., Dublin 1, wondered what theological
qualifications McEnroy had, to go against the Pope in this matter.[6]

Unmarried mothers and sex education

Birth control concerned married people only; discussion of unmarried mothers
and the difficulties they faced was entirely separate. Most correspondents on
this topic, which surfaced in 1967 in response to an article, directly linked this
problem with the lack of sex education. Mrs P. D., Tullamore, Co Offaly, reacting
to an article on the subject in the magazine, was typical:

> How this article should shake up some of my smug friends who still labour
> under the misapprehension that all a girl needs is proximity to a Roman Catholic
> Church and three Hail Marys after the family Rosary to keep her on the straight
> and narrow.

Nuala Lynch, Ballyvourney, Co Cork, invoked Mairéad Ní Ghráda's play, *An
Triail* (*The Ordeal*), which concerned an unmarried mother, while K. M. D., Co
Dublin, called for prison sentences for unmarried fathers because her adopted
daughter had the fact of her adoption 'thrown at her constantly'. The lack of sex
education, according to Mrs R. K., Co Armagh, and M. McDermott, Cavan,
was directly responsible for unmarried mothers, but Mrs Rita Johnson, Rathgar,
Dublin, a mother of four daughters, did not believe that 'any girl attending
a city convent' was ignorant of sex education; pregnancy is 'the incidental

penalty a girl must suffer when she deliberately flouts the teaching of the sixth commandment'. Five readers – D. W. from Portarlington, Co Laois; Brigid Ryan from Kilkenny; Miss N. R., Birr, Co Offaly; Mrs P. D., Tullamore (again); and Mrs E. M., Wicklow – disagreed strongly with her. K. F., Cork, however, believed that unmarried mothers found it too easy to 'take the boat to Fishguard'.[7] This point of view, expressed again by a 'problem' in 1969, written in to Angela Macnamara claiming that there were no unmarried mothers twenty-eight years before, made Mrs Alice Drennan, Dublin 8, 'smile'; 'Perhaps my part of the country was different [she was obviously a rural migrant in the city] but we had quite a large number and it was the same in my mother's day'. W. F., Mallow, Co Cork, however, who pointed out some time earlier that the 'illegitimate child' brings 'heartbreak to some and joy to others' (the others being adoptive parents), was expressing the 1960s' best-possible scenario outcome of unmarried motherhood, a view also expressed by correspondents to the British *Woman's Own* in 1966. The unmarried mother walked away and picked up the pieces of her life; the childless couple joyfully adopted her baby.[8]

Politics and labour

There was not much discussion of women in politics, despite editorial urgings. 'Stay-at-Home Kilkenny', who wrote in 1965 in mild support of mothers who elected not to go out to work, nonetheless believed in the need for women in public life, citing Mrs Frances Condell, who was held up as an example to girls everywhere in that decade. 'Party worker', Bray, Co Wicklow, thought it 'dreadful' that so few women went into politics or took an interest in the government of their country, and some weeks later, M. K., Ballon, Co Carlow, pleaded for more women TDs, deploring the fact that most existing female deputies were relatives of dead male politicians. But, unlike the two previous issues discussed, this one did not escalate over time, and this is probably why Mrs B. D., Mallow, Co Cork, believed in 1967 that the lack of female politicians was entirely due to women's political apathy. Mrs P. D., Tullamore – who contributed on a number of other issues (see above) – wondered in 1968 why women could not be on juries; they had been 'exempted' from this duty in 1927, and it would not be restored to them until 1971. The inevitable maleness of politicians was taken for granted by Miss B. H., Rosscarbery, Co Cork, in 1967 when she urged that greater teenage interest in politics would result in the election of younger *men* instead of the 'doddering old men' already there, and by Esther Hurley in 1968, when she wondered why there were no women on the Commission for Constitutional Reform but went on to say that the higher education of girls was a necessity:

> If we don't educate the mothers of the future who will *rear the sons* who will one day control our lives? [italics not in original]

However, this woman's ideas had evolved somewhat by 1969, when she won a prize for declaring that women would never be equal until they got involved in politics and government.

Labour issues did not feature much. Mrs Margaret Shiel, Dublin 9, in a letter in April 1968, took strong issue with an article that complained about strikes:

> You even go so far as to say that 'men on strike are men out of work. They're disagreeable, not easy to get on with' …. We are reminded, after all, when other domestic problems arise, that marriage is a partnership.

However, a prize-winning letter some months later from Mrs S. D., Dublin 14, attacked strikes for the inconvenience they caused to women as consumers and asked 'Who is going to start a campaign to improve the hours and conditions of those who work hardest of all, the housewives?' This view of bread-and-butter issues as the only ones that should be of political relevance to housewives would have been supported by Mrs R. McG., Wexford, who commented early in 1969 on the need to have a Minister for Housekeeping, a woman who had reared a large family on a wage of not more than £10 a week and spent some time on unemployment or sickness benefits. This was a common theme in women's magazines on both sides of the Irish Sea.[9]

Women on the land

All magazines had and have an urban, even metropolitan bias; an extreme example of this was an article by Berenice Russell in *Young Woman* in 1967 entitled 'Country Girls – do we want them in Dublin?' *Woman's Life*, as we have seen, did its best to include farm women from time to time, but they were firmly established readers of *Woman's Way*. 'Stay-at-Home', Athy, Co Kildare, in 1965 was what the census called an 'assisting relative in agriculture' and one of a dying breed. She was twenty-one years old 'and could not be happier than I am, living and working on the family farm'. She was also a member of the ICA and Macra na Feirme. 'Farmer's Wife', Kilkenny, noted in January 1966 that there were 'no letters from farmers on your page' and gave 'city readers a run-down of a woman's work around the farm'. Her letter – which had not been framed as a complaint or anything like it – provoked a sour response from two urban readers, Y. Kelly, Dublin, and regular Cork letter-writer Sheila O'Farrell; farm women had it easy, they believed. But this hostility did not stop farm women from using the letters page to talk to each other. 'Flabbergasted', west west Cork (*sic*), in 1967, told of the questions she was asked by a young farmer on a first date: her age, occupation and pay, her cooking ability and whether she would object to working out of doors, whether she dyed her hair or shaved her legs, whether her family would be classed as 'respectable', the cause of her mother's early death and, significantly, whether she could keep on her job after she got married. J. R., Dublin 6 (probably the 'flatland' of Rathmines, Rathgar or Ranelagh – she was from a farming background), told of her experience of 'doing a line' (going steady) at home with a young farmer who 'coolly informed me that the wife he chose must be nice-looking, have a good personality and a dowry, and agree to live with his parents'. She hated criticizing farming people but had to tell readers of another young farmer's question on a date: 'Is your position in Dublin good enough to save for a dowry?' A week later C. L. C., Co Limerick, told of how, on a first date with a young farmer, she was asked directly what her father did for a living and if he had any land, and what each of her brothers and sisters did for a living: 'He was 19 and I am 16.' Later that summer M. M. D., Rathcoole, Co Dublin, deplored such snobbery; her father, a farmer's son, had married a labourer's daughter 'and we had a wonderful mother'. Criticism of farmers as mercenary caused 'Thirty-acre Happiness' (the editors asked him to send on his address) to put pen to paper; he had married a 'working-class' city girl who had no dowry:

> We have a family of 8 and after 18 years are still very happy and still have no money in the bank but children, health and happiness are better than wealth … not all farmers are the same.

Mrs K., Midleton, in big-farming east Cork, was one of the few dissenting voices when she pointed out that a farmer had to be careful choosing a wife because she was part of the business. M. B., Co Longford, complained that there were nine bachelor farmers, all comfortably off, in her townland. These men may have missed their chances in the 1940s or 1950s, when their potential spouses emigrated to Britain or migrated to towns for work, but some authorities in the 1950s and 1960s believed that they had dodged marriage deliberately because they were 'selfish'. 'Hurry Hurry Hurry', Cloyne, Co Cork, did not agree:

> The bachelors are not to blame
> It is the dame
> Who is not game
> To do the same
> As mother did before her.

M. G., Co Roscommon, in the same year was not amused but 'angry and perturbed when I hear young women complaining about the boredom and slavery of life on the land'. Their mothers and grandmothers, she pointed out, did not have water and electricity, and they were happy. But three years later Mrs M. T., Co Mayo, gave sober background evidence for the flippant Cloyne verse: Knock Marriage Bureau was finding that farmers' daughters were refusing to marry farmers because they did not want the hard lives their mothers had. A farmer's wife herself, she wanted to assure single women that life had changed and improved, with modern houses, electricity, water and cars, and 'Nobody makes a better or truer husband than a hard-working farmer.' But Mrs T. M., Dublin 4, won a prize in 1968 for asking why the ICA was not training women in public life. The magazine's approval for this badly informed comment – the ICA, right through the 1950s and 1960s, prioritized teaching women how to conduct meetings and speak in public – highlights the magazine's lack of knowledge of rural organizations.[10] (Would *Woman's Life*, in the previous decade, ever have made such a fundamental mistake?) Still, *Woman's Way* gave farm women a forum and showed that they were articulate, opinionated and by no means all the same.

Pregnancy, birth and childcare

Given the large families of the period, childbirth, infant care and feeding and childcare (other than education) did not feature as often as might be imagined. The previous decade had seen great changes in the place of birth: a third of all babies in Ireland were born at home in 1955, and this fell to just over a fifth (20.3 per cent) in 1961 and continued to fall. All the more striking, then, that an exchange of letters to *Woman's Way* showed a preference for having babies at home. Mrs R. N. Scully, Dublin 9, wrote in to say in 1966 that she had had her first two babies in hospital and her third at home, 'and I can state that I got far more rest at home, even though I had only my not-very-domesticated husband to look after me'. Mrs E. R., Waterford, wrote in to tell of her experience three years before in the maternity ward of a large hospital with her first baby; left alone in labour from 10.00 pm until 'the baby was nearly born at 8 am', she was 'abused' when she asked for gas 'and the few times I rang the bell caused another lecture'. 'Once-bitten-not-twice-shy', Dublin, described the twenty-eight hours she spent in labour in a maternity hospital, as 'the most harrowing experience of my life', but nursing homes were expensive and home births risky, so what could she do? Mrs Teresa Walker, Dublin, in 1969, called for some kind of maternity home help; she had given birth to three babies at home and would have loved someone to come in even just for the day after to help with the housework, instead of 'hopping back into bed when the doctor or midwife's car was heard approaching'.

Infant feeding was never discussed in the letters page. The 1950s and 1960s were the decades when most Irish mothers switched definitively to bottle-feeding, and the absence of any discussion of this change suggests that it was entirely uncontroversial. Apart from the comical 'Things They Say', children's doings were no great novelty to readers, who had enough of them at home; child-rearing (as opposed to vocationally orientated education and training) was rarely discussed, and E. H., Bray, Co Wicklow, probably spoke for many people when she commented in 1967 that parents who could talk only about their children were boring.[11]

Single women and widows

A light-hearted debate about what to call single women appeared in the letters page during 1963–4. Miss Mary Howard, Navan Rd, Dublin, who did not like being called a 'spinster or bachelor girl', wondered when 'the experts' would coin a new term. 'Unclaimed Treasure', again from Dublin city, agreed that spinster was 'corny', old maid 'obsolete' and bachelor girl 'silly' and suggested the name 'unclaimed treasure' for herself: 'Only the mugs are taken down for use: the best china is left on the shelf!' Louise Dennis, Co Wexford, however, believed that women stayed single because there was nobody 'good enough for them', reflecting a common belief in Ireland in the 1950s and early 1960s that the single state was eagerly embraced by people too comfortable in their standard of living to take on the sacrifices of married life. But as ideals and aspirations of the married state evolved to become more companionate and romantic, those staying single were coming to be seen more as failures than as opters-out. A sign of the changing values was Mrs Sheila O'Farrell's letter in 1969, which asserted that single women 'are not freaks, but wonderful women who make the world a better place to live in'. Such a patronizing 'defence' or explanation would not have been necessary ten, or even five, years before. It was brave of M. R., Waterford, to take issue with married women who complained about undemonstrative but otherwise good husbands:

> If I and many more single women like me had good, kind and considerate husbands we'd be down on our knees thanking God ... what are boxes of chocolates compared with the happiness and security (and I don't mean financial) of a good, decent if inarticulate man?

But another Waterford woman, N. B., was more cynical. Reacting with scorn to a *Late Late Show* participant who claimed that Irish girls could not talk on any serious subject, she asserted that if an average Irishman heard a girl converse on anything other than the price of lipstick 'he takes off so fast that even Arkle couldn't catch up with him'. (Arkle was a world-famous Irish racehorse.) N. B. was 'planted firmly on the shelf and likely to stay here' because she was not afraid to express her opinions, but if she had her time over, 'I'd act the dumb cluck with the best of them', and she knew one or two highly intelligent girls 'who worked this stunt with great success'. Her comments reflect some single women's belief, first, that underhand wiles were necessary to catch a husband, and second, that such strategies were beneath their dignity.[12]

Resistance to the idea that husbands were to be caught, like fish, flared up in response to one letter in 1968. Mrs B. MacC., Co Leitrim, wrote in to advise mothers not to cheapen their daughters by 'throw[ing] them on the rubbish heap, namely the dancehall'. Her four daughters had never 'gone dancing', but she had 'placed them in good positions'. Two daughters were doctors and had married doctors, one was a bank clerk and married a bank official and the air hostess (of course) married a pilot. Four indignant replies were printed. Mrs Miriam Luby, Co Dublin, reacted strongly to the idea that mothers 'sent' their daughters out to 'look for' husbands: 'The only place my mother ever "sent" me was to school.' Married with six children, she had met her husband at a dance. M. G., Dublin 2, wondered how any woman whose daughters did not go dancing could possibly know what went on in dancehalls; A. O'G., Carrick-on-Suir, first met her good, steady boyfriend at a dance; and Five Foxtrotters, Dublin 7, protested at the 'narrow-mindedness' of Mrs B. MacC., arguing that three of them were engaged and two 'doing steady lines' with 'well-educated' men they had met at dances.

This reader reaction was not just an objection to anti-dancehall snobbery, but a very modern appeal for some element of chance in courtship. Mrs B. MacC might have been modern in her insistence on girls' education, but in advocating the strategic placement of daughters for the securing of husbands she was adhering to older ideas about the 'good match'.[13]

An article on widows in 1968 prompted Mrs Rhona Williams to comment that *Woman's Way* was the only publication to bring the plight of the widow to the notice of the general public: 'Wake up, Irish widows … write to Mr Flanagan [Minister for Social Welfare Oliver J. Flanagan] and ask if he could feed a 15-year-old on 8s. a week.' Mrs M. H., Dun Laoghaire, drew readers' attention the following year to her mother, widowed with eight children aged four to twelve, who had educated them all to Leaving Certificate standard. Earlier, H. C., Co Mayo, praised her mother who reared six children, having been widowed when the eldest was eleven and the youngest only a few months old:

> Now we realize how wonderful she was. She seldom went any place except to Mass on Sundays but now she can go places and is happy. Women with their husbands should be happy and thankful.[14]

But were they?

Marriage and husband–wife relationships

Throughout the decade the general tone on marriage and courtship was light-hearted. 'A Longford Lady' wrote in 1963 to tell of a man she knew who picked his wife by the way she peeled vegetables (presumably not wasting anything); Mr J. McA., Co Dublin, fell in love when he saw his future wife sewing buttons on a shirt. The husband of F. S., Waterford, in 1965 proposed to her after he met her mother: 'He reasoned that with such a wonderful mother, I would surely make a good wife and mother myself.' There were sentimental moments: 'Happy as Larry', Co Kilkenny, wondered about one of the magazine's articles about loneliness in marriage – she had never experienced it; Mrs M. E., Dun Laoghaire, opined that the richest woman was the one with love and affection from husband and children; while Mrs B. M., Monkstown, Co Cork, agreed, pointing out that grandchildren added 'compound interest'. Other readers were more specific: the husband of Mrs B. Darcy, Leeson Park, Dublin, was always giving her 'little surprises'. 'Five Years Married', Co Cork, always polished her husband's shoes and got him his breakfast, but when he came home in the evening he helped her 'to make the supper and wash up'. Some notes of scepticism were sounded; Mrs A. B., Kilrush, wondered if 'Five Years Married' would still be saying 'she isn't a doormat' after another five years. Married for thirteen years with six children, this correspondent always had breakfast brought to her in bed, and her husband always helped with the children too. But Mrs D. M., Castleknock, Dublin, believed that wives should not be brought tea in bed because, unlike their husbands, they could have tea at several times during the day. Given the variety of opinion on this, it is hard to know whether Mrs M. T. B., Longford, was complaining or boasting when she wrote that she was married ten years and had never got a cup of tea in bed in the morning. J. W., Kilkenny, however, heartily agreed with one of the columnists that women should be 'allowed' to keep the change out of the housekeeping money – 'it is time Irish wives copped themselves on and began to be heard'. This was about as serious as it got, and Mrs P. T., Drogheda, in 1969, struck a discordant note when she referred to a catchphrase from the popular quiz show *Quicksilver*:

> Everywhere men are throwing cold water on any project that their wives try to undertake. 'Get down', they say. Perhaps one man in a hundred encourages his wife, and then you see a successful woman.

This was unusual and, significantly, was near the beginning of a new decade that would see far more public attention paid to women's unequal status in marriage. The recommendation by K. M., Dublin, late in 1969 that 'wifely subjugation' be left out of the marriage ceremony was also timely.[15]

Conclusion

The women who wrote to *Woman's Way* on women's status often disagreed strongly and confidently with the magazine and with each other. People in favour of change are probably more likely than others to write letters to the press, but the number of good and well-argued letters against, for example, contraception and in favour of the Catholic Church's authority on this and other matters indicates an ownership of the magazine by a wide range of women, not just those who were committed to change. The nuances of agreement and disagreement about certain issues show a readership that was imaginative, intelligent and independent-minded, albeit within certain limits. And rural women had come in from the cold to talk with each other, making their voices heard across the protests of some of their urban counterparts.

But it is, of course, impossible to know on what basis letters were selected, or rejected, for publication. Caroline Mitchell, as a Protestant, was probably super-conscious of reflecting the opinions of the faith of the majority, in the letters page as well as in the editorial content. Nonetheless neither she nor her correspondents (Catholic or Protestant, it seems) were shy about criticizing the teaching of the Catholic Church on certain issues. It is striking, therefore, that there were no letters at all in the 1960s about the lack of divorce legislation and few, if any, about marriage breakdown. Commentators in the succeeding decades would often talk about 'divorce, contraception and abortion' as if in ascending order of gravity, but while *Woman's Way* letter-writers expressed themselves freely in favour of contraception, not one advocated divorce. Indeed, it was hardly mentioned at all, and when Mrs H., Dublin 9, expressed dismay at the prospect of it ever being introduced, she may have been responding to Monica McEnroy's very negative article on it some months earlier. Abortion was beyond the pale – 'Britain's Bloody Mistake' was what McEnroy called it in a feature-length article in 1969 – but she linked recourse to abortion directly to lack of access to, or information about, birth control.[16]

Moreover, while, as we have seen above, sex education was welcomed by most correspondents, and unmarried mothers more pitied than censured, there was never any questioning of the authority of the Catholic religious orders who ran mother-and-baby homes. Neither was there any suggestion that the unmarried mother and her child be welcomed into the community. In 1968, 'Irish Unmarried Mother' wrote (in response to an article in the magazine about Irish unmarried mothers going to England), pleading with Irish girls to stay and have their babies in Ireland. She praised Sean Ross Abbey, Roscrea, Co Tipperary, one of the mother-and-baby homes run by religious orders: the nuns were 'helpful, friendly and modern', and the housework was light. She even asked that her prize money be sent to Sean Ross if the letter was published. Memories of Sean Ross that have appeared in recent years, most notably the book and film about Philomena Lee, are far more negative. Were negative letters about mother-and-baby homes written to *Woman's Way* and not published, or would Irish unmarried mothers themselves have dared to challenge the authority of those who 'helped' them at this time? An article about unmarried motherhood in the rather more challenging (and short-lived) *Young Woman* magazine in 1967 praised St Patrick's Mother-and-Baby Home in Cabra, Dublin, which it had inspected, and dismissed the common belief that you had to 'give two years to the nuns' – mothers could leave after six weeks. Two women – one who gave up her baby for adoption, another who kept hers – described the nuns as kind and humane and supportive in both cases; another article some weeks later, also very sympathetic to unmarried mothers, quoted an unmarried mother who described the nuns in the same home as 'kindness itself'. Likewise, the very modern and taboo-breaking Monica McEnroy in 1967 suggested that there was no need for pregnant unmarried Irish mothers to go to England when mother-and-baby homes in Ireland were such a great improvement on the notorious county homes, the sight of which 'kept many a wayward girl on the straight and narrow'.[17] Definitions of kindness can change from generation to generation, and what is accepted as normal in one era can be viewed with horror when it is remembered. What should be noted, however, is that women's magazines and their readers were fully aware of mother-and-baby homes and that no voice of either journalist or reader was lifted against them.

Another noteworthy aspect of the discussion on women's status is that male correspondents' views were only challenged when they trod on particular ground. Their criticism of women's housekeeping skills aroused a storm of protest. P. F., Athlone, responded indignantly to a male correspondent who suggested that modern women were lazy: 'There is no such thing as a shorter working day for women. It is a man's world.' Harry Howard, who suggested in 1967 that babies would be healthier if more women baked their own bread, provoked two angry responses, one very eloquent from S. P. F., Castleblayney:

> Instead of writing that letter he should have been baking a cake of bread, throwing a bucket of bran in it and it might have helped his digestion.

However, when two male correspondents (cranky Corkman Noel P. Collins and Jim Trahy of Swords, Co Dublin) wrote in, in 1964 and 1966, respectively, to argue that women's place was in the home and to urge women to 'cut out all this talk of equality', no female correspondent took issue with them.[18] (Would they have, in later years? No man wrote in like this, so it is difficult to say.) And as we have seen in this chapter, there was little enough interest expressed in politics, compared to other issues, in this magazine's letters page. It should be pointed out that the British women's magazines looked at, for half of 1958 and for the full year 1966, had very few letters on political matters either, and they had a much smaller proportion of letters on women's status generally than *Woman's Way*. There was no readers' letters page in *Woman's Life*, so letters to *Woman's Realm* from July to December 1958, as well as letters to *Woman's Own* in 1966, will be looked at for comparison here (see Tables 4.1 and 4.2).

Table 4.1 Letters to *Woman's Realm*, July–December 1958

Subject	Number	Percentage of all letters
Handy Hints/Why Don't They/ Things They Say	105	40
Miscellaneous	79	30
Family/Friends (Praise)	60	23
Houses/Furniture	19	7
Total	262	100

Table 4.2 Letters to *Woman's Own*, January–December 1966

Subject	Number	Percentage of all letters
Miscellaneous	297	43.7
Hints/Things They Say/Why Don't They	172	25.4
Marriage, Extended Family	87	12.9
Paid Work NOT Women's Status	42	6
Community, Neighbours	40	5.9
Women's Status	23	3.4
Unmarried Mothers/Adoption	18	2.7
Total Letters*	679	100

*Missed December 24, last issue of year.
 Women's status includes the work versus home debate for married women, and women's status as
 housewives, and women and politics.

There were far more female local and national politicians in Britain than there were in Ireland, and a much higher proportion of single and married women in the workforce there too, but one would think from reading the letters pages of *Woman's Realm* during 1958–60, or *Woman's Own* in 1966, that all married British women were engaged in domesticity and all single women aspiring to it. One can understand, even from reading the letters pages of only these two magazines, how Marjorie Ferguson concluded that women's magazine discourse did not favour married women working outside the home.[19] Table 4.2 looks at letters to *Woman's Own* for 1966.

But the message that working for wages is somehow of secondary importance in women's interests is not implicit or explicit either in the editorial content or in the letters page (or indeed in the problem page) of *Woman's Way* in the 1960s. Perhaps because more married women in Britain than in Ireland had the option of going out to work, were those British women who bought women's magazines more likely to have chosen to stay at home (or to aspire to stay at home after marriage) and therefore to be more domestic in their interests? Women in Ireland, at every social level, did not have the same opportunities, and *Woman's Way* letters page was one of the few public forums they had for expressing themselves on issues that concerned women. Rural and urban, middle-class and working-class, farming and non-farming, married and single, young and old, Catholic and Protestant, from the four provinces of the Republic and occasionally from Northern Ireland, they made full use of it.

'He Didn't Seem At All Pleased As I Was Leaving The Car': *Woman's Way* Problems 1: Sex Education and Birth Control

Introduction

From April 1963 to December 1969, there were approximately 1,186 problems written in to *Woman's Way*. All the caveats and cautions already mentioned in the chapters on problems in *Woman's Life* apply here: these problems cannot be taken as representative of the problems that Irish people – mainly girls and women – experienced in the 1960s. They can, however, be taken with all due caution as representative of the problems that some people felt they could articulate and write about to a magazine and that a magazine could publish.

The categories of problem are slightly different from those in *Woman's Life* in the previous decade. Courtship in its emotional (as opposed to sexual) aspects made up 31 per cent of all the problems; extended family (mainly parent/adult 'child', teenager or small child) generally made up 10.8 per cent; work and education constituted 6.7 per cent; and miscellaneous accounted for 13.6 per cent. Marital conflict made up only 6.3 per cent of all the problems written in, but queries for information about sex, pregnancy and birth control – a category almost completely absent from the 1950s – made up the largest category of all, just slightly bigger than that of courtship, at 31.5 per cent of all problems published (see Table 5.1).

The problems were answered for the first few months by Maura Laverty and from the end of October by Angela Macnamara. Maura Laverty (1907–66) was a well-known novelist, broadcaster, cookery writer, journalist, playwright and TV scriptwriter. Angela Macnamara (1931–), who took over from Laverty in late 1963, had written a number of articles on family themes for the very popular Jesuit periodical the *Irish Messenger* between 1960 and 1961, was a sought-after public speaker on family issues and answered problems in the *Sunday Press*, as well, from 1963 to 1980. When the magazine went through a brief period when

Table 5.1 Problems in *Woman's Way*, 1963–9

Subject	Number	Percentage of all problems
Sex Educ/Info	374	31.5
Courtship (not Sex)	367	30.9
Miscellaneous	162	13.8
Extended Family/Parent-child	128	10.8
Work/Education	80	6.7
Marital Conflict	75	6.3
Total Problems*	1,186	100

*About three issues were missing over the six years and eight months from April 1963 to December 1969, inclusive.

every second issue was edited in Belfast, from 21 October 1966 ('Hello Ulster and Welcome') to early 1967, the problems in the Belfast issue were answered by Sylvia Grace, who gave roughly similar advice to that of Angela Macnamara.[1]

There were other advice columns in the magazine too, which could dispense counsel at variance to that given by Angela Macnamara. For example, Macnamara dissuaded a correspondent from marrying her first cousin while Your Health could see nothing wrong with it, unless there was a hereditary illness.[2] (The marriage of first cousins was legal but was not allowed by the Catholic Church without a special dispensation.)

Sex, pregnancy and birth control

Macnamara never refused to answer a request for information. In her answer to a question from a fourteen-year-old who wanted to know what venereal disease was, for example, she deplored the fact that the girl's mother had turned off the television when it was being discussed. She was trying to avoid the absurd ignorance expressed by one correspondent in 1968: 'I am going to America and want an answer to this question. Can a girl get pregnant love-making in a car?' When asked by one problem if it was possible to get pregnant from 'heavy kissing and hugging', Macnamara's usual mild manner left her:

> Letters like this make me wonder what parents and schoolteachers are doing about sex instruction. No girl over 13 years of age should have to ask such questions.

Another girl, also in 1967, wanted to know if 'courting' would make her pregnant – having spent '6 years in a convent' she knew little about 'dating boys'. Macnamara recommended a book but described her ignorance as 'scandalous' though not her fault. 'Four girls aged 13–14' who wrote, in the same year, wondering if they could become pregnant by talking to boys provoked the same reaction. A mother who would not tell a sixteen-year-old daughter the 'facts of life' was strongly criticized in 1968. Later the same year, parents wondered if telling a nine-year-old boy about sex and babies would 'destroy his innocence'; Macnamara retorted that ignorance and innocence were not the same thing, and she reiterated this in response to a number of similar queries. Asked in 1969 what she thought of children habitually seeing their parents nude ('as in the recent film *Helga*'), Macnamara responded that it did not necessarily do any good but did not much harm either and advised that parents practise 'reasonable modesty while showing no shame or shock if caught unawares in his or her birthday suit'.

In detail and without any obfuscation, Macnamara answered queries such as what is the hymen, what is an embryo, what is a miscarriage, what are French letters ('This is a name given to a device which should not be used'), what is French kissing, what is an abortion. Two 'secondary school students who know nearly all the facts of life', almost incredibly, did not know what breast feeding was. Was it possible to get pregnant without having sex (no), to get pregnant the first time one had sex (yes), to have sex without knowing it (probably not). Asked if tampons, 'immodest touching' or 'passionate kissing' took a girl's virginity, she responded that only having sexual intercourse could do this. For those entirely ignorant about sex and reproduction, she recommended books, usually written from a Catholic standpoint.[3]

However, almost as numerous as the simple requests for information were the questions about whether something was wrong or not. These could also have been requests for information from people who did not know how to ask about sex apart from the context of morality, and there is no guarantee that those who wrote in followed the advice given. One writer objected very articulately and confidently (in 1965) to Macnamara's response to a previous problem in which she had stated that bikinis were immoral:

> As one of the 'bikini set' I hotly resent your implication that I am immoral and immodest. You should avoid sweeping generalizations. I am 20 and my sex life is beyond reproach. I never indulge in petting and prolonged kissing. Every man I have dated has respected me.

Macnamara's response that the bikini-wearer was causing men to sin in their minds probably made no difference whatsoever to the reader's preferences in swimwear.

As far as kissing and what was popularly called 'courting' were concerned, Macnamara was firm – anything other than a quick kiss on the cheek or lips was dangerous. She wrote this in 1964 and held the line firmly throughout the rest of the decade. In 1965, for example,

> A boy should not kiss a girl to arouse his own passion. If he kisses her just to show affection, finds he is aroused but still continues, he is again wrong.

A repentant correspondent wrote in to tell of how she and her boyfriend had nearly died in a motorcycle accident; she linked this to the 'passionate love-making' that they had engaged in previously. Macnamara was sympathetic and solicitous but, deserting her usual rationality by implying that there was cause and effect between the two incidents, commented that they had 'learned the hard way'.

Like all agony aunts of her time everywhere, Macnamara believed that it was up to the girl or woman to exercise control on dates. A girl who complained that boys were only interested in 'sex experience' was told:

> If many more girls refused to be guinea pigs for teenage boys who want to play at being in love, the boys might change their tune. So many girls have not the character to refuse these boys.

A man complained about girls putting their heads on his shoulder in the cinema and leaning up against him 'most provocatively'; in response, Macnamara exhorted girls to be more careful with their behaviour on dates. Three years later, a young man of twenty who was 'sick' of girls 'seducing men by wearing mini-miniskirts' was evidence, Macnamara commented, that 'there are good men left, but they depend on the help they get from the girls to keep on the right road'. A man who wrote in the same year complaining about girls who encouraged necking and kissing and were too forward was told: 'Fellows are as bad, girls tell me.' But she had a harsh response for a boy of seventeen who was finding it hard to meet 'nice' girls because they all let him go too far, and he was 'pretty hard to tempt'. Macnamara told him: 'Perhaps they don't date you again because you try to tempt them and then sit back and criticise them.' Less self-righteous and more idealistic was the 27-year-old bachelor who told Angela Macnamara that most 'boys' only wanted to 'shift' (i.e. to get to a situation where they can kiss) and applauded her insistence on sex education.[4]

The boyfriend pressurizing the girlfriend to go further than she wanted was inevitably the most common complaint, and Macnamara gave the standard advice that a boy who went beyond what a girl permitted had 'little respect' for her; this theme was returned to again and again. But the girl whose boyfriend told her he had got another girl into trouble but would not do the same to her because he 'respected' her was advised to drop him for his 'abuse' of the other girl; respect was not just for those who 'deserved' or 'earned' it but for all women. A girl whose medical student boyfriend threatened to break off if she did not 'go further' and who did not want to lose him because she herself had not proceeded beyond the Intermediate Certificate examination was advised to give him up and, if she felt inferior, to read more books and join clubs and meet people. This was good advice, because she could have ended up like the exploited seventeen-year-old whose thirty-year-old doctor boyfriend never took her out but brought her in his car to 'lonely places' where they behaved 'immodestly'. He said he loved her, but Macnamara (realistically enough) told her that he probably did not. The escalation of this kind of letter over the decade is a sign of the greater freedoms being experienced by young people living and working away from home or able, in cars, to escape supervision. The worried eighteen-year-old in 1967 whose 21-year-old boyfriend had bought a car and 'now we've had 4 affairs [*sic*]' made the connection explicitly. The girl in the bedsitter who wondered if she should ask a boy who walked her home to come up for a cup of tea was advised to make some excuse not to do so until she knew and trusted him (and herself) better. The fifteen-year-old working far from home (perhaps in a hotel, like the Sligo girl who wrote the letter about low pay), who had made love in a car and had missed a period, was an example of the two risk factors coming together – allied with the one of extreme youth and vulnerability. A country girl alone in the city and pregnant was given advice but consoled:

> Being lonely in a city I am sure it is hard to resist the affection and friendship a boy might offer you. As you say, it is very easy for an uninstructed girl to let things get out of control.

Sometimes she could be caustic; a pregnant eighteen-year-old who had been going out with a 33-year-old who gave her expensive gifts and was 'very kind' was told: 'I hope he will continue to be "very kind" to you after this event which is no kindness to anyone.' But at least there was the prospect of marriage. In a worse quandary was the nineteen-year-old who had not known her 26-year-old boyfriend was married, and she was referred to the Catholic Protection and Rescue Society. Referred to the same organization was the sixteen-year-old who was pregnant by a forty-year-old married father of four who had offered to leave them and bring her to England, and an eighteen-year-old made pregnant by a married thirty-year-old who had got two other girls 'into trouble'. Women made pregnant by married men featured much more often than those pregnant by single men, and one can only conjecture that in many of the latter situations marriage ensued, and there was no 'problem'. But anticipating the wedding was not taken lightly by either young couples or their parents. A mother wrote in that her twenty-year-old daughter, engaged to a 'very good boy', was already pregnant by him. She and her husband were not only disappointed and shocked but anxious to keep this from their other daughters. Macnamara was very sympathetic and asked this correspondent if she had left the couple alone too much, or tolerated too long an engagement, and although she concluded her response by hoping the marriage would be a happy one, it is evident that she understood and shared this mother's dismay.[5]

The extreme youth of some sexually active or exploited girls does not seem to have aroused alarm in itself; a fifteen-year-old who had had sex with a 22-year-old in 1966 was told she had sinned against the law of God. Another fifteen-year-old who had been kissed by a 27-year-old was urged to get some sex education, but no comment was made on the twelve-year age gap and extreme youth of the girl. A fourteen-year-old who had had a 'bad experience' with a married man at the age of eleven was implored not to let this put her off men and advised not to dwell on it. A girl of unspecified age whose parents' friend kissed her and said he was in love with her, after which his wife spread rumours about her, was advised to stop 'weaving romantic dreams' and to get to know boys of her own age. The fifteen-year-old in 1968 whose father's friend kissed her and 'made love to her' (she found it hard to resist him) was asked 'Have you no pride?', though Macnamara also urged her to tell her parents or the police: 'Show this man you are not a weak child to be made use of so cruelly.' Another girl whose parents' friend came to the house every night and touched her 'immodestly' (her mother was in bed sick, her father working) was told to tell her parents. Some girls' living situations rendered them virtually defenceless in the face of both attention and abuse. The sad story, in 1969, of an exploited young waitress in a country town deserves to be quoted in full:

> I work in a café in a village and some of the local men come in regularly for meals. One of them left me home a few nights and two months ago he courted me. After that experience I wouldn't like to go with him again. We did not have intercourse but as a result of what he did I am wondering if I am still a virgin. …

I smoke very heavily and I am 17. Also I am 5'3" and weigh 10st 7 lb. Am I too heavy? This man is getting married in September so he doesn't care about me!

Macnamara advised her to look after her health and to see a doctor but commented rather unsympathetically: 'Well, you have learned not to allow yourself to be used to satisfy a man's sexual desires.' Surely this girl (who seems to have been alone in the world) should have been advised to try to get some training or mentoring or at least to move out of the village before she was abused by some of the other men? A sixteen-year-old farmer's daughter told of how working in a hotel had made her despise married men, one of whom had offered her 'a roll of notes if I would do wrong with him', and others who 'kept after her'. Less vulnerable, though slightly older, was the nineteen-year-old in a bedsitter in Dublin who had let the fifty-year-old landlord make love to her because she was 'lonely and depressed'. She wanted to finish it and move out but he threatened to tell her mother. Macnamara told her to report him to the police for intimidation, and added, 'Other girls in similar situations please note', which suggests that the situation was not unheard of.[6]

The correspondent who asked whether it was possible to get pregnant from having sex with a member of one's own family was advised that it was and told that incest was 'a grave matter, morally and socially'. A month later (sometimes a letter on a particular topic sparked another one), when another asked if it was wrong to have sex with a 'near-relation', Macnamara replied briskly that it was wrong to have sex with anybody other than one's spouse.[7] Child victims of intra-family sexual abuse, we now know, were often unaware that what was being done to them was unlawful and wrong as well as unpleasant and cruel. Maybe these correspondents were referring to brother–sister relationships, and one or other party needed Macnamara's authority to put a stop to it. We will never know.

Although firmly opposed to extra-marital sex, Macnamara did not believe that women were tainted for life by sexual transgression. She assured several correspondents that they were under no obligation to tell boyfriends or fiancés if they (the women) were not virgins, and two correspondents who wanted to enter the religious life were assured that lack of virginity was no impediment to doing so, once the sin (if sin it was – in one case virginity had been taken by abuse at an early age) had been confessed and forgiven. A correspondent whose 'pal' was getting engaged to 'a most attractive girl' who had 'things about her past' that the 'pal' did not know about, and who wondered if he (or she, it is not clear) should enlighten him, was told to say nothing unless s/he knew for certain that the friend's fiancée was actually already married to somebody else.[8] Women who had given babies up for adoption should probably tell fiancés/husbands about it, but were under no moral obligation to do so. One woman who was going out with a 'very decent boy' for four weeks wondered if she should tell him about having had a baby through being assaulted two years previously. (The assailant had been in the newspapers for assaulting another girl since, whereupon this girl's parents had 'forgiven' her.) Presumably the baby had been adopted. She was advised not to tell him yet, to let the relationship develop a little first and then, if he was any good, he would not let it affect them. A year later a girl whose boyfriend had dropped her when he found out she had had a baby was advised that he was not worth keeping, and a woman whose boyfriend dropped her because she had a seven-year-old illegitimate son was told she was better off without him – her son was her priority. Macnamara was quite sharp with a woman whose children were all 'exemplary' except for the eldest girl who had borne a baby at twenty-five, in England, with a man of another race 'and we would never have approved'. The baby had been adopted. Macnamara assured her that her oldest daughter was 'every bit as good' as the rest of the family and reminded her that 'inter-racial marriages between mature people can be very successful'; she hoped that the daughter had not given up her child on that account alone. Two married women, in 1967 and 1969, whose babies were not their husbands' and who were no longer involved with the biological fathers, were told that they were not morally obliged to tell their husbands about this. In all of this Macnamara was consistent with her religious beliefs, which held that there is redemption once a sin has been forgiven in confession and the sinner resolves to do right. It was probably for this reason that she scorned, in several responses to queries from readers, the popular belief that pregnant or non-virgin brides should not wear white. When challenged about this by a correspondent who said it was a 'mockery' for non-virgins or pregnant brides to wear white, she reproached the writer for such a 'holier than thou' attitude, observing that 'we are all sinners one way or another'.[9]

Emphasis on the need for self-control by young women rested on the assumption that women's sexual desires were quite strong. Feeling no sexual desire at all was, therefore, a problem too. The engaged woman who was not interested in the 'physical side' was advised to let her boyfriend know how she felt, to read up about it and to see a doctor and check if she was run down. Another woman who had gone out with two men neither of whom had 'aroused the slightest physical emotion' was also advised to talk to her doctor. The woman (and there was only one) who wrote in to say that she was strongly attracted to her own sex and could not tolerate the idea of a man, even though she got on well with men, was advised very sympathetically to get skilled medical advice 'to help you cope with this emotional difficulty'. Another woman who described herself as a 'carefree' thirty-year-old did not like men kissing her but wanted to get married and have children. She was told that faulty or inadequate sexual education was probably to blame for this, though she, like the other woman, was probably either lesbian or asexual.[10]

Lack of sexual desire in husbands or wives will be dealt with under the husband–wife section; birth control might seem to be something that would come into that category rather than into this one, specifically, but it pertains directly to sexual knowledge and the provision of information, so it will be discussed here.

Birth control

Although *Woman's Way* published articles supporting contraception and allowed free discussion of it in the letters page, the magazine's agony aunt was unequivocally opposed to artificial methods of birth control for married and, it need hardly be added, for single people. She held this line throughout the decade, modifying it somewhat in later life. However, she was even wary of recommending natural birth control. An engaged woman in 1966 who inquired about the safe period because she wanted to postpone childbearing to keep her job for at least a year after marriage was admonished:

> Since one of the primary purposes of marriage is to have children, it is not advised to use the safe period until such time as you are spacing the number in your family. I would advise you to approach your priest or clergyman. Having heard the full circumstances, he will be better able to judge it.

Spacing, rather than delaying, was what natural family planning was about. The following year, a couple with a similar query was told: 'The purpose of marriage is not merely to legalize lovemaking and to surround yourselves with comfort,' and was strongly advised to reconsider. Another couple with an identical question a few months later was urged: 'Do have a baby soon … it's what you married for, isn't it?' Before the year was out, however, Macnamara simply recommended a book on natural family planning to a couple intending to get married, and two years later a woman whose husband did not want children yet, and who asked if there was anything she 'could get in the chemist', was advised, without comment, to get personal advice on the fertile and infertile periods and the temperature method.[11] Perhaps the mention of the chemist (and the wider availability of the Pill on prescription for menstrual regulation) brought Macnamara to a belief that delaying a first baby by natural methods was the lesser of two evils.

Married couples who wanted to put off having another baby did not write very often into Macnamara's page, as she had no solution to offer, for example, to the married woman of twenty-eight with four children already who wrote in in 1967 that her husband just 'has to have intimacy' and that the safe period therefore did not work for her. However, another woman who wrote in around the same time for advice about planning only four children because she could not afford any more was asked how she knew she could only afford four. A woman married eight years who had just had her fifth baby and wanted to know if it was safe to have sex during menstruation was advised to get the full information about the infertile period: 'People say this doesn't work but that is because they haven't implemented it properly.' Rough instructions and recommended reading were given some time later to a woman with a 'large family' who did not want any more children. The question of birth control of any kind for unmarried people only came up once. A seventeen-year-old girl, pregnant by a man of forty-four she met at a party, wondered if it was too late to take the Pill. Macnamara blamed this girl's predicament on the contraception she had not used:

> A situation like this (and there are many) underlines the Pope's concern about the increasing disrespect that would be shown to women, if contraceptive devices were approved.

As in her responses to some other letters from under-eighteens quoted in this chapter, Macnamara did not express shock at the age difference, as such. It is true, as Dyhouse tells us, that girls, and not only in Ireland, were considered adult (in the sense of being marriageable) in their mid-teens in the 1950s and 1960s, but one wonders if the greater freedoms (living away from parental supervision) and rapidly changing social and occupational scene (more young women in male-dominated workplaces, for example, and more girls living away from their families) enabled some unscrupulous middle-aged Irishmen to prey on teenage girls in an unprecedented way.[12]

Conclusion

The seventeen-year-old referred to in the preceding section was rendered vulnerable by her ignorance about contraception and, probably, about sex too. Whatever her views on the former, Macnamara was determined to remedy ignorance about the latter, defying even a threat from one of the staff of Dublin's redoubtable Archbishop, John Charles MacQuaid. It is hard to believe, now, that Irish girls and women were really that ignorant about the mechanics of reproduction, but this seems to have been the case. One correspondent who did not think so, and queried the need for 'sex instruction' on the grounds that the previous generation had managed fine without it, was (sharply? wearily?) told that he or she 'should see the letters' Macnamara received.

But this agony aunt's insistence that women should know both what sex entailed and what it could lead to could be interpreted by her readers in ways she did not intend. One letter in 1967 was not so much a problem as a cry from the heart, from a young motherless woman:

> Please keep on advising parents to instruct their children so that teenagers who know nothing about marriage will not keep on getting married. I don't think men have any conscience about right or wrong before or after marriage – no matter how good their education. We are three girls none of whom has any inclination towards marriage. Our mother died in childbirth at the age of 44.

Macnamara's response deftly avoided engaging with these girls' central concern that sex could lead to pregnancy, which could occasionally be fatal:

> Girls sometimes have the idea that because men's sexual urge is much greater than that of women, that men are 'bad' in this respect. Girls must understand that this is the nature of a man. If they exercised control on dates and helped the men to control their strong sexual drive, the men would learn to be considerate and unselfish (as women must be too), both before and after marriage.

And sex, or lovemaking, was sometimes disappointing – even baffling, as in the case of one correspondent:

> I didn't get any pleasure. Did he get any pleasure? He didn't seem at all pleased when I was leaving the car. How do I tell this in Confession?

Anybody with a Catholic education would have known the vocabulary to tell a priest that she had committed 'impurity' or 'sinned against the sixth commandment'. The very incoherence of this 'problem' conveys the reader's incredulity – and perhaps exasperation – that an experience so mutually unsatisfactory could have broken any commandment or be in any way transgressive.

The British *Woman's Own* in 1966 did not have anything like the same volume of queries simply requesting information. Mary Grant, like Macnamara, insisted that boyfriends putting pressure of any kind – to have sex, to get engaged – were to be resisted and that mutual respect was vital. (For Clare Shepherd in the earlier British magazine examined, *Woman's Realm*, sex either in or outside marriage barely existed.) And, like Macnamara, the English 1960s agony aunt did not believe that a woman was obliged to tell a man about her sexual past. But, unlike Macnamara, Grant was equivocal towards the correspondent who asked if 'petting' (sexual behaviour short of intercourse) before marriage was wrong; this really was up to every couple to work out for themselves, she said. She advised another couple, however, who had a long engagement and did not want to 'get carried away', not to isolate sex from other aspects of the relationship and to expand their horizons and develop their interests. A British National Marriage Guidance Council leaflet in 1961 was advising engaged couples to kiss and touch without 'going all the way', to reinforce their intimacy.[13] When it came to married couples' requests for information, the British agony aunt had no objection to artificial methods of birth control. She dispensed addresses and book titles to those who asked for information, and her reply to a correspondent who wrote in to ask about the safe period began thus: 'Well, if you have an objection to the more reliable methods of birth control …'[14]

Paul Ryan has argued that Angela Macnamara's advice columns in the *Sunday Press*, while they upheld Catholic teaching on issues of sexual morality, provided vital information and sympathy to men and women, especially gay people, who were bewildered, troubled and confused. In *Woman's Way* she fulfilled this role for girls and women of all ages, in all situations. The idea that even knowing about sex was shameful had been picked up by a thirteen-year-old who felt guilty for knowing the facts of life without her mother having told her. She might have been afraid of her mother finding out, like the fourteen-year-old who wrote in some time later whose mother would not tell her anything and threatened to 'kill' her (punish her severely) if she got a book about it. Macnamara's strongly worded disapproval of both mothers would have been seen as abhorrent by many Irish people of her time. Those who wrote to her on sexual matters, however, were looking for moral guidance, even permission, as well as information and sometimes defiantly anticipating her response. 'I would like to know if you object to close dancing,' a correspondent asked with what must have been sarcasm in 1968 (Macnamara gave her usual response); earlier another reader who had 'got carried away' on a date and engaged in 'heavy petting' wrote in defiantly:

I think that in 1968 *we should be let* [i.e. allowed] indulge in more passionate love-making on dates. *You don't allow much.* [italics mine]

Macnamara's response that these were not her rules but God's probably had limited impact; many of her readers were making up their own rules. Engaged couples who wrote asking if they could have greater freedom to indulge in lovemaking short of sexual intercourse had obviously picked up this idea from their peers and may have disregarded her advice that they should be more careful than ever not to go too far. However, it is significant that they felt they could raise the matter at all. The fact that she was fairly relaxed about nudity, strongly in favour of sex education and usually against corporal punishment already placed Macnamara in opposition to many of the dominant values of the parent generation in Ireland. Even if dissenting and 'daring' letters were published mainly so that she could refute them authoritatively, the fact that they were written in the first place shows that she was not feared. 'At least you let us voice our opinions, thank you,' a young woman wrote in; that 'at least' is revealing. Angela Macnamara's refusal to allow girls and young women to go on believing that 'heavy petting' or 'necking' caused pregnancy meant that those who wrote in to, or read, her page were able to make their own decisions about sexual behaviour, based on information she either provided or recommended. A baby could not be conceived except through 'union' in the 'marriage act', she assured a reader in 1964 (in euphemisms that would soon be out of date), but 'grave sin' could be committed.[15] Whether they committed this 'grave sin' or not – or indeed, considered it to be grave – was left up to readers.

'And Then They Wonder Why Their Wives Are Cold': *Woman's Way* Problems 2: Courtship and Marriage

Courtship

As we have seen in Chapter 5, questions about sex, because they concerned respect, affection and, not least of all, attraction, shaded naturally into questions about courtship. But there were problems about relationships with boys and men that had nothing to do with sex, as such. Many young teenage girls were anxious to embark on courtship. 'I am 15 and would like to know how to go with a boy', ran a typical letter from a young hopeful in 1967; other teenagers wondered 'what to do' on a date and how to talk to a boy and how to kiss (not how much kissing was 'permitted' – Macnamara, however, soon told them). Quite common were letters from 'two girls' who were looking for boys, or were hoping particular boys would notice them, or were in love (unrequited) with two boys, or were hoping to break off with two boys without hurting their feelings, or who did not know what to 'do on a date' or who never got dances. Girls and boys under eighteen were constantly advised not to go steady but to make as many friends of the opposite sex as possible. There were also many of the mad about the boy/he does not know that I exist love problems, which had featured in *Woman's Life* and the British magazines also and were a staple of the teen magazine *Jackie*'s Cathy and Claire page and have been a feature of problem pages since they began. With these, Macnamara was both sympathetic and firm. A correspondent who asked if it was wrong to send a boy she loved cards without signing her name (helpfully adding that she knew all the facts of life) was advised that it was not wrong but was a little foolish, and elsewhere the agony aunt expressed shock that girls were telephoning boys they did not know and asking them out. When a correspondent criticized her in 1969 for her callous dismissal of young love, citing Romeo and Juliet, Macnamara gave the irresistible response that those two lovers were hardly an example of a happy outcome. Maura Laverty in her brief tenure as agony aunt in 1963 advised a nineteen-year-old, unsure about which boyfriend she loved most, that she obviously did not love either of them. Angela Macnamara was not quite as brutal. A very typical problem came from a 28-year-old woman who had 'two prospects' – a 29-year-old 'lovely fellow' in the city (where, presumably, she was working) and a 37-year-old businessman 'at home'. Beyond advising her not to marry without love, there was little that Macnamara – or indeed, anybody – could tell her.[1]

Readers could not be told what their own feelings were, but both Laverty and Macnamara, like Mrs Wyse before them, had no doubts about what constituted bad boyfriend behaviour. The boyfriend of two years who had never asked his girlfriend to meet his family should be dropped, as should another boyfriend who sulked, and a boyfriend who wanted to be free to meet other girls but who did not want the problem-writer to meet other boys. Boyfriends who drank were dead ends, and one nineteen-year-old in love with a 39-year-old who drank and hit her was strongly advised to listen to her parents' warnings and drop him immediately. A correspondent whose boyfriend of four years would marry her only on condition that she had a £500 dowry, did not want an engagement ring, could cook and housekeep on £5 a week including fancy dishes and did not smoke was advised to give him up immediately. But some kinds of immaturity could be challenged. A 'plain and rather fat' girl of nineteen whose twenty-year-old boyfriend was 'completely selfish' and never did anything she wanted to do was advised to go out on her own with her friends or join some club, to improve her confidence and to insist on her own way with her boyfriend, because 'a selfish marriage partner can make life utterly miserable'. At the other end of the spectrum, women rearing children outside marriage were as entitled as anybody else to be treated properly by boyfriends. Her current boyfriend drank and was often unpleasant, an unmarried mother rearing two children by two different fathers told Macnamara, but she needed someone to provide for her family. Macnamara told her strongly not to let anybody 'use and abuse' her and advised her to get a job (getting her mother to mind the children) so that she would not have to depend on a man. She told the unmarried mother of 'two coloured children' who was having an affair with a married man who threatened to kill her if she broke it off to stand up for herself and to go to the police. Women rearing children (especially multiple children) outside marriage were unusual in Ireland at this time, but they were not afraid to ask Angela Macnamara for help, and her advice to them held no tinge of judgement or condemnation.

Age difference, even on the man's side, was more inclined to cause objection to than in the previous decade. A nineteen-year-old engaged to a man twenty-three years older, who still had not introduced him to her parents, was advised that the fiancé was irresponsible to have allowed the situation to develop. A twenty-year-old whose 45-year-old boss had asked her out and then asked her to marry him, wanting a 'quick answer', was more or less advised not to. Another twenty-year-old whose parents were 'furious' because she had got engaged to a man of forty-four (he gave her many presents and had a car) was unsure of her own feelings; she was advised to break it off too. In contrast to the previous decade, the matter of the female older than the male came up only twice, with the small difference of three years in the early twenties. But some differences were more serious than others. A 25-year-old in love with a 47-year-old of a different religion, whose parents disapproved of the marriage for both of these reasons, was advised that religion rather than age was the more serious difference. Four years earlier a sixteen-year-old going out with a seventeen-year-old boy of a different faith, whose parents forbade it, was advised to break it off now, because the longer she left it the harder it would be:

> The different churches agree that mixed marriages are unwise, because they often cause a clash in fundamental ideals between husband and wife.

Macnamara told a widow of twenty-seven with three young children, who had met a non-Catholic aged thirty (with 'his own car'), that the failure rate was three times higher in mixed marriages. However, a young woman who wrote in asking if she should convert her Protestant boyfriend was told that he should only convert if he wanted to and not so that he could marry her. The question of Protestants converting to marry Catholics (and whether they converted or not, being obliged to rear their children as Catholics) was openly discussed by an alarmed Protestant population in the 1960s, and Macnamara would not have wanted to be seen to (or might genuinely not have wanted to) proselytize.[2]

Racial difference came up very rarely. We have seen already from one of her responses to the mother of an unmarried mother that Macnamara did not believe interracial marriage to be unacceptable in itself. Two girls (again, the hunting in pairs) in their late teens wrote in because their parents did not want them to get married – one because she was too young and the other because she was 'in love with a Negro'. Angela advised both girls, as she always advised teenagers thinking of marriage, to wait until they were twenty-one, but while she said that racial prejudice was wrong, she asked the girl who was in love with the 'Negro' if she was prepared to go and live in Africa. This was probably realistic, as most black people in Ireland in the early 1960s were African students or interns/trainees of some kind. A woman in love with a 'coloured boy' wondered if she should forewarn her parents before bringing him home to meet them; Macnamara said she should. Class difference did not surface very often. A woman worried that her manners would not be acceptable to her higher-class boyfriend's family was assured that there was as much 'ignorance and ill-breeding' among the wealthy as there was among those who were 'less fortunate'. A woman in a similar predicament who was afraid to bring her wealthy boyfriend home to meet her family because of 'the poor circumstances in which I was reared' was told that he would not be put off if their love was 'the real thing'. Another 'girl' (as she described herself) whose father was 'well-known and well-off' wondered if she should marry 'a man with a trade, house, and money' or another who was a labourer. Her parents said they would disown her if she married 'beneath' her. She was advised to marry the man she loved but, as she was well-off, to consider what it would be like not to have any money. Like all the other agony aunts, Angela Macnamara had little patience for those who looked down on other people, although she was gentle with the woman who now regretted rejecting a man she was 'desperately in love' with because of his social background, only to see him going out with her friend and getting on very well in life. A woman in her mid-thirties, who had met a 'nice man' and was trying to improve his speech and table manners ('He is quite willing but keeps slipping back'), was told tartly: 'He must be most humble to have accepted your efforts to improve him.'

A slightly different problem came from a woman of twenty-four, 'crazy about' a 'boy of 25' who was 'not all action like other boys', whose mother objected to him because he was not 'respectable'. Macnamara said that if her mother objected because the man was from 'a district known to be rough, then that's snobbery', and it should be discounted; but maybe, she suggested, the mother's objection was because the man was disreputable in other ways, for example drinking. (Perhaps, too, that was why he was not 'all action', i.e. constantly trying to get her to go further sexually.) A more bizarre problem needs to be quoted in full, in order for it to be understood:

> I am 19 and have been living with an aunt for the past 10 years. A local farmer of 40 is interested in me and my aunt wants me to marry him. She even encourages me to have an affair with him. She invites him to the house and then leaves us alone together. He hits me if I do not do as he wishes.

Macnamara's reaction to this story of coercion, and perhaps rape, was surprisingly mild; the girl was advised to leave her aunt's house immediately and to go somewhere; anywhere. But the violence was not addressed at all, and there was even an attempt to let the aunt off the hook: 'Perhaps you have given your aunt the impression that you like him.'[3]

This was unlike Macnamara, because, as we shall see below in the section on parent–extended family–child/adult offspring relationships, she usually took the young person's part. But first we must look at husband–wife relationships.

Husband–wife relationships

Angela Macnamara differed quite a lot from *Woman's Life's* Mrs Wyse, from *Woman's Realm's* Clare Shepherd and even from Maura Laverty in her first few months of answering problems for the magazine. But all three women who answered problems for *Woman's Way* – Laverty, Macnamara and, for a brief period, Sylvia Grace – sympathized with the over tired and over burdened woman of the house. Laverty told a correspondent in 1963:

> There is a malady from which many mothers suffer after about ten or twelve years of married life. Psychiatrists probably have a name for it. As a laywoman I am acquainted only with the symptoms. These include fatigue, irritability, regret that the honeymoon shine has been dimmed, discontent and lack of interest in the home of which, at one time, they were so proud. A Glasnevin reader offers a typical example of this malaise.

The Glasnevin (Dublin) reader – whose husband was 'unsympathetic' – did not even have a particularly large family, by the standards of the day: five children, though their ages were not stated, and the prospect of another five probably loomed large. Laverty recommended iron injections and two or three evenings of freedom every week when the husband would take over. Although it is tempting to see this 'problem' as akin to Betty Friedan's 'problem that has no name' – Laverty's description invites such an analogy – it certainly had a name, and that was exhaustion. (It is not beyond the bounds of possibility that Laverty had seen an American edition of Friedan's book, which had been published there the previous February.) All 1960s agony aunts, however, insisted upon women's right to have time to themselves. Another mother of five children, whose husband had insisted she give up all her work and hobbies when they got married, was suffering with her 'nerves'. Her husband, though very good with the children, never paid her a compliment or gave her a present and hated visitors and visiting. Laverty advised her to 'startle your husband out of his present apathy by having a straight talk with him' and to insist upon having at least one evening off a week with her friends: 'Every woman, no matter how much she loves her family, needs friends and outings.' However, when a woman wrote in who was trying to do something about over tiredness by getting her husband to help with the housework, mentioning that her neighbour's husband always did the evening meal wash-up, Laverty was appalled: 'Your neighbour is either unique or lazy and selfish.' She seemed to lose her temper completely with another woman who complained about a similar situation, commenting, 'There are women who are more to be pitied than the *bean a' tighe* who, however hard-worked, has compensations.'

But Laverty as agony aunt gave way to the far more sympathetic Angela Macnamara when the magazine was six months old, and the latter, much more modern, assured a fiancée appalled at the years of housework ahead of her that her husband would and should help 'which adds to the feeling of togetherness'. A woman working outside the home herself, whose husband expected everything laid on for him, was told to persuade him nicely to help, and another woman, also working, who ended up rushing around getting dinner was told to be sure to sit down when she came in 'and let him see how tired you are'. Macnamara insisted more than once that boys should help around the home, because 'spoilt sons become spoilt husbands'. The wife whose husband wanted detailed accounts of how she spent the housekeeping money was told to remind him of his marriage vows. Wives whose husbands would not go out with them or make friends were advised to go out themselves and make friends. One woman, new to an area, with six children ranging in age from eighteen months to thirteen years, had no friends, and the woman across the road seemed 'snobbish'. Macnamara advised her to give the woman across the road another chance and to join some club; her view that this woman's lack of friends was a real problem to be addressed would have been scorned by some of the older generation at this time.[4]

Early married life was expected to be difficult and even perplexing; Sylvia Grace told a bored young wife that she was suffering from 'bride's blues', and Macnamara gently reminded a 21-year-old, married three years with two young children in 1964, whose husband was no longer a charmer and who wished she was free again, that she would have to work to make a success of her marriage. There was very little that could be said to the woman who wanted more 'romance' in her marriage, but another woman married for five years with two children, whose husband called her 'Mammy' even when they were alone, elicited the following comment:

You are only one of hundreds of women who yearn for a little affection and tenderness from their menfolk. Men in this country are brought up to feel that to show tenderness is not masculine. ... Then they wonder why their wives are cold when it comes to marital intimacy.

This husband was not physically or verbally abusive, just unromantic, but Macnamara encouraged women to expect more than this. However, the 'coldness' of wives was a problem for some husbands, one of whom, sixteen years married, wrote that his wife only allowed him sex once a week when he insisted. Another was only allowed sex every three months or so. Macnamara could only advise these men to have sympathy and understanding and, if necessary, to see if there was a medical problem. More common, of course (as this was a women's magazine) were the letters from women who did not like sex. A woman with an 'undemonstrative husband' who only made love for his own satisfaction was advised to give him a few 'carefully dropped hints'. Another woman aged nineteen, married two years, who could not bear her husband to touch her since the baby was born was advised to get medical help, as was a woman who had not 'adapted to the intimate side of marriage' after two years. But medical advice did not always help; a woman with a 'wonderful husband', who had been to see two doctors who said there was nothing wrong with her but who still did not like sex, was advised to get some Catholic marriage guidance on the issue. A wife who wrote that she never enjoyed sex, whether pregnant or not, was told that the greatest pleasure is when one sets out unselfishly to make it pleasurable for others. (The reference to pregnancy is obscure – was sex supposed to be more or less pleasurable at that time?) There was really no solution to this problem, but the fact that some women themselves saw it as a problem indicates that the emotional revolution that Langhamer suggests happened in twentieth-century Britain was happening in Ireland too, gradually, in the post-war decades. The man who asked if it was all right to have sex with his pregnant wife, and if she could enjoy it at that time, was told it was and that she could enjoy it – provided he made the effort. But one woman complained that her husband was only interested in 'the physical side' and commented,

I now agree with what you said some months back that if a girl allows a boyfriend liberties before marriage he'll look for those and nothing else afterwards.

Macnamara held this up as a warning against pre-marital sex, arguing that couples who did not share interests other than each other's bodies before marriage would have trouble developing interests in common afterwards. But also implicit is the very modern suggestion, both from the correspondent and from Macnamara herself, that men who imposed sex on their wives were making unreasonable demands rather than claiming what was theirs by right.[5]

Downright unhappy marriages featured from time to time. A woman married for ten 'stormy' years with five children asked 'How does one bring out the best in men, even difficult ones?' She was advised to contact the Catholic Marriage Advisory Council. Another mother of five (the oldest in her twenties), whose husband beat her, would not let her go out and called her terrible names in front of the children, was advised to get a social worker, a priest and the Irish Society for the Prevention of Cruelty to Children involved: 'You cannot let him treat you like that.' One correspondent wrote in not only to compliment Macnamara on the fact that she never gave 'smart-alec' responses but to ask if she ever got 'unfaithfulness problems, that we see so much of in English magazines'. Macnamara replied that this problem did turn up, but rarely, and that 'while all marriages have their ups and downs, Irish married couples seem to work at honouring the vow "till death do us part"'. This might have been news to the many unmarried teenage girls who wrote in desperation when they were made pregnant by married men, and to the seventeen-year-old girl whose sister's husband (the couple was living with her family) was always trying to kiss her, despite her having begged him to stop. Adultery was probably less common in Ireland than in Britain for various reasons – lack of anonymity due to rural and small-town residence; lack of opportunity due to fewer mixed-sex workplaces – but it was not unknown. A woman who complained to Maura Laverty in 1963 that her husband had 'gone cold' and that she was afraid he was having an affair was asked if she had neglected him when the children were small, and Sylvia Grace said something similar to a woman who was sure her husband was having an affair in 1966. This was the classic 1950s women's magazine response to the woman whose husband strayed, used by Mrs Wyse, as we have seen, and by Clare Shepherd on the British *Woman's Realm*. While Angela Macnamara never blamed the wife like this, she could not offer any solution. A woman whose husband had been having an affair 'after many years of happy married life', had kept his wife short of money during this time and had come back to her when the affair was over, unrepentant, telling her this was 'common' could only be sympathized with and advised to call up 'all her reserves of patience and love'. A year later a woman who wrote in did not have this option; her husband had left her to go to another woman after many years of happy married life – 'my husband's heavy drinking [was] our only serious problem'. He refused to give her any money and she was having nightmares about making ends meet. This problem had passed out of the realm of emotion, and she was advised to see a solicitor about the maintenance, a doctor about her anxiety and a priest about a separation. In a very pathetic situation was a young married woman whose 'very cruel' husband had left her to go to England after only six weeks: 'He wouldn't let me buy fuel (and it was very cold weather), nor would he let me read a newspaper.' She and her mother were now living with a tyrannical female relative: 'She strikes me if I stand up for myself.' A very sympathetic Macnamara advised her about getting a legal separation but counselled her to get somewhere to live for herself and her mother as a matter of priority.[6]

Women could be unfaithful too: a mother of six children, having an affair for two years with her best friend's husband, was afraid her friend suspected something: 'I would not like to hurt my friend as I have a great affection for her.' Macnamara was scathing:

> What an extraordinary way to show affection for your best friend! You know perfectly well that this affair is wrong and utterly selfish. You are risking the happiness of two families.

Another woman, married twenty-seven years, whose husband showed her 'no love physical or otherwise', was having sex with another man, also married; Macnamara asked: 'How will you feel about all this when your life passes before your eyes and death approaches?' She was also firm with a married woman of twenty-three with two children, who was in love with a 21-year-old 'boy' and had been 'intimate' with him. A young married woman in love with a married man at work and wondering if she should tell him how she felt was dissuaded from doing so. But apart from the woman sleeping with her best friend's husband, she was gentler with these women than she was with unmarried people who wanted to have sex or even to 'go far' in 'necking and petting'.

There was no divorce in Ireland at that time, and then, as now, Catholics were not permitted to marry divorced people in a church ceremony. There were grey areas, however. A 23-year-old going out with a 27-year-old divorced Catholic who had been previously married in a registry office (not a church) was told that keeping company with a divorced person was a mortal sin unless that person was not married in the church. This couple was lucky because he was technically unmarried in the Catholic Church. Not so fortunate was a woman of twenty living with a married man who left his wife for her; he had been married in the church, and they were expecting a child and did not want it to be illegitimate. Across the water, agony aunt Mary Grant in *Woman's Own* in 1966 was advising women in common-law second unions to take the men's names, wear wedding rings and act to all intents and purposes as a married couple. In Britain, hasty first marriages contracted during and after the war and some of the very-early-teen marriages of the 1950s resulted in a significant number of these second unions, because not every party to a break-up agreed, or agreed immediately, to a divorce.[7] This predicament was not as common in Ireland, but second unions certainly existed. Possibly the reason why so few of these problems featured in *Woman's Way* was because people with this problem knew the answer they would get. This might be the reason for the low representation of marital problems generally in the magazine. Expectations of spousal behaviour were certainly rising, but divorce and the break-up of families was unthinkable, except in very extreme cases of violence and abuse.

Conclusion: A comparison with a British magazine

The near evenness of the breakdown of problems published in *Woman's Own* in 1966 suggests that it might have selected problems to appeal to all readers (see Table 6.1). Comparing quantities of problems in this year with those of *Woman's Way* over the seven-year period would not make much sense, therefore. However, it is useful to compare the kinds of problem, and the varieties of agony-aunt response, for the sample year of 1966 in this British market-leader with the problems in *Woman's Way*.

As far as marital problems were concerned, Grant in the British magazine, like Macnamara in the Irish one (but unlike earlier agony aunts in either country), rarely blamed husbands' affairs on wifely 'neglect'. However, like Macnamara, Grant urged wives to accept pragmatically that husbands had the advantage in this situation. (She had to deal with many more of these problems that did her Irish counterpart, and in this way, the correspondent who pointed this out to Macnamara in 1966 was right. It is not clear whether this means that there was

Table 6.1 Problems sent to *Woman's Own*, January–December 1966

Subject	Number	Percentage of all problems
Marital	124	29.8
Miscellaneous	123	29.5
Courtship	104	25
Extended Family/Parent-child	65	15.7
Total	416	100

more marital infidelity in Britain or that women were better able to articulate it as a problem there.) A husband who went away temporarily with a 'girl' while his wife was expecting their second baby came back; she must make every effort to keep him, Grant said. A wife who found out her husband had been seeing another girl for two years (he came back) and who had lost all hope and interest in her house and her children as a result was firmly advised to snap out of it, and similar advice was given to another woman in the same situation. Such advice was given in a time and place when divorce was legal and not prohibitively expensive, but for women who had given up work and independence to get married, ending a marriage entailed economic hardship. But if husbands wanted to impose this hardship on them, wives had no option but to let them. A 'reasonably happy' twenty-years-married woman was upset when her husband fell in love with another woman and begged her for a divorce. She (the wife) did not want to leave her home so they were living separate lives in the same house. Grant advised her to 'stop the cold war' and to give her husband a divorce. She gave identical advice to another woman in the same situation whose husband had gone off with another woman six years previously. 'Why should I lower my standard of living?', the woman asked, but Grant believed she would have to. Nor could she assure a woman married thirty-four years, with two married sons and four grandchildren, whose husband had fathered two children by another woman during a fourteen-year relationship, that she would not lose her home. Grant did occasionally counsel divorce – to a woman who had endured twenty years of a brutal, mean-with-money husband, and who had no children and who wanted to know if it was too late to get a divorce and start again at forty-seven, for example. However, another woman who had divorced a violent husband and who worried that she would never find somebody else was urged to give herself time and not to rush into another relationship too soon.

As in the Irish magazine, domestic violence did not feature very often, possibly because women who experienced this might have been too ashamed, frightened or inarticulate to put pen to paper about it, or because they might have accepted it as a natural if unpleasant part of life. Those who complained about it to the British magazine were always, significantly, young women, and the 22-year old married for two years ('but it feels like 52') with a baby, whose husband hit her, and a nineteen-year-old in a similar situation were urged by Grant to seek marriage guidance. The fiercely jealous husband who would not allow his wife to see any friends and the woman whose husband humiliated her in company were advised to seek similar help. This was like Angela Macnamara and in stark contrast to the 1950s agony aunts who always urged correspondents to try and see how they were provoking their husbands into bad behaviour. Neither were women to put up with husbands who were mean with money and would not tell wives what they earned.

Non-enjoyment of sex also featured occasionally in the problem pages of the British magazine, in terms remarkably similar to the way it was expressed in *Woman's Way*. A young married woman was upset because her otherwise good husband never said any 'loving words' during sex. The chief worry another woman had about the fact that she did not enjoy sex was that this would prevent her conceiving; she was assured that it would not. A woman of fifty-five whose husband was sixty asked if it was right for herself and her husband to keep having sex because they both enjoyed it. Grant assured them that it was. Macnamara, in the Irish magazine, likewise commended a 66-year-old married woman who was worried because her sexual desires were 'stronger than ever'. Mutual enjoyment of sex was the ideal in marriage, and when lack of interest by husbands hurt or bothered their wives, this was a problem that needed to be addressed.[8]

While the marital problems written in to the British magazine usually consisted of disappointment and disillusion, the courtship problems were sometimes characterized by desperation. Time and again, the British agony aunt had to tell correspondents that the boys they were mad about were simply not good husband material, whether they were violent, jealous, bad-tempered or petty offenders. She also had to damp down over-enthusiasm for early marriage in a way that her Irish counterpart did not. (Perhaps Irish people were more accustomed to postponing marriage?) A young woman whose boyfriend had a chance to work abroad but had to be unmarried to do so was advised strongly not to stand in his way, and a female student who wanted to marry a male student was counselled to wait until they had both graduated, which was what the man wanted. A mother wrote in worried about her daughter who had announced her intention of 'catching' her boyfriend by getting pregnant; not only was this wrong, Grant pointed out, but it might not work – the boy could refuse to marry her. Pretending to be pregnant to 'test' a boy who had made love once and then not contacted her again was, Grant told another correspondent, 'wrong-headed and desperately sad'. She was also firm with a woman who had been proposed to by a married man. Could she sue him for breach of promise? (She could, but it would not bring him back.) She and others in love with married men were always advised to give them up, such as a woman had been going out with a married man for two years, in which time his wife had had two children, and several others in similar situations: some of the girls, as in Ireland, were in their late teens, and one of the men was the inevitable parents' 'friend'.[9]

The problem of being pregnant and single hardly featured at all in the British magazine. One of the very few was an Irish girl of eighteen, living in Britain and going out with a boy for eight months. He had not asked her to marry him 'and I don't think he will'. Grant did not think he would, either; gave her the address for the National Council for the Unmarried Mother and her Child; and urged her to tell her parents, or at least her brother, who lived in England. She had less sympathy for another correspondent, engaged and pregnant, who did not want to get married for another year and wondered if she could 'end it' (the pregnancy). Abortion was still illegal, but even had it not been, Grant's advice might have been the same – the baby comes first, bring forward your wedding if necessary.

Grant's tone was similar to that of Angela Macnamara – sympathetic but equally tough on the self-deluding and the self-righteous. When one woman wrote in indignantly asking why 'unmarried pregnant girls' get 'so much sympathy' while girls 'skimping and saving for marriage' got no help at all, and concluded: 'It doesn't make sense, does it?' Grant's reply was, 'No, not the way you put it. But you put it so bitterly, don't you?' Kind-hearted, open-minded and pragmatic though she was, her response to one 'problem' (really a letter) shows the limits of the British agony aunt's social imagination. An eighteen-year-old male student, obviously a regular reader, wrote in to advise her that men were put off by girls desperately seeking boyfriends and that girls who 'couldn't care less' were not only more attractive but lasted longer as friends. For this piece of advice he was taken to task quite strongly by Grant, who told him his advice was 'not remotely connected to what most people look for in relationships'. She could only interpret his recommendation that girls and women relax into real friendship with men (rather than chasing them for marriage) as advice to them (the women) to 'play hard to get'. Macnamara, in the Irish magazine, would probably have upheld the young man's sentiments as support of her constant exhortations to girls and women to treat men like friends and to go out with several people before settling down. Likewise, in the British magazine, Grant's assurances to older single women about the validity of their state of life (when they expressed doubt to her about it or annoyance at other people's attitudes to them) rang a little hollow in the light of her response to an engaged woman of twenty whose thirty-year-old unmarried sister had told her she was a 'cabbage' for wanting to get married so young and give up her job. The sister was jealous and bitter, Grant told her; there was no suggestion that the older sister was so fulfilled in her own job and state of life that she might have worried about her younger sister throwing all this away.

The courtship and marriage problems that some Irish women were able to articulate in the 1960s were somewhat different to those that British women articulated – requests for sex and birth control information, for example, and a constant appeal for judgement about sexual behaviour. But the whole question of attracting and keeping 'boys' often shaded into more unfocused appeals in this decade of change and heightened expectations in Ireland, expressed in heartfelt letters like the following:

> We are three teenage friends who don't know the facts of life, have no personality and can't make conversation. Life is an awful strain.[10]

Part of this 'strain' was dealing with the older generation, and it is to these problems we now turn.

'Everything I Do Is Criticised': *Woman's Way* Problems 3: Extended Family/Parent–Child and Miscellaneous

Parents and teenagers

A mother wrote in to the problem page in 1964 to say that she had three teenage daughters and had almost forgotten what the bathroom looked like, and another mother wrote the following year to ask how she could stop her teenagers hogging the telephone. Irritating teenagers were probably more common in middle-class urban homes where their labour was not essential to the running of the farm/business and where there were modern communal facilities to be abused. But most parent–child problems written in to *Woman's Way* in this decade were in the form of complaints from young teenagers about parents. Not all of them were as reasonable as the fifteen-year-old whose mother would not allow her to go out with a 24-year-old man: 'I am trying very hard to be patient with my mother as I know she is going through the change of life.' (Menopause or not, the mother, Macnamara told her, was right.) She also supported the mother who would not, her daughters complained, permit them to marry before they were twenty-one. A seventeen-year-old asked Angela Macnamara if she was still obliged to obey her parents, even though she could see clearly the mistakes they made. (She was.) But Macnamara was usually on the side of youth, and although she told a fifteen-year-old whose 'fuddy-duddy' parents would not allow her out to dances that she was 'most disrespectful to speak of your parents in this way', she believed young people from the age of fifteen upwards should have pocket money, some kind of social life and friends of both sexes. 'Parents must wake up to the fact that teenagers are growing up and need to get out and have recreation suitable to their age', she commented in response to a sixteen-year-old burdened with housework, who was never allowed out; she also believed that students should be allowed to keep the money they earned from part-time jobs, if family finances permitted, because it taught them responsibility and budgeting. She sympathized with a seventeen-year-old who had to sneak out on dates – should not her parents tell her just what they were worried about? A 21-year-old student in a small town whose parents would not let her (or him) make friends and who wished s/he were dead was advised to defy the parents, take a firm stand and get out and meet people. Macnamara even took it upon herself to lay out standards about curfews, in a response to a problem from a sixteen-year-old junior clerk:

> Home at 11.30 p.m. or at 12.30 for a dance – I think two dates a week and one dance a fortnight would be plenty for you. (This of course would not be the rule for a girl still at school). Other evenings stay in with your parents, or ask some of your friends to come over, or take up some sport, hobby or class.

Her comment about the girls still at school being kept on a stricter timetable indicates that she knew her advice would be read keenly by parents of daughters still at school, as well as by teenagers themselves. To many teenagers, this was still probably unimaginable freedom.[1]

Parents and adult daughters

The most striking change in agony-aunt advice about the parent–adult child relationship between the 1950s and 1960s was on the question of the adult daughter as carer. When a twenty-year-old wrote proudly to the problem page that she had, since the age of fourteen when her mother died, reared her brothers and sisters ('not all teenagers are the same!'), Macnamara praised her but advised her strongly to get some education or training for herself as soon as possible. An eighteen-year-old girl still rearing her younger, motherless brothers and sisters, whose father would not let her go out or give her any freedom, was urged to try to get out of the situation, as was a nineteen-year-old with an identical problem, whose father was 'awful'. One reader wrote in about her twenty-year-old friend, top of the class in school, who had been forced to leave when her mother died and who would not be free until the youngest (seven at the time of writing) was reared. Macnamara advised the writer as a matter of urgency to get her own parents to talk to the father or to seek the intercession of the local priest or clergyman or some aunt or uncle. Getting away from what she considered unreasonable family demands was so urgent, for Macnamara, that it overcame her objections to early marriage, as in her response to a twenty-year-old going out with a boy who wanted her to get married and move to Canada. Her mother was dead, and there was nobody to take charge of the four younger siblings if she went. Macnamara was firm: the father should pay a housekeeper or get some adult friend to help, but the twenty-year-old should get married and go away. An 'only girl', living out the country, whose father wanted her to stay at home and help with her arthritic mother was advised to get a job not too far away; her duty to her parents was recognized 'but you also have a duty to yourself'.[2]

Sometimes the problem was exacerbated by elders' apparent lack of gratitude for youngsters' efforts. A seventeen-year-old had left school without her Intermediate Certificate and was at home cooking, cleaning and caring for her younger brothers while her mother was at work. She was supposed to be getting £1 a week for this but rarely did, and 'everything I do is criticized'. Maura Laverty – this was in 1963 – asked her to get another family member to mediate and (perhaps with a view to continuing her schooling) to talk to the headmistress of her old school. (If she was, indeed, the same person as Mrs Wyse who had answered problems on *Woman's Life*, she had changed her mind on this topic.) A 21-year-old working for no pay in her parents' shop ('Nothing I do is right') had a boyfriend against her parents' wishes; Macnamara advised her to keep going with him and to insist her parents meet him. A forty-year-old woman caring for her parents told Angela Macnamara that she would like to marry but also to join some club or evening class to develop her interests. She was given the addresses of Knock Marriage Bureau and the Institute for Advanced Education and wished well. Ways of living that might have been common a generation before were now becoming unusual, and this was one of the reasons why, in 1969, a woman with a good job, living with her widowed mother, sometimes got very lonely and depressed: 'I feel so different from everybody else.' Macnamara was sympathetic, advising her to join some organization or do something to meet people. One correspondent told of a 'friend', a woman in her thirties, completely alone in the world except for an arthritic, alcoholic uncle with whom she lived; she had no job, and her late mother's illness had prevented her from fulfilling her dream of entering the religious life. The response was to get help for her and get the old man into a home, if possible. There were either a lot of arthritic alcoholic uncles in the country, or else this woman's situation did not resolve itself, because less than two years later there was another letter about a 35-year-old 'friend' who was living with an 81-year-old alcoholic uncle with arthritis. She was lonely and depressed and had spent time in a mental hospital, and she found her uncle a 'terrible strain', although he was going to leave her the house. The writer wanted to know: 'Is she being selfish thinking of herself?' House or no house, she was not, came the emphatic response, and practical advice was given again.[3]

Over protective parents were also to be resisted. A 24-year-old with a heart complaint whose parents would not let her get a job in the city was told that they had no authority over her – she was an adult. A 'partial invalid' who was always 'fussed over' by her parents and would like to be more independent was given addresses of supportive organizations and lots of encouragement.

Parents and small children

Questions of disciplining children came up rarely, which suggests that readers were already following time-honoured methods. A mother of four teenage boys aged fourteen to eighteen who wondered if she should use 'a cane or a strap' was told that the father should punish them but that the punishment should fit the crime and that the child should be given a chance to defend himself. Corporal punishment was common practice in ordinary, loving families in Ireland in the 1960s, and Macnamara was by no means outlandish in endorsing it. However, she agreed with the mother, in 1965, who felt that it 'wasn't right' for her husband to 'wallop' two of her children (aged twelve and fourteen) for telling lies – the more he hit them, the more terrified they became, and the more they lied. In the same year a mother who worried that her husband was too severe with their boys was told that excessive severity was very bad for children. When asked to recommend books to a woman expecting her first baby in 1965, Macnamara recommended Grantly Dick-Read's classic on natural childbirth, a BBC publication *Having a Baby*, and 'it would be hard to beat Dr Spock's *Baby and Child Care*'. She also recommended Fr Urteaga's *God and Children*, but her endorsement of Spock at a time when his very name was (however inaccurately) a byword for permissiveness, and of two other non-Catholic publications (one emanating from the BBC), shows her openness to modern approaches to child-rearing in a decade where family advice originating abroad was viewed with suspicion and derision by many.[4]

Adopted children

Adoption was, as we have seen, discussed in the letters pages, and there were several articles on it or profiles of parents who had adopted children in the magazine throughout the decade. Always portrayed in a positive light, it surfaced rarely in the problems. A couple married five years with no children – she was twenty-nine, he was thirty-two – were advised to seek medical advice and then to consider adoption. An adopted person (the gender was not clear) wrote in to say that although s/he was very happy, s/he would like to contact his or her natural mother. The advice was the standard counsel given in all women's magazines in Britain and Ireland at the time: leave well enough alone, do not contact her, or, as Macnamara put it, avoid 'needlessly hurt[ing] her now'. (The women referred to in the previous chapters, who wondered if they should tell current boyfriends or fiancés about babies, must have had these babies adopted or absorbed into their families of origin.) A mother who found out that her 21-year-old daughter had gone to England pregnant and wondered if they should help her to keep the baby was advised that it was 'usually wiser to have the baby adopted'. Consistent with Macnamara's insistence on children knowing the facts of life, she believed adopted children should be told the truth about where they came from, and she recommended a pamphlet by Fr Colleran CPRS, *Telling The Child*, to a couple who wrote inquiring about this.[5]

The extended family

Vertically extended family problems featured very rarely. A woman whose live-in mother-in-law was 'buzzing around my house all day' was advised to 'arrange her [the mother-in-law's] bedroom as a bedsitting room where she could have a cosy fire'. (The large house which would allow such a solution was taken for granted, as was the older woman's willingness to be banished from the family hearth.) There were a few other domineering mother/mother-in-law problems of this kind, mostly in the early years – they faded away after this. The problems of horizontally extended family featured not at all after 1964, but two such problems featured in the magazine's early months. A Roscommon woman with 'the best husband in the world' and a beautiful baby, on a good farm, was annoyed that her husband's sister ran the house and criticized her (the young wife) 'all the time'. Maura Laverty's advice was uncompromising – get her out! She said the sister should be set up in a business or a farm of her own. (This was unrealistic; a farm that could support three adults and any number of children might not have much left over to launch somebody in a separate farm or business.) Some of the entanglements of obligation and accommodation are difficult even to explain. A woman of thirty-seven who had looked after her mother until the mother died was now being made to feel she was in the way by her widowed sister who shared the house with her. She (the 37-year-old) had fallen in love with a man of forty-one, whose 56-year-old sister, in turn, had always looked after him and was against his marriage. If they married, what would become of this man's sister? Having been made to feel unwelcome in her own house herself, the 37-year-old woman sympathized with her future sister-in-law, but Laverty assured her that independence might be good for the older woman, without specifying how the latter was expected to support herself. As sibling households aged and died out, problems like this became less common. However, it remained the norm for a single grandparent in particular to continue to live with or near married offspring and their families, on and off farms, while many single aunts and uncles (urban and rural) were absorbed into a complex web of part-time nephew- and niece-rearing, whether they were co-resident or not. If these relationships did not feature much as a problem in the Irish magazine in the 1960s, it was probably because they were still taken for granted and not seen as something that needed to be changed or challenged.[6]

Work and education

There were not as many inquiries to the problem page about training and work as there had been in the previous decade, which suggests that teenagers were finding careers advice elsewhere – at school, or in the career advice columns of newspapers and the magazine itself. There were, especially in the early years, requests for information about nursing, dressmaking, drama school and what to wear to an interview. Several people throughout the decade asked how they would go about becoming lay missionaries.

The religious life featured from time to time. A fourteen-year-old in 1964 who believed she had a vocation was advised to wait till she was older and then to talk to a sympathetic nun or priest. The practice of attracting teenagers as young as twelve to novitiates was still going on in this decade, but a modern Catholic like Macnamara deplored it. In 1969 a woman of twenty-eight who wondered if she was too old for a 'vocation' (to the religious life) was assured that she was not and advised to get in touch with Good Counsel Bureau, Seville Place, Dublin – a national clearing house for the various religious congregations at a time of high religious recruitment. Parents wrote in quite upset that their daughter wanted to enter the religious life; Yvonne McKenna has described this phenomenon of parental opposition to the religious life, even in a highly clericalized culture. Macnamara tried to talk them round to letting their daughter follow her dream. However, she firmly discouraged those who wanted to enter convents because their hearts were broken. The convent would not take them on this basis, she assured them.[7]

Miscellaneous

These are the problems that do not fit into the other categories. A woman worried about her new husband's unhealthy eating habits was not given much hope by a cynical Maura Laverty in 1963: 'The lifetime eating habits of a man are next to impossible to change.' A young woman wrote in 1965 to complain that two 'girls' at work were making her life a misery, teasing and belittling her. Macnamara answered: 'Very few girls are so unkind and perhaps you are over-sensitive.'

Many of the questions about sex discussed in Chapter 5 were coded or direct requests for moral/religious judgement, but Macnamara also fielded questions about Catholic religious practice per se. A woman wrote in 1963 that her husband would not join in grace before meals and family prayer and that she was afraid this would set a bad example for her son. She was advised that she should 'gently remind' her husband that if her son did not see him praying, he would think prayers were for females only. A correspondent calling him- or herself 'Anti-Square' wrote in protesting at this 'unrealistic' advice two weeks later, and it is unlikely that his/her mind was changed by Macnamara's other-worldly response: 'A saint sees the only purpose in life is to get to heaven. Surely he is being realistic?' She sometimes had to deal with what was known in popular theology as the disorder of 'scruples' – baseless worry that sin was being committed. Asked if it was a sin to receive Communion after not having been to confession for two weeks, she gave the standard advice that it was not, unless her correspondent was in a state of mortal sin. A woman who asked if it was a sin to have sex when pregnant was also reassured. A woman married four years with no children was afraid she had been preventing conception by undertaking sporting activities and driving on bumpy roads: 'My confessor does not seem to understand my difficulty.' Macnamara shared the spiritual adviser's puzzlement as she attempted to reassure this woman; we can only hope she was more successful. A boy in his early teens who was afraid he had 'sinned already' was told that he had not, as was a correspondent (gender unclear) who was afraid of touching him- or herself immodestly while washing. It has already been mentioned in the section on courtship that a Catholic was dissuaded from trying to convert her Protestant boyfriend. Macnamara herself did not try to proselytize either. A sixteen-year-old Protestant girl, who wrote that she wanted to convert because she was going to a Catholic convent school and had a cold home life and all her friends were Catholics, was advised strongly to try to understand her parents better and to talk to a clergyman of her own faith: 'The important thing for any of us is to belong to the church which we feel can bring us closer to God.' The belief that every life had to have a governing religious belief would have been shared by most readers. One correspondent who worried about the meaning of her life would not have been unusual:

> Is the single life a vocation? I try to make the best of it, but I cannot see that there is anything special about it as there is about marriage and the religious life.

A woman who did not know whether or not she should marry a particular man, however, was supplementing religious consolation with a demand for practical advice when she confided in Angela Macnamara: 'Except for the fact that I am a daily Communicant [i.e. attending Mass and receiving Holy Communion daily] I would be out of my mind worrying about this.'

Like Mrs Wyse before her, Angela Macnamara warmly applauded the single life. A 24-year-old who wrote in wondering if there was something wrong with her because she did not want to get married ('I find other girls pity me') was commended for avoiding 'the mad rush into matrimony'. Three years later a single woman in her forties also wondered if she were 'odd' for being happy in her own home with a good job, and again, her choice in life was supported by Macnamara.[8]

Other advice columns

There was some overlap between the kind of problems answered on Macnamara's page and those written in to the other advice columns, especially the medical, career and legal ones. Each of these would merit a study of its own. The 'lifestyle' questions and answers give a clue to the changes in social life and material culture in some parts of urban Ireland in this decade. Jean Begley, who answered 'Social Know-how', was asked at various times about who should pay for the flowers for a wedding, how to invite people to a christening, how to organize a dance in one's own house ('we have three large reception rooms'), whether a widow could wear white at her second wedding, how to cancel a wedding at short notice and how soon after getting to know somebody should Christian names be used. Begley's responses were a blend of contemporary etiquette and tradition, as in this response to a query about proper death protocol: 'Blinds and curtains are drawn as soon as a member of the family dies. They are raised after the funeral.'[9] The modern and the traditional also featured in the cookery column, 'Check-pot', which was asked about croutons, omelettes and iced coffee but also about barmbrack, mock cream and sheep's heart. The reader who wanted to how to store cheese, however, was probably not asking about the popular foil-wrapped blends, Galtee or Calvita, that graced most formica-topped tea-tables in this decade.[10]

'Counsel's Opinion', begun in 1967 as an occasional column, fielded queries about land, property and planning, consumer and employment issues. Family issues featured occasionally. Somebody who had worked for fifteen years on the family farm and was never paid wages saw the farm signed over to a brother and, being left with nothing, was wondering if s/he could claim wages. No, was the answer; living, eating and sleeping on the farm was considered payment enough, unless there was some agreement, and even if there was an agreement, wages could be claimed only for the previous six years. This, like the Roscommon sister-in-law problem mentioned above, underlines the precarious position of many 'assisting relatives' and explains more clearly than any other evidence the reasons for the much-lamented 'flight from the land'. The legal advice column, 'Counsel's Opinion' also advised that a woman who broke off an engagement was obliged to return the ring, which should be seen legally as a deposit or down payment of the husband's promise to maintain her for life.[11]

The magazine also offered career information aimed at teenage readers (male as well as female) and anxious parents. From March 1965 it provided information on the career fields of nursing, beauty, radiography, teaching, medicine, social science, occupational therapy, teaching and hairdressing; the occupations of *bean garda*, au pair, rail hostess, poultry instructor, waiter/waitress, and ship's radio officer (boys); and Guinness clerkships. Advertising and public relations were recommended to females for two reasons – most consumers were female, and when it came to market research, people talked more readily to a woman than to a man. Although some careers were still gendered, there was no attempt to dissuade girls from medicine, for example. And a girl who wrote in to say that she did not want a career, just a husband, and that she had tried dances and parties and just wanted the name of a marriage bureau was strongly advised to take up a career.[12]

The medical columns gave advice on all kinds of problems. A single 'Your Health' column in 1964 answered questions on the change of life, pimples, plastic surgery, electrolysis for hair removal and varicose veins. As time went on there was more of an emphasis in this column (renamed 'Patients Postbox') on problems to do with menstruation, sex and pregnancy, which could indicate a younger age profile of readers. One column in 1969 carried queries from, among others, a woman who did not enjoy sex, a woman who wondered if she could postpone a period that would coincide with an important appointment and a girl who worried about the short interval between her periods even though she was careful never to wash her hair or feet while menstruating. This last comment reflects a folk belief that was still current in the 1970s, and she was disabused of it. Another worried correspondent wanted to know if having been treated for tuberculosis with streptomycin was making it difficult for her to conceive. The answer given was no, but this was also a popular folk belief. A correspondent in 1968 who had a large family and wondered if her doctor would prescribe the Pill for her was told that she should try, because he might prescribe it for menstrual regulation. Angela Macnamara would never have advised this.[13]

The questions sent in to Sister Eileen SRN in the Young Motherhood Bureau had to do with pregnancy, childbirth and infant feeding. Sister Eileen promoted breastfeeding, but before her column started, in 1964, it was more or less dismissed by the magazine. She ran full articles on it in 1965 and 1966 and supplied plenty of information and encouragement thereafter. The Young Motherhood Bureau also promoted home birth and supported mothers having the choice to work outside the home and, in one article in 1969, gently deplored boarding schools. Sister Eileen's advice in 1966 that the only risk of smoking ten cigarettes a day was that coughing might cause miscarriage was of its time. It was not until the 1970s that the dangers of smoking in pregnancy were widely known.[14]

Conclusion: Comparison with British magazine

The category of parent–child problems was larger in *Woman's Own* in the sample year looked at, 1966, than it was in *Woman's Way*, although, as has been explained, British magazines might have published a quota of different kinds of problems to appeal to a broad readership. Still, there is no reason to suppose that problems were not genuine, either, and the larger category could indicate a greater number of letters written in to the British magazine on this topic. (See Table 6.1, Chapter 6.)

Like the Irish magazine, the British one had the problem of teenagers straining at the leash. Values were changing so quickly that some mothers and daughters had to be told firmly by *Woman's Own* agony aunt Mary Grant that age twelve to fourteen was too young to be going on exclusive dates with boys and that even sixteen was pushing it. Like Angela Macnamara, however, Grant believed that young people needed some freedom, and a mother who asked if 10.30 pm was too late for her seventeen-year-old daughter to be home was gently asked what she was afraid of for her daughter. Although legal majority was still twenty-one, adulthood began around seventeen or eighteen, and the age of consent was sixteen; therefore, a twenty-year-old whose parents had forbidden her to see her fiancé was advised to leave home if she could.[15]

While the co-resident extended family had featured a lot in the problem page of the other British magazine looked at, *Woman's Realm*, during 1958–60, it hardly featured at all in *Woman's Own* in 1966. The chronic overcrowding of the earlier period had eased somewhat; single-family occupancy houses, and better accommodation generally, removed some of the strain. (There was still a problem with emergency accommodation and family homelessness in Britain – this was the year of *Cathy Come Home* – but people with this kind of overwhelming, life-threatening problem would probably not have been in a position to write into a magazine about it.)[16] However, many asked advice about the practicalities of managing extended family. In Britain, two decades of early marriage had narrowed the generation gap, and many grandparents of the 1960s were young and vigorous – a fact that aroused amused comment in the letters page about granny on her scooter. This is probably why the worries of two grandmothers, who wrote in at two different times that they feared their daughters-in-law were mistreating their grandchildren, were not dismissed; the extended family still had a recognized role in the rearing of children. David Kynaston argues that everyday patterns of family living in Britain, whether in old or new towns, suburbs or countryside, changed a lot less over the decade of the 1960s than one might imagine, and, reading the very family-conscious letters and problem pages of *Woman's Own* in the middle of the decade, one can well believe it.[17]

It is also striking that despite the widespread social anguish in Britain about 'new town loneliness' (the sundering of extended family ties due to the relocation of some inner-city residents to local authority housing in new towns and suburbs), there were no problems, as such, written in to *Woman's Own* in 1966 from young married women pining away for the everyday support and companionship of their mothers. Nor did even one of the thousands of countrywomen who went to work in the cities of Dublin, Limerick and Cork and settled and married there write to Angela Macnamara about her loneliness for home ties, though in both the British and the Irish magazine there was at least one letter, to the letters (not the problem) page, about coping with such a move. A woman in one of the most notorious British 'new towns', Harlow, described how 'new town loneliness is banished' by networks of friendship and mutual support among the young mothers, and M. M. in Limerick city explained that people like herself who loved the country had to leave it to make a living for themselves, because only one child could inherit:

> I ... loved every stick and stone of my native place. ... There are so many memories – the rearing of young fowl, the Christmas turkey market in the nearest town, the sight of a shiny newborn calf beside its mother ... . One of the saddest days I remember was when I said goodbye and took the train to the city.

M. M.'s 'home-house' might have been anything from twenty to two hundred miles away from her, but her break with it was complete.[18] Perhaps these women in both countries, staking a claim for the families they founded away from their families of origin, were experiencing a freedom they considered unproblematic, apart from the practical difficulties of finding ready help at hand or the nostalgic backward glance. Or perhaps they experienced this movement as a grave and terrible rupture, a problem to which no possible solution existed: a problem that therefore did not find its way into magazine agony columns.

Conclusion: Hearing Their Own Names Again: Magazines and Irish Women in the 1950s and 60s

A Dublin factory worker was one of the few early letter-writers to express disappointment at *Woman's Way*, in verse:

> Hurray Hurray Hurray,
> Three cheers for *Woman's Way*,
> But dear oh dear I am deluded,
> For US poor girls have been excluded!
> Models, typists and shopgirls too,
> Romance, cookery and dressing for you.
> To make our Irish magazine completely satisfactory
> Please please DO remember the girl in the factory.
>   – letter from Miss Jean O'Hanlon, Markievicz House, Pearse St, Dublin.[1]

By the early 1960s, Irish domestic living standards were arriving at that rough homogeneity that makes magazine discourse – especially in its service articles – both appealing and applicable (if only in an aspirational way) across classes. So it is difficult to understand Miss O'Hanlon's complaint; why would the 'girl in the factory' need 'romance, cookery and dressing' that was any different from girls or women in any other occupation? Markievicz House, where she lived, was a modern, serviced local authority flat complex, and the household advice in the magazine would have been adaptable to her circumstances. Her letter, however, is typical of communications to *Woman's Way* in this decade, in its confidence that the magazine should belong to her – an urban working-class woman – as much as to anybody else. And as we saw in the introduction to this volume, rural readers were also insistent that the magazine reflect their experiences of life.

Jean O'Hanlon probably expected the new magazine to pay the same conscientious attention to women in the workforce and to female achievers in general as did its predecessor *Woman's Life*. But *Woman's Way* was a different publication for a different era. It was not that female public achievement was firmly established and unremarkable in Ireland by the 1960s – it most certainly was not; it was that in the 1960s magazine, the service articles, the opinion columns, the features and the letters, as they trickled in, took wholly for granted that women's lives were of abiding interest, whether situated within the home or outside it. Women achievers and women in public life were often mentioned and celebrated, but they were not considered to be any more worthy of remark than women of the house. Besides, with new facilities and services (or the prospect of these) within the home and outside it, and changing uses of the domestic space and changing expectations of the relationships that played out in and around it, there was more than enough to explain and discuss in everyday life without having to seek out the unusual and the exemplary for editorial copy.

In the previous decade, the popular and accessible *Woman's Life* was certainly less attractive and less glamorous than either its main Irish competitor, *Model Housekeeping*, or its successor, *Woman's Way*. However, as an Irish magazine, it catered for the growing number of female consumers – women working in schools, in offices, in shops and on factory floors – and offered its single and married readers an important networking tool in the Buy-and-Sell Service Club. The diary pages provided a platform for women who wanted to avail of it (paying them for the publicity), and its problem pages enabled, and probably encouraged, some women to articulate their dissatisfactions with life. The 1950s was not a glorious dawn even for Irish single women, but it was the brightening sky before the dawn, and *Woman's Life* held up a mirror to it. Some editorial articles throughout the decade hinted at financial difficulty, but the fact that this magazine was bought and shut down by a large British magazine publisher in 1959 is one indication of its value – Odhams was not a charitable organization.[2]

The changes of the 1960s brought a new cohort of readers – opinionated, baffled, defensive, confident, tentative, creative – who not only wanted a magazine to be part of their familiar media world but needed to be able to talk to each other in a readers' letters page and to be guided on questions of private morality and personal freedom in the problem page. It is true that nearly 45 per cent of the letters to the editor of *Woman's Way* during 1963–9 fall into the familiar women's-magazine category of 'Hints/Why Don't They/Things They Say', but this leaves 55 per cent – over half of all the letters – belonging to the other varied categories, including the miscellaneous group (25.5 per cent), which usually concerned current affairs. In the British magazines looked at for comparison, *Woman's Realm* in four discrete periods in 1958–60 had nearly the same proportion of letters in this 'Hints' category (42 per cent), but another 24 per cent of its letters

Figure 5 19 May 1951. Independence was more strongly emphasized than domesticity in both decades.

Courtesy of the National Library of Ireland.

praised and expressed thanks for family (including step-family and in-laws) and neighbours. In *Woman's Own* in 1966, only a quarter of the letters came into the category 'Hints', but another 18.6 per cent praised family and community. Whether musing and philosophical or fervently grateful, this kind of letter, found in abundance in two different British magazines some years apart, was almost wholly absent from *Woman's Way* in the 1960s. A male correspondent to the British *Woman's Own* in 1966 drew attention to that magazine's letters page as an example of exemplary writing, commenting that many letter-writers, 'if they could escape the day-long tasks of home and family, would blossom into first-class novelists and writers'. Another, from a woman resident in England who was either Japanese herself or married to a Japanese man, told of how the reader saved the letters pages to show to her Japanese female friends an example of the wit and wisdom of Englishwomen. Mrs M. L., Cork, envisaged rather a different function for the *Woman's Way* letters page in 1969 when she suggested that it should be compulsory reading for 'every priest, bishop and Dáil deputy [TD] in the country'.[3]

Perhaps linked to the absence of emotional outpourings about family and community in letters to the Irish magazine in the 1960s (or perhaps not) was a comparative silence in both decades, in both problems and letters, about emigration. It has been mentioned in Chapter 2 that letters and problems about emigration featured quite often in British magazines, especially *Woman's Realm* during 1958–60, when the number of descriptive letters from British people settled abroad in these years, noted earlier, was treble to the bass rhythm of the problems (featured on the problem page) that such exile posed to women who were very attached to their own families of origin. Irish levels of emigration in the 1960s had slowed down since the high point of the 1950s, but it was still quite common, well into the early 1970s, for young single people and for fathers of families from both urban and rural areas to go to Britain for work. Also in the 1960s, those who had emigrated in the 1950s were settling down in their new country without losing touch with the old one. The 1960s saw Irish- and British-domiciled lives connected in a way in which they had never been before, when nearly every family, community and neighbourhood was familiar with people 'home from England' (temporarily, on holidays) or 'back from England' (permanently, after some years across the water). It has been mentioned in Chapter 1 that a good proportion of the babies whose photographs were featured in *Woman's Life* in the 1950s had English addresses, testifying to some emigrants' desire to keep in touch with home. But moving to the problem pages, the problems in which emigration featured in *Woman's Life* and *Woman's Way* were either 'courtship' ones, where residence in 'England' fostered uncertainty about relationships (and even these were rare), or the (very) occasional 'refuge' problem, where the neighbouring island was a real or imagined place of recourse for delinquent husbands, absconding adulterers or unmarried mothers. Clare Shepherd told a seventeen-year-old Irish girl living in England in 1958 who wrote in to *Woman's Realm* with a problem that she was 'rather young to be so far from the people you know'. Mrs Wyse in *Woman's Life* never gave this kind of advice; she was never asked for it.[4] There was, we have seen, a series of shocked letters on *youth* emigration to *Woman's Way* in 1967–9, as if this were a recent phenomenon,[5] and the ongoing reality of Irish female emigration to Britain was brought home by a letter from A. Dillon, Surrey, in 1967:

As a ward sister in a London hospital I say thanks a million to Irish mothers who allow their daughters to train and work as nurses in this country. Where would we be without their beaming faces and their friendly smiles? ... Mothers and dads of Irish nurses – may God bless you, one and all!

This was unusual (if gratifying); correspondents to the letters page of *Woman's Way* tended to avoid this subject. Even its editorial content paid more attention to the far less statistically significant issue of unmarried motherhood than it did to the fact that such a large proportion of Irish-born people were living across the water. Not only was there no debate about whether life was better for women in Ireland or 'England' – a topic that must surely have been discussed around many an Irish table or fireside – there was not even any neutrally expressed correspondence on the different customs and terrain of the adopted country. There were occasional correspondents from British addresses. Mrs V. Burriss, Warwickshire, told the magazine proudly that her thirteen-year-old son wanted to learn Irish, and her younger sons loved Irish legends. Some six months earlier this same correspondent, appending the title SRN to her name (another Irish nurse in Britain), congratulated the magazine on its short-lived experiment of having every second issue emanate from Belfast, asking 'May a Donegal exile draw up a chair at your fire of friendship?' But towards the end of the decade, Maureen Gogarty, Dundalk, asked why (not if) Irish people emigrating to England were 'scorned by their neighbours and called ne'er-do-wells' while those emigrating to North America and Australia were given parties and wished well. And Joyce Peck, Goole, Yorkshire, wrote in exasperation to correct an impression given by an earlier correspondent that England was all smug suburbia: she lived on a farm, as did many English people; there was nothing wrong with suburbs anyway; and if there were, why were so many Irish people content to live in them in England?[6] These two letters stood out starkly in their direct confrontation of Irish attitudes to emigration to England in particular, but even the happy-wistful letter of the kind often published in the late 1950s in *Woman's Realm* from English people settled abroad was quite rare; Mrs Burriss was exceptional.

'Silence' on emigration might have been partly because *Woman's Way* was quite self-consciously helping to forge a new and distinctively Irish female identity in this decade. Mrs Rosemary Lucas, Co Kildare, in the readers' discussion of birth control, congratulated

Our own intelligent magazine that does not have its head buried in the sand of women's outer decoration and adornment. ... You seem to have achieved a beautiful balance between mind and body. [italics mine]

Women like Mrs Lucas who bought an Irish magazine in preference to a British one were probably already committed to supporting Irish industries and businesses and buying Irish goods. Although they were not slow to complain trenchantly about many aspects of Irish life, they would have been uncomfortable using Britain as a comparison. When M. Attard wrote from Colchester to *Woman's Way* about how good it was for her as a married woman to be able to work outside the home, she refrained from making the point that she would have found it quite difficult, as a hospital nurse, to do this in Ireland at that time. And although no Irish women's magazine published readers' letters at the time she was writing, one wonders if Irishwoman Mrs E. M., Derbyshire, would have dared opine some years later to *Woman's Way*, as she did to *Woman's Realm* in 1959, that Englishmen made the best husbands.[7]

Another topic in letters to the editor that was quite common in the two British magazines looked at, but hardly to be found at all in the Irish magazines, was housing. Praise for new houses, or pride in making-do in old ones, made up 7.2 per cent of all letters to the British magazine in the second half of 1958 and a considerable number in 1959–60, and several letters like this featured in *Woman's Own* in 1966 as well. Letter-writers to the Irish magazine rarely told personal stories about housing; one or two have been quoted in Chapter 3, but as in the case of letters about relationships, these were more likely to be general rather than personal – Mrs T. D., Kilkenny, for example, wondering what was the point of rural people spending so much money on children's education, if adult children were ashamed to bring friends home to a house without a toilet and running water. Her letter was unusual, and it did not spark any debate. Yet, 1960s Ireland saw huge changes in housing – the widespread modernization, with water and electricity, of existing housing stock and, running parallel with it in the 1960s, the biggest public housing programme in the history of the state. This lack of comment on housing cannot have been because *Woman's Way* readers were from solidly comfortable, well-housed backgrounds. At this stage it should be obvious from the letters and problems discussed that its readership was far more broad-based than that, and besides, even middle-class people in rural Ireland were often inadequately housed in this decade. Were Irish people in general and Irish women in particular not as house-proud as British women? In a recent work, Judith Flanders suggests that European societies can be divided into those that have separate words for 'house' and 'home' and those that do not. The 'home' countries, mainly northern Europe, she argues, cherish and nurture homeliness and cosiness, while the 'house' societies are more community-based with less emphasis on the interior. Her analysis conflates the Irish experience with that of the English, but had she looked at the Irish language, she would have seen that while the Irish for house is *teach*, and hearth is *tinteán*, the phrase 'at home' or 'home' in Irish is '*abhaile*' or '*sabhaile*' – which means, literally, in the townland (i.e. nucleated or dispersed village); Ireland, if Flanders' theory holds, would be a 'house' rather than a 'home' country. Does this lack of a specific word for 'home' mean that even mainly Anglophone twentieth-century Irish women had less interest in 'homemaking', in its literal sense, than British women? It is true that the 'Hints' section in *Woman's Way* letters page was bigger than those in both British magazines looked at (only slightly bigger than one of them), but hints can be as much about short-cuts and cutting down on work as about making things homely or cosy or doing things properly. This subject would benefit from further research, which could throw new light on the material culture of each island. A more likely explanation for the comparative silence in Irish magazines, from Irish readers, on housing issues might be that Irish people, newly conscious of modern standards, feared being seen (even by each other) as 'backward'. They were, perhaps, more ashamed than British people of poor accommodation and less likely to share either details about coping with it or joy that such coping was no longer necessary. Mrs C. N., Tralee, Co Kerry, who wrote proudly to the British *Woman's Realm* in 1958 describing (in detail) how she improvised without water or electricity in a 'little, old-fashioned cottage', was almost certainly a 'blow-in' to the area – and her neighbours would just as certainly have resented her drawing attention to their community's lack of a water scheme, had they read it. Letters like this rarely, if ever, appeared in *Woman's Way*. When Mrs Mary Morris, Dublin 6, commented in the letters page in 1966 on how the word 'cottage' had 'come up in the world', to mean a holiday house instead of a local authority dwelling, nobody wrote in to agree or disagree; many country people would have regarded her observation as snobbish in the extreme.[8]

It has already been noted that *Woman's Way* letters page rarely carried letters praising individual family members (except, occasionally, husbands, in a light-hearted way) and that such letters were a staple of both British magazines looked at. Neither, however, did it have extended-family *problems* framed in an emotional rather than a practical (lack of 'permission'/curtailed independence) way. A problem that came up in the British *Woman's Realm* in 1958–60, and had no exact parallel in either Irish magazine, was not only (as mentioned above) the emotionally demanding family of origin that objected to married daughters emigrating even temporarily, but mothers objecting to single daughters marrying. A very hurt woman wrote to the British magazine that her single middle-aged daughter, who had always seemed happy at home, was now going out with a widower and 'says … [that] I cannot rule her life'. Another mother complained that her newly married daughter of thirty-six 'has cut me out of her life. She never comes to see me or writes'. And, from the other side of the problem, a newly married woman wrote in despair that although she brought her aggrieved mother gifts every week to try to make her happy, nothing worked. Naturally the agony-aunt advice was to put the marital relationship first.[9] Problems like this never featured in either Irish-produced magazine. Were emotionally demanding mothers of daughters in Ireland so taken for granted and obeyed that their daughters did not recognize their own bondage? This can hardly be so; the 1950s and 1960s were decades marked by serious family ruptures, as not only massive emigration (especially in the 1950s but to a lesser extent in the 1960s) but a heavy migration of women to towns and cities for work and for marriage moved mothers and daughters far away from each other. The rising numbers of women described by the census as 'engaged in home duties' in their own houses suggests a move away from the extended family. Perhaps the 'emotionally demanding mother' problem did not arise as much in Ireland because Irish families were usually big enough to always have a spare daughter (or son) at home or nearby for emotional and practical support. Or could it be, national stereotypes to the contrary, that Irish people in general, and women in particular, were not as emotional as English people? This is another question that could be more fully researched by using an oral history approach.

Other differences between both problems and agony-aunt responses in the two decades and the two countries – Ireland and its nearest neighbour – have already been discussed. What we will never know is how readers – whether they were the ones who sent in the problems or were those with similar problems who appreciated the advice – read and understood the responses. Certainly some agony-aunt 'solutions' in the 1950s in both Britain and Ireland, especially those offered to unhappily married women, were, as we have seen, brutally unsympathetic. But even the sympathetic advice, in both decades, was unrealistic. Where was an over burdened and house-bound wife and mother going to make the 'friends' with whom she was urged to have regular 'outings'? Where was she going to go, in a small town with perhaps one cinema, or a rural area with no transport? And (the most important point of all, blithely ignored by agony aunts) where was she to find the money? But people do not always take published advice literally. Deborah Cameron has shown that women who read the self-help books popular in the past three decades or so do not necessarily follow the advice in these books but are reassured nonetheless to find that their 'grievance' is both real and recognized.[10] The same could have been true for the very busy and put-upon woman of the house. Even if she never made a friend or went on an outing, being told authoritatively that she was entitled to such luxuries might have given her a much-needed negotiating tool in her marriage. And, of course, this would apply not just to the woman who wrote the problem but to others, similarly situated, who read it. The same was true of other kinds of problem and other kinds of advice. There is no doubt that Angela Macnamara gave downright impracticable advice to courting couples, even to those who were engaged: 'Once kissing is introduced into a steady line [long-term relationship leading to marriage] the companionship is no longer a completely happy one,' she commented in 1964 in one of her responses, yet she advised another correspondent whose boyfriend had no interest in kissing and who said they were 'doing wrong when we aren't' that he was 'scrupulous'; there were no reassurances about his respecting her.[11] As in wives' rights to leisure outside the domestic sphere, it was an ideal of non-sexual companionship that was being upheld. Marjorie Ferguson suggests that British magazines' predominant emphasis on the virtue of 'self-control' (and its corollary, self-help) for their readers from the 1940s to the 1970s empowered women rather more than it constrained them. Irish girls and women who wanted to avoid sexual intimacy that might lead inevitably to pregnancy could have used the edicts of Angela Macnamara to hold off importunate boyfriends and thus give them (the women) a few extra years of earning and freedom. In the 1960s, many Irish people still objected to young women having education, good jobs, independent living, friends outside the family and sexual information. Macnamara robustly defended young people's rights to all of these things; the strictness of her advice about sexual conduct has to be understood against this background. 'If we teenagers had a woman like you in every town we would be a lot better educated than we are', wrote one grateful girl in 1967 – not better-behaved, the reader should note, but better *educated*.[12]

It is significant, nonetheless, that two Irish girls'/younger women's magazines that appeared in this decade did not flourish. *Miss* was inaugurated in 1965 by the publishers of *Model Housekeeping* (which would wind up the following year) and incorporated into *Young Woman* in May of the following year; this, in turn, folded in 1968. Both were attractive and interesting publications that solicited readers' letters and responded to problems. *Miss* concentrated on models, films, fashion and music – everything from the Royal Showband to the Yardbirds – and had a lively letters page, a problem page and a 'serious' discussion about young people's issues chaired by television personality

Thelma Mansfield. There were no knitting patterns, and cookery columns concerned 'fun' catering for occasions like Halloween. *Young Woman*, edited by Clare Boylan from October 1967, like *Woman's Way* had celebrity-media columnists (presenter Terry Wogan and actor Rebecca Wilkinson from RTE's weekly drama *The Riordans*), and it carried at least one 'serious' article per issue on the preoccupations of the decade, already explored in the *Woman's Way* letters page – sex education, relationships, country girls in Dublin, corporal punishment in schools, unmarried mothers, married women working outside the home, child psychology. The advice given in the problem pages was almost identical to that of *Woman's Way* – no sex before marriage, beware of heavy petting, no 'going steady' too young, stick at your marriage as long as you can. The short life of these magazines (which deserve a study of their own) suggests that young Irish women who wanted to read magazines aimed specifically at them – aged sixteen to twenty-five – either bought a British magazine (one of the modern ones like *Nova*, on sale in Ireland) in preference to an Irish one or were already satisfied with *Woman's Way*.[13]

Women's magazines in every era tell women how to do certain things: how to sew, knit, cook, look, dress, manage their relationships and rear their children. Not all readers appreciated this in the period under discussion. Mrs W. E. S., Ghana, writing to the British *Woman's Realm* in 1960, commented:

> Fashion, cookery, childcare, to say nothing of the psychology of pleasing our menfolk – all these we learn from women's magazines. But does there exist a magazine which teaches the average male how to treat and appreciate us hard-working females? ... This knowledge is supposed to be inherent in men, and women are the ones who must strive so hard to supplement their home education.

Patricia Burke, Portlaoise, writing to *Woman's Way* in 1966, responded sharply to an article advising women not to let themselves go after marriage by turning the criticism back on the male sex:

> How gallant, suave, debonair and courteous men are – when single. ... Collars and suits immaculate, hair and nails likewise. ... Then marriage, honeymoon ... a complete metamorphosis. Hair barely combed, shoes unpolished, any old suit. ... The men are disappointing and it's time they were told what's wrong and made to see what's wrong![14]

These two 'resisting readers', worlds apart, represent a submerged stratum of cynicism about the whole magazine project. Jennifer Scanlan's classic description of the women's magazine striking a balance between the fostering of anxiety that draws readers to seek out advice and the offering of positive meanings that encourage them to return the following month[15]

can be applied to all the magazines looked at in this book, but for Irish readers in either decade the most 'positive meaning' in their own home-produced magazines might have been the chance the magazine gave them to read about, and hear the voices of, other women like (and indeed, unlike) themselves, as letters or problems, or to communicate directly or indirectly with them through letters, competitions and 'buy-and-sell' clubs. And however it was framed, the magazines' insistence that women (married or single, young or old, mothers or not) were individuals in their own right and that they deserved care and attention and leisure was welcomed by women themselves. *Woman's Life* readers were invited to identify with the remark made by a Galway delegate to the 1957 ICA fête in Termonfeckin, Co Louth:

> What I find most enjoyable about coming here for a course … is hearing myself addressed by my Christian name. When you're the mother of a family, and even your husband addresses you as Mammy, it makes a nice change to hear your own name again.

Eleven years later (as seen in Chapter 6), a woman whose husband called her 'Mammy' would frame this as a problem and write to a very sympathetic Angela Macnamara about it.[16] The Galway woman in the 1950s did not find this form of address by her husband something to be worried about; she just liked to get away occasionally from all the people who called her Mammy. Emotional expectations of husband and family changed over the following decade, but both Irish magazines in both decades gave voice and space to real women's satisfactions and dissatisfactions, whatever they were and however they evolved.

Appendix One: Political, Social and Economic Developments in Ireland 1951–69

Ireland underwent several changes of government over this twenty-year period, but the most important political/economic event of these two decades was the First Programme for Economic Expansion devised by civil servant T. K. Whitaker in 1958 and implemented by Taoiseach Seán Lemass in the years that followed. Ireland in the 1960s saw the gradual winding down of emigration, the creation of many new industrial and service jobs, a rise in public spending on housing and the provision of universal free secondary education from 1966. In rural Ireland, the modernization of existing housing stock (with the provision of water and electricity) and the building of new houses escalated demand for consumer goods, giving a boost to manufacturing and retailing. A rise in car ownership and improved public transport helped to keep families in the countryside and to mitigate the effects of migration somewhat. The very stringent censorship that had prevailed over the previous thirty years was relaxed in this decade, and many Irish people had a chance, for the first time, to read the work of Irish authors whose books had been banned.

But the 1950s was not a complete wasteland, although chapters devoted to it in general histories tend to have words like 'malaise' and 'drift' in the titles.[1] Alarm about population decline and ongoing emigration led to the setting up of the Commission on Emigration and Other Population Problems in 1948; by the time the panel made its report in 1956, an average of 40,000 Irish people a year were emigrating, mainly to Britain. The commission focused attention on rural depopulation in particular, and some of its recommendations were effective; the lifting of the marriage bar on female National teachers in 1958 might have been a response to the commission's recommendations to encourage as many people as possible to earn a living in rural areas. The 1950s, as mentioned in the Introduction, also saw a steady increase in the numbers of women in extra-domestic (i.e. not on farms or in other people's houses) paid work and in organizations of various kinds (see Appendix 3). However, the percentage of married women in paid work remained quite low, though it rose slightly in the 1960s. The marriage bar against civil and public servants (including secondary teachers, nurses, psychiatric nurses and office employees) was not lifted until the early 1970s, and although there was no marriage bar operating in industry or in many of the service occupations, wages were comparatively low, families large and childcare costs too difficult to manage. Women in business for themselves, however, whether as hoteliers, shopkeepers or small-scale manufacturers, were a significant presence, especially in the smaller cities and towns.[2]

Emigration – mainly to Britain, but with a steady number still departing for North America and Australia – was the overarching reality of Ireland between 1947 and 1958, and for at least a decade thereafter emigrants, though nowhere near as numerous as before, continued to make their way to the ports. The numbers going were about evenly divided by gender, with more of one sex or the other going from different regions, depending on the work available in Ireland. The popular stereotype of the men going into the massive building works of the post-war period and the women going into nursing and other caring service work has some basis in reality, but many Irish men and women obtained work in transport, commerce and industry as well. Crossing the Irish Sea was not as devastatingly final as transatlantic or transhemispheric emigration, and relatives in 'England' usually came home on annual visits and for family occasions such as funerals. Nonetheless, numbering about 400,000, most of whom never returned permanently, they were a huge loss to Ireland.[3]

Ireland was developing many of the features of the modern welfare state from the mid-1940s. In 1944, children's allowances were introduced: 2s 6d per week for every third and subsequent child, payable to the father. From 1952, these were payable for every second and subsequent child, but the allowances were not payable directly to the mother until 1973. (In practice, many husbands seem to have signed this payment over to their wives; however, this was their choice to make.) In 1945, a dedicated Department of Health with its own minister was set up – previously, responsibility for public health had been collapsed into local government. Tuberculosis, which had returned to make a last devastating stand in the 1940s, was finally routed and defeated in the early 1950s. Various developments from then until 1953 (including a massive confrontation between the Catholic Church and the medical profession on one side and the Minister for Health on the other in 1950–1) resulted in the provision of free medical care, regardless of income, for all pregnant and parturient mothers and for all children up to six weeks of age. A hospital-building programme in the early 1950s provided nearly 8,000 new hospital beds and spurred the vigorous development of specialist medical services – orthopaedic, maternity and children's. Maternal and infant mortality rates began to plummet from the early 1950s and 1960s, respectively. This modern health service continued to develop into the 1960s and culminated in the setting up of regional health boards in 1970.[4]

There were some legal improvements in women's status in the 1950s and 1960s. In 1956, the Married Women's Status Act gave women equal legal rights in marriage with their husbands; in 1964, the Guardianship of Infants Act gave a mother equal rights with her husband to custody of her children; and the Succession Act of 1965 ensured that husbands could not disinherit wives and leave them homeless. These acts were a long time coming, and those that happened in the 1960s took place against a backdrop of intensified discussion and debate about people's rights generally – a debate spurred by rapid social change and facilitated by television and radio. A native television station from January 1962, Teilifís Eireann, enabled countrywide debate on many social issues; the ongoing march of rural electrification ensured its penetration to the most rural and remote parts of the country by the end of the decade. Women's political participation remained quite low, however, until well into the 1980s.[5]

The power of the Catholic Church remained strong throughout these decades, although it would never again attain the heights it had scaled at the time of the Marian Year in 1954. Still, bishops and male clergy remained respected spokesmen on moral and social issues throughout the 1960s and well into the succeeding decades. Legislation prohibiting birth control reflected Catholic beliefs. Divorce was not available and would remain unavailable until 1995.

Appendix Two: Other Women's Magazines in Ireland in the 1950s and 60s

Circulation

There are few reliable sources on newspaper or periodical circulation before the 1980s.[1] A small clue about circulation in the 1950s comes from a response to a Dáil question on revenue from government advertising in newspapers and periodicals in 1955. Neither *Woman's Life* nor *Woman's Mirror* supplied any numbers, but *Model Housekeeping* claimed a circulation of 27,000 to 28,000. (The very popular *Ireland's Own* and the satirical *Dublin Opinion* had circulations of 37,958 and 38,746, respectively.) Putting this into perspective, the two major daily newspapers (except for the *Irish Times*, which had a smaller readership than either of those periodicals) had readerships of 167,224 (*Irish Press*) to 195,588 (*Irish Independent*), while the two popular Sunday publications, the *Press* and the *Independent*, claimed readerships of 383,716 and 380,995, respectively.[2] *Model Housekeeping* was probably not the most popular woman's weekly in Ireland at this time, judging by the higher levels of advertising in, and apparent reader engagement with, *Woman's Life*. But even assuming that *Woman's Life* had something like 32,000 (halfway between *Model Housekeeping* and *Ireland's Own*), this still represented a low level of readership per head of the population compared to that of British magazines in Britain.

While this study is not a history of Irish women's magazines, it looked at a number of magazines other than the ones that were intensively scrutinized, and these are described below.

Woman's Mirror 1951–6

CAROL-ANN: if you worry too much about the lines on your face you will only make them worse.

> – 'In Reply to Yours', *Woman's Mirror*, March 1951

Not many Irishwomen speak it but we have all toyed at times with the idea of learning Esperanto.

> – 'We Halt the Passing Pageant' (Diary/editorial page),
> *Woman's Mirror*, May 1951.

Woman's Mirror, with an address at 270 North Circular Road, Dublin, was older than *Woman's Life* by three years, and it ceased three years earlier, which gives the two magazines exactly the same life span. Its content, as illustrated by the two quotations above, sometimes read like a parody of women's magazines' blend of self-evident advice and wild fantasy. At 3d, it cost a penny less than *Woman's Life*; it appeared monthly rather than fortnightly and was much thinner than the other magazine as far as editorial content was concerned. It was mainly interested in film stars, whose photographs were often placed in the middle of features to which they had no relationship whatsoever; for example a short story by Nancy Dingle entitled 'Wedding Dress' was accompanied by a photograph of Gene Tierney walking her dog, and a story called 'Pity is Highly Dangerous' by Rosemary Timperley had a photograph of Tyrone Power, while a snap of Barbara Bel Geddes pouring tea was stuck into another story in October of the same year. Sometimes, however, film-star pictures were relevant to the article: 'Give Your Home the Lived-in Look' had a picture of Rosemary Clooney (presumably a reference to her hit, 'This Ole House') in 1954. The beauty of short hair was illustrated by a picture of Audrey Hepburn, and in the same issue, 'Baby on Holiday' in 1955 was accompanied by a photograph of Humphrey Bogart, Lauren Bacall and their infant. Photographs of Joan Crawford and her children accompanied several articles on childcare and motherhood, including one entitled 'Habits are Formed Early and Easily'. In an article about beauty through the ages in 1955, Glynis Johns was presented as somebody who 'typifies the modern beauty' – very little attention was given to the previous ages. Jeanne Crain and Doris Day featured a lot, with an identical piece about the latter appearing twice.[3] Fashion features were almost always accompanied by photographs of film stars.

Readership

Woman's Mirror did not have as many competitions as *Woman's Life*, so it is difficult to establish a geographical profile of readers. However, four of the six winners of a competition in 1952 came from urban addresses in Tipperary, Kildare, Offaly and Cork – the other two may or may not have been urban addresses in Co Cork and Co Wexford, but they were all from Munster and

Leinster, and they were all 'Miss'. The competition was for household hints, and the prize was nylons. It can be speculated that most readers of *Woman's Mirror* – in keeping with magazine readership in general at the time – were town-based and more likely to be single than married. The magazine did, however, carry knitting patterns for children's clothes (featured on the cover occasionally) and articles on children's health from time to time and, once, an article on husband–wife communication.[4]

The diary pages (called, variously, 'We Halt the Passing Pageant' and 'Mirror of the Month') sometimes featured Irish women and men and their activities, but they did so less often than did *Woman's Life* and without the same self-conscious intent to promote and support women's activities. The years 1951 to 1953 were the best for this, with photographs of, and snippets about, folklorist Bríd Mahon, broadcasters Marie O'Connell and Una Linehan, playwright Louise Murphy, actors Maureen Cusack and Pepita Keating, comedian Paddy Dunlea, soprano Mollie Brazil, popular Dublin dancing troupe the Royalettes, and national and local organizations like An Oige (a youth hostelling organization), the Dublin Marionette Group, the Fr Mathew Players, the Irish Esperanto Group and the Old Belvedere Musical Society. As in the case of *Woman's Life*, these organizations/groups might have sent in press releases.[5]

Surprising items of local and national interest surfaced here and there. In November 1951, the diary mentioned that new local authority houses in Ennis, Co Clare, had glass panels by the front door and that the architect was 'a lady'. (These houses, in Clarecastle, outside Ennis, are indeed distinctive and very attractive.) The diary in March 1952 quoted a letter from a young wife who resented the suggestion that she should be as good a cook as her mother-in-law, but this was never followed up. The same month brought a reference to John A. O'Brien's milestone volume about population decline in Ireland, *The Vanishing Irish* (though this full-length edited volume was described as 'a little booklet' – perhaps the magazine was sent an offprint of the eponymous article), and readers' opinions on the low marriage rates were solicited. The following month, reference was made to the 'big pile' of letters on this topic received from both urban and rural addresses, though the letters themselves were not published. Reference was also made in July 1952 to the inauguration of President Sean T. O'Kelly for his second term in office, and his wife's mauve outfit (designed by her niece) was praised, but neither the fact that the president's wife, Phyllis Ryan, was a chemist in her own right and a veteran of the War of Independence nor the name of the niece, up-and-coming dress designer Neilí Mulcahy, was mentioned.[6] In October of the same year, reference was made to a book about

Dublin in 1728, *The Life and Character of Harvey*. However, while Women's Christmas, a particularly Irish tradition relating to 6 January, was noted in that month in 1952, St Brigid's Day in February 1953, and Samhain (Halloween) in October 1953, by 1956 the magazine was drawing attention to Little Christmas and to St Agnes Eve on 20 January, neither of which was a particularly Irish feast. An occasional feature on 'If His Name Is …', which inferred male partners' personalities from their first names, in January 1951 discussed the name 'Guy' – a name rarely, if ever, heard in Ireland. The national festival An Tóstal, widely promoted in *Woman's Life* in 1953–4, was never referred to at all in this magazine, but even within its own narrow ranges of interests, the magazine ignored Irish events. When actor Virginia McKenna was interviewed in August 1955, neither her Irish ancestry nor her convent education – both of which would have been of interest to readers – were mentioned. The magazine noted that Maureen O'Hara was in Mayo shooting a film in 1951, but there was no mention of *The Quiet Man* when it appeared in 1952, despite the fact that it was directed by a celebrated Hollywood director, had two Hollywood stars in leading roles, used mostly Irish actors in minor roles, provided six weeks' work for Galway and Mayo extras and showcased the west of Ireland for an international audience as never before. (*Woman's Life* did not mention the film either, but *Woman's Life* rarely discussed films.) Other films like *Three Coins in a Fountain* and *The Robe* were mentioned in more than one issue of *Woman's Mirror*, which confirms the suspicion that the film news provided was all syndicated and none of it solicited or generated by the magazine or its journalists. In March 1955, 'Mirror of the Month' claimed that 'our own capital city has become quite a centre of world fashion with amazing rapidity', but there was no mention of the designers, male or female, who had helped to make it so. Sybil Connolly and Irene Gilbert, who featured regularly in *Woman's Life*, might as well not have existed, though there was a mention in October 1955 of male designers Digby Morton and John Cavanagh.

Unlike *Woman's Life*, *Woman's Mirror* did not pretend to the slightest interest in politics, and, indeed, it opined in 1953 that women could have no such interest beyond the personal:

> Women in particular are more intrigued by whether the president of Utopia prefers pyjamas to a night-shirt than they are in his views on the current political situation. … This attitude of ordinary people does not suggest that international affairs do not interest them or that they are unimportant, but … that the day-to-day lives of these people are usually not only more interesting, but every bit as important.

This was followed by a photograph of Deborah Kerr illustrating 'Now is the Time for a New Winter Coiffure'.[7]

Yet the magazine continued until February 1956, when it ceased without warning. It must have had enough readers to justify its advertising budget up to then.

Model Housekeeping

Model Housekeeping commenced publication in 1927 and ran until 1966. By the mid-1950s it was a colourful and well-laid-out publication (far more attractive than either *Woman's Life* or *Woman's Mirror*), and it cost 6d, rising to 9d in the early 1960s. From September 1962 it began to be known as *Woman's View and Model Housekeeping*, but 'Woman's View' was printed in smaller, less obtrusive type, and the incorporation was never explained in the magazine.

Model Housekeeping, like *Woman's Life*, had diary pages filled with news items about prominent Irish or Irish-domiciled people (not just women) in the arts or in public life generally. There were far more photographs in *Model Housekeeping's* diary pages than in *Woman's Life's*, but *Model Housekeeping* rarely carried news items from women's or community organizations like Macra na Feirme or Muintir na Tire or from amateur drama groups around the country. The Irish Countrywomen's Association was occasionally mentioned through profiles of individuals involved in it, but the magazine does not appear to have solicited news items and press releases as *Woman's Life* did.

The service articles in *Model Housekeeping* comprised cookery, gardening, medical matters, 'mother and baby' and quite a lot of fashion and beauty. Like 'Brian' in *Woman's Life*, a male columnist, Ralph Tone (surely a pseudonym, perhaps a pun on Wolfe Tone?) dispensed bracing and astringent advice to women from the man's point of view. Fiction was represented by two short stories in each issue, and the default setting of these stories was Britain or the United States. In the eight years I looked at, I came across only one story that was set in Ireland. (*Woman's Life* had a higher proportion of stories with an Irish setting by Irish authors, but there too, the bias was in favour of the English or American setting.) The greatest contrast with *Woman's Life*, however, was in the extensive arts coverage in *Model Housekeeping*. At least eight and usually about ten books were reviewed in each issue, and there were reviews of plays, operas and other Dublin shows, with attention paid even to the smaller theatres like the Pike. This magazine was definitely aimed at a more affluent readership than *Woman's Life*. Articles about travel to foreign lands appeared in it, even in the 1950s, with regular features on Mediterranean and African destinations, at a time when many Irish people could not afford even domestic holidays – as correspondents to *Woman's Way* in the following decade were not slow to point out. Photographs of foreign places even accompanied ordinary articles, for example a photograph of Sacre Coeur in Paris illustrated an article on spring cleaning, while two photographs from Dalmatia and the Canaries accompanied an entirely unrelated article of a miscellaneous nature. Another hint of the slightly wealthier readership of this magazine are the regular advertisements for Bond's marking ink – for the clothes of children going to boarding school.

But the biggest difference between *Model Housekeeping* and the two magazines that are the focus of this study, *Woman's Life* and *Woman's Way*, was that *Model Housekeeping* did not have a problem page (which both of those magazines had) or a readers' letters page (which *Woman's Way* had). Neither did it have a buy-and-sell club, or regular competitions or other kinds of reader engagement. Another difference between it and *Woman's Way* (rather than the earlier magazine) was that it did not carry full-length features about current affairs. Nor did it have columns by, or articles about, TV and radio personalities – there might have been mention of them in the diary pages, but only occasionally, and they were not the axis of the magazine's editorial content in the way that they were in *Woman's Way*. Even *Woman's Life*, in 1956, had radio personality Maxwell Sweeney on board for a brief time.

When *Model Housekeeping* finished, its publishers attempted to replace it with *Miss* and then *Young Woman*. Both magazines, which have been referred to from time to time in the main text, had all the features of the modern mass-market Irish/British magazine – readers' letters, agony columns, topical discussions and media celebrity columnists. Dolores Rockett, who had edited the diary column in *Model Housekeeping*, emerged in the new role of agony aunt in *Young Woman*. But there must not have been a market in Ireland for two similar magazines; some correspondents, as we have seen, wrote to both, indicating a shared readership. *Young Woman* ceased publication in 1968.

Although attractively produced and carefully laid out, with attention to the arts as well as to 'women's concerns', *Model Housekeeping* was not a modern magazine that could compete with British market leaders. But neither was it distinctively national enough to offer Irish readers a real alternative to imported publications. *Woman's Way*, a self-consciously Irish magazine that appealed to women of all ages, classes, geographical locations and creeds, seems to have hit the winning formula.[8]

Irish Tatler and Sketch

Irish Tatler and Sketch was founded in 1890 as *Lady of the House*, changing its name in the early twentieth century. Renamed *IT* magazine in 1979, it was bought by Harmonia publications in 2004 and is now known, again, as *Irish Tatler.*[9]

In the 1950s and 1960s, *Irish Tatler and Sketch* was subtitled *Ireland's Premier and Sporting Monthly*, and cost 1s 6d, making it three times as expensive as *Model Housekeeping* and four times as dear as *Woman's Life*. Printed on high-quality, glossy paper, its front cover right into the 1960s featured advertisements for items ranging from Moet et Chandon or Mumm's champagne to more mundane products like Sunbeam Wolsey fabrics or Lyons Tea. The magazine contained three or four diary/social pages; articles on motoring, tennis, 'rugger', golf, the hunt and the turf (horse-racing); book and theatre reviews; a letter from London and many other regular features. It was not a women's magazine as such, although there were regular fashion and beauty columns. Many upper-middle-class and professional Irish people had their social engagements or weddings recorded there: Miss Rita Dudley's reception prior to her marriage to Mr Erskine Childers, Angela Little's engagement to Mr Peter Geoffrey Macnamara, the engagement of the Honourable Andrew Bonar Law and Miss Joanna Margarette Neill and the wedding of barrister Brian Lenihan and dentist Ann Devine. There was, however, no fiction, no readers' letters page, no problem page and, it is hardly necessary to add, no buy-and-sell service for readers.[10]

Appendix Three: Women, Paid Work and Marital Status in Ireland 1946–71

Table Appendix 3.1 Percentage of adult females who were gainfully occupied and percentage of each marital status to the total number gainfully occupied, Ireland.

Total AF	Total FGO	Single	Married	Widowed
1946: 1,081,362	334,862	269,207	22,609	43,046
	(30.9)	(80.3)	(6.8)	(12.8)
1961: 1,001,095	286,579	229,223	24,288	33,068
	(28.6)	(79.9)	(8.8)	(11.6)
1971: 1,055,707	287,867	235,403	39,214	25,000
	(27.2)	(77)	(13.6)	(8.6)

Key: AF = adult female population (over fourteen). FGO = females gainfully occupied. The single, married and widowed percentages refer to females gainfully occupied, not females as a whole.

Statistics are crude instruments and need some explaining. The figures above show a smaller percentage of the adult female population 'gainfully occupied' in 1961 than in 1946 and a smaller percentage in 1971 than in 1961. The decline between 1946 and 1961 can be explained mostly by the huge decline in the numbers of two categories of worker who had previously made up about half of all 'gainfully occupied' females: those who were 'assisting relatives' in agriculture, that is working and living on the family farm; and those working in domestic service. The decrease in their joint numbers between 1946 and 1961 totalled 77,926, while the decline in the numbers in paid work over that period added up to 48,283. Numbers of females in these two sectors fell again, by 62,541, in the period 1961–71. Numbers of women in industrial, commercial, white-collar and professional work rose by 31,574 between 1946 and 1961 and by a further 75,356 in the succeeding decade. The reason for the lower percentage of adult females (over fourteen) in gainful occupation in 1971 compared with 1961 has to do with the rising numbers remaining at school until their later teens and, the census commentary suggests, a rising marriage rate and consequent abandonment of gainful occupation. However, these figures also show a rising number and percentage of married women in the female gainfully occupied category, with the most marked rise happening in the 1960s.

The numbers and proportion of employed widows fell significantly over this period, possibly due to improved welfare provisions for them and a growing tendency on farms for the farm, and thus the occupation of farmer, to be passed on directly to the heir – usually a male – rather than to the widow.

But what about the percentage of married women per se who went out to work? A greater percentage of the workforce than in previous decades was made up of married women in 1961 and again in 1971, but does this mean that more married women were actually in the workforce, or is it due to other factors?

Table Appendix 3.2 Percentage of married women who were gainfully occupied, Ireland, 1946, 1961 and 1971

Year	No. of Married Women	No. of Employed Married Women & Percentage of All Married Women
1946	451,331	22,609 (5 %)
1961	468,228	24,288 (5 %)
1971	523,075	39,214 (7.49 %)

This table shows that there was a small but undramatic rise in the number of married women who went out to work and that this increase happened in the 1960s. Using the UK – as the nearest neighbour and the temporary or permanent residence of hundreds of thousands of Irish people in these decades – as a rough comparison, married women made up about 25 per cent of all female workers in 1951, 35 per cent in 1961 and around 40 per cent in 1971.[1]

Notes

Introduction

1   Interview by the author with Josephine E. (pseudonym), Galway, 10 July 1995. Josephine was born in rural Mayo in 1933 and emigrated to England in the early 1950s, returning to Ireland in 1958. She died in 1999.

2   *Woman's Life* Service Club (readers' buy-and-sell column), 3 March 1956.

3   Joke Hermes, *Reading Women's Magazines: An Analysis of Everyday Media Use* (Oxford: Polity, 1999), pp. 143–52; Penny Tinkler, *Constructing Girlhood: Popular Magazines for Girls Growing Up in England 1920-1950* (London: Taylor & Francis, 1995), p. 59. C. Clear, *Women of the House: Women's Household Work in Ireland 1922-1961* (Dublin: Irish Academic Press, 2000), pp. 68–95, 216–18.

4   A person with a 'hardship narrative' could, of course, have experienced a very hard life. I explore this more fully in C. Clear, 'Hardship, Help and Happiness in Oral History Narratives of Women's Lives in Ireland', *Oral History* 31, no. 2 (Autumn 2003), pp. 33–42.

5   Paul Ryan, *Asking Angela Macnamara: An Intimate History of Irish Lives* (Dublin: Irish Academic Press, 2011), p. 30; Janice Winship, *Inside Women's Magazines* (London: Pandora, 1987), p. 7. Most people – and not only academics – are amused and indulgent when I tell them I am writing a book about women's magazines.

6   Betty Friedan, *The Feminine Mystique* (New York: W. W. Norman, 1963), especially Chapter 2, 'The Happy Housewife Heroine'; Cynthia White, *Women's Magazines 1693-1968* (London: Michael Joseph, 1970); Irene Dancyger, *A World of Women: An Illustrated History of Women's Magazines* (Dublin: Gill & Macmillan, 1978); Brian Braithwaite, *Women's Magazines: The First 300 Years* (London: Peter Owen, 1995); Marjorie Ferguson, *Forever Feminine: Women's Magazines and the Cult of Femininity* (London: Heinemann, 1983); Janice Winship, *Inside Women's Magazines*; R. Ballaster, M. Beetham, E. Frazer and S. Hebron, *Women's Worlds: Ideology, Femininity and the Woman's Magazine* (London: Macmillan, 1991); Jennifer Scanlan, *Inarticulate Longings: the Ladies' Home Journal, Gender and the Promises of Consumer Culture* (London: Routledge, 1995); Nancy Walker, *Shaping our Mothers' World: American Women's Magazines* (Jackson: University of Mississippi, 2000); Linda Korinek, *Roughing it in the Suburbs: Reading* Chatelaine *Magazine in the 50s and 60s* (Toronto, ON: University of Toronto, 2000).

7   Claire Rayner, *How Did I Get Here From There?* (London: Virago, 2003), p. 333.

8   'Pen to Paper', *Woman's Way* (hereafter *WW*), M. M., Kildare, 14 August 1963.

9   Other letters implying that *WW* was the first of its kind were from
    Mrs K. Barrett, Clonmel, Mrs M. E. Clarke, Mullingar, 26 April 1963, and many
    more were referred to by the editor in his column, the same issue. Thanks to
    Norah Casey, publisher of *WW* among other titles, for her information on the
    genealogy of the *Irish Tatler*. See Appendix 2 for discussion of some of these
    titles.

10 Noliwe Rooks, *Ladies Pages: African-American Women's Magazines and the Culture
    that Made Them* (Newark: NJ: Rutgers, 2005), pp. 143–6.

11 'Young Queen', *Woman's Life* (hereafter *WL*), 7 February 1953; Tóstal number,
    4 April 1953; Maire Comerford, 'Carve Their Name in Pride: the women of 1916',
    WW, 1 April 1966.

12 Rooks, *Ladies*, p. 144.

13 The classic textbook on Irish media is John Horgan, *Irish Media: A Critical
    History Since 1922* (London: Routledge, 2001), which mentions *WW* once.
    Chris Morash's, *A History of the Media in Ireland* (Cambridge: Cambridge
    University Press, 2010) does not mention them at all, but neither does it
    mention other popular magazines like *Ireland's Own*. Other books on Irish
    media that pay no attention to women's magazines are Paul Lindsay (ed.), *The
    Media and Modern Society in Ireland* (Celbridge: Social Study Conference,
    1993); Mary J. Kelly and Barbara O'Connor (eds), *Media Audiences in Ireland*
    (Dublin: UCD Press, 1997), Damien Kiberd (ed.), *Media in Ireland: The Search
    for Diversity* (Dublin: Four Courts/Open Air, 1997) and J. Horgan, B. O'Connor
    and H. Sheehan (eds), *Mapping Irish Media: Critical Explorations* (Dublin: UCD
    Press, 2007).

14 *WW* letters page, 14 May 1966. Al Byrne's article to which it reacted, 'Home For
    Tea', 15 March 1966.

15 Ruth Schwarz Cowan, *More Work for Mother: The Ironies of Household Technology
    from the Open Hearth to the Microwave* (New York: Basic, 1982).

16 There are so many books attesting to these changes that only a sample will be
    given here: J. J. Lee, *Ireland 1912-1980* (Cambridge: Cambridge University Press,
    1989); Ruth Barrington, *Health, Medicine and Politics in Ireland 1900-1970*
    (Dublin: IPA, 1987); Michael Sheils, *The Quiet Revolution: The Electrification of
    Rural Ireland* (Dublin: IPA, 1974); C. Clear, *Women of the House*, pp. 96–142.
    Appendix 1 goes into more detail on the social and economic changes of these
    decades and refers readers to specific authorities.

17 The reference here is to William Trevor's short story 'The Ballroom of Romance',
    first published 1972, in William Trevor, *Collected Stories* (London: Penguin,
    1983) and to the award-winning RTE drama by Pat O'Connor 'The Ballroom

of Romance', which appeared in 1982 and starred Brenda Fricker and John Kavanagh. It is not clear whether the short story or the film is cited by Lee in *Ireland*, p. 335, when he used it to make a rather general point about single women's miserable lives in post-1945 Ireland. The sociological literature of the 1950s and 1960s, particularly John A. O'Brien (ed.), *The Vanishing Irish* (London: W. H. Allen, 1954), promoted a view of Irish singleness as rural, lone and pathological. This was developed in a number of influential anthropological studies in the following decades, notably Nancy Scheper-Hughes, *Saints, Scholars and Schizophrenics: Mental Illness in Rural Ireland* (Berkeley: University of California, 2001). This point of view is gently but effectively questioned by C. Curtin and A. Varley, 'Marginal Men? Bachelor farmers in a west of Ireland community', in C. Curtin, P. Jackson and B. O'Connor (eds), *Gender in Irish Society* (Galway: Officina Typographica, 1987), pp. 287–308.

18   Katherine Holden, *The Shadow of Marriage: Singleness in England 1914-1960* (Manchester: Manchester University Press, 2007). On the origins and development of the over parented family, see C. Clear, *Social Change and Everyday Life in Ireland 1850-1922* (Manchester: Manchester University Press, 2007), pp. 81–2.

19   'She's Leaving Home' by John Lennon and Paul McCartney, *Sgt. Pepper's Lonely Hearts Club Band* LP (London: Parlophone/Apple, 1967).

20   On emigration, Enda Delaney, *Demography, State and Society: Irish Migration to Britain 1921-1971* (Liverpool: Liverpool University Press, 2000), pp. 112–225; on women in the workforce, see figures in C. Clear, *Women of the House*, pp. 14–15.

21   Marianne Heron, *Sheila Conroy: Fighting Spirit* (Dublin: Attic, 1993); Aileen Heverin, *ICA: The Irish Countrywomen's Association: A History* (Dublin: Wolfhound, 2000), p. 92, 108, 129. Heverin describes the 1950s as 'a productive, lively and forward-looking decade' for the organization (p. 129).

22   *Rural Ireland: Muintir na Tire Rural Publication* (Tipperary: Muintir na Tire Publications, 1950), pp. 131–41; *Rural Ireland: gach pobal ina mhuintir* (Tipperary: Muintir na Tire Publications, 1964), pp. 153–68.

23   On women TDs and senators, see the indispensable Medb MacNamara and Pascal Mooney, *Women in Parliament 1919-2000* (Dublin: Wolfhound, 2000); on Sheila Conroy nee Williams, see Heron, *Sheila Conroy*, p. 65.

24   John Horgan, *Irish Media*; Robert Savage, *A Loss of Innocence? Television and Irish Society 1960-72* (Manchester: Manchester University Press, 2010).

25   See the works cited in note 11. This writer remembers the long-promised green-and-cream-bakelite-surround television arriving in our house in time for these celebrations and commemorations, and watching, with the whole family, a very

thrilling and occasionally frightening dramatized version of RTE's play about the 1916 Rising, *Insurrection*, by Hugh Leonard.

26 Linda Connolly, *The Irish Women's Movement: From Revolution to Devolution* (Dublin: Lilliput, 2003), pp. 7–13 and 56–86.

27 R. Ballaster and M. Beetham, *Women's Worlds*, p. 176.

28 Mending children's clothes, Mrs N. O'B, Sligo, *WW* 1 August 1966; and majority never having holidays, E. N., Clondalkin, Co Dublin, 30 June 1967.

29 Over this period of six years and eight months, three issues were missing.

30 Korinek, *Roughing It*, pp. 71–101. Selective analysis of problems and letters can lead the historian into untenable generalizations, for example, M. Richards and B. Jane Elliott, 'Sex and Marriage in the 1960s and 70s', in D. Clark (ed.), *Marriage, Domestic Life and Social Change: Writings for Jacqueline Burgoyne* (London: Routledge, 1991), pp. 33–54, make very selective use of Mary Grant's problem page in *Woman's Own* in the 1960s to argue that unsympathetic recommendations of stoicism in the face of marital conflict characterized Grant's advice to those in difficulty. This is simply not borne out by an intensive week-by-week study of the problem page in 1966.

Chapter 1

1 I have discussed *Woman's Life*'s changing content elsewhere, in C. Clear, *Women of the House*, pp. 68–95.

2 *Woman's Life* (hereafter *WL*), 2 May 1953.

3 Hugh Oram, *The Advertising Book* (Dublin: MO Books, 1986), p. 164, shows Mrs Lily Murray, the owner/editor (the magazine did not have a masthead, and the editor was never identified in it). Oram also identifies a Hilda Carron, at a conference in 1957, as belonging to *WW* (photograph, p. 184). *WW* did not begin until 1963, and *Woman's Mirror* had ceased publication in 1956, so he must mean *WL*.

4 *WL*, 19 April 1952; 15 October 1955.

5 *WL*, 24 March 1951.

6 *WL*, 8 January 1955; 7 January 1956; 26 May 1956.

7 *WL*, 6 July 1957.

8 *WL*, 17 April 1954.

9 *WL*, 12 June 1954.

10 *WL*, 10 July 1954.

11 Just a sample is given here: ICA summer school, *WL*, 8 August 1953; Muintir na Tire Carlow, 9 January 1954; ICA Letterkenny, 9 January 1954; ICA Dunfanaghy, 6 February 1954; Portlaoise Macra na Feirme, 20 February 1954; ICA Gort, 11 June 1955; ICA Termonfeckin, 22 June 1957.

12   Again, just a sample: WNHA, *WL*, 17 May 1953; SSC, 16 June 1953; IHA, 25 June 1955; 7 July 1956, 23 November 1957, 6 December 1958; JCWSSW, 30 April 1955; Red Cross, 3 September 1955.

13   Carlow Arts, *WL*, 8 August 1953; Carlow Fashion, 3 April 1954; Glasnevin, 29 October; South Mayo, 28 April 1956; Colleen Bawn, 29 December 1951; Elizabethan, 7 January 1956.

14   E.g. *WL*, 21 July 1956, Shadeine, Orlex Compound and Shadeine again, 27 September 1958.

15   Ballaster and Beetham, *Women's Worlds*, pp. 146–7.

16   *WL*, 8 August 1953.

17   E.g. Weddings, *WL*, 7 August 1954, 21 January 1956, 9 June 1956, 5 January 1957, 7 December 1957 and *passim*. Children's party, 19 February 1955; coming of age, 20 March 1954. Contrast with *IT & S*, January 1952–December 1960, any issue.

18   *WL*, 10 January 1953. The Sisters of Mercy in Galway, as elsewhere, ran a free 'secondary top' secondary school for girls whose parents could not afford school fees.

19   Smith, *WL*, 10 March 1951, 19 May 1951 (see also obituary *Sunday Independent*, 12 May 2013); O'Sullivan, 10 January 1953; Hobson, 10 March 1951, 18 October 1952; D'Alton, 4 September 1954; McKenna, 10 March 1951, 26 May 1956, 25 May 1957; Ryan, 3 March 1956; Cusacks, 24 February 1951, 1 March 1958, 11 October 1958; Potter, 3 August 1957. Caffrey, 13 January 1951, 14 November 1951; Bourke, 14 July 1951; Long, 12 May 1956; Lynch, 1 March 1958. Taibhdhearc, 10 January 1953; Doolin, *WL*, 15 September 1956; Collins, 12 May 1956; JDM, 17 April 1954, 7 July 1956; Swift, 5 January 1957. O'Hara, *WL*, 1 October 1955; Watkins, 17 March 1956; Ledwith, 27 December 1952; O'Grady, 31 March 1956; Ní Scolaí, 2 March 1957. O'Brien, 19 March 1955, 14 May 1955, 11 June 1955; Laverty, 25 October 1955; Boland, 25 June 1955; Troy, 7 June 1955; Purcell, 14 May 1955; Lynch and de Valera, 21 July 1956. Thomas Davis Lectures, 12 November 1955.

20   Shannon, *WL*, 7 January 1956, 14 September 1957; Ballsbridge, 28 April 1953; ICA, 5 January 1957.

21   Connolly and Gilbert featured so often that only a sample of references is given here: *WL*, 6 March 1954, 18 September 1954, 10 September 1954, 19 February 1955, 21 January 1956, 16 February 1957, 17 August 1957, 2 August 1958; Mulcahy, 4 February 1956. Keenan, 24 March 1951, 20 October 1951; Carroll, 19 May 1951; Brady, 3 April 1954; Swift, 26 April 1958; Phillips, 10 November 1956; James, 6 March 1954, 18 September 1954. Dorene, 27 September 1958; Melina, 23 April 1957. Woodbyrne, 25 May 1957; Whelan, 20 July 1957; Carty, 8 December 1956; Fisher, 13 September 1954. Griffin, 14 July 1951; Ross, 10 January 1953; Hickey, 4 January 1958; Gallagher, 4 January 1958; Advertising,

31 March 1956; Hugh Oram, *Advertising*, pp. 132–270, confirms that these
women were working in advertising in their own right in Ireland and were not
spouses of 'ad men'.

22 Receptionists, *WL*, 5 May 1951, 26 July 1952; saleswoman, 21 April 1951; radio
workers, 25 June 1955; young Esso workers, 18 February 1956; farm, 26 May
1955.

23 Thanks to Therese Moylan for this information, which she found in 'A Family
Affair', *Irish Independent*, 4 February 1963.

24 Cassidys, *WL*, 25 July 1953; Reckitts, 11 December 1954; Greenmount, 14 April
1956; Stork, 21 March 1953; 17 April 1954. *The Report of the Commission on
Emigration and Other Population Problems 1948-54* (Dublin: SO, 1956, R. 84) and,
before it, books like John A. O'Brien (ed.), *The Vanishing Irish* (London: W. H.
Allen, 1954).

25 CIE, *WL* 12 December 1953, 23 July 1955, 24 May 1958; Kellys 4 October 1952;
Monks 3 September 1955; Gannon 12 November 1955; Cullen 7 April 1951;
Cronin 14 May 1955.

26 Cammon, *WL*, 20 March 1954; trainees, 26 July 1952; other references to air
hostesses, 26 January 1953; 31 October 1953; 18 May 1955; 20 August 1955;
19 October 1955; 21 January 1956.

27 Williams, *WL*, 23 July 1955; Hederman, 23 June 1956; O'Connor, 21 March 1956;
O'Carroll, 25 June 1955; ITGWU conference, 21 July 1956. For more on Tuairim,
the organization of which Hederman was a member, see Tomás Finn, *Tuairim:
Intellectual Debate and Policy Formation: Rethinking Ireland 1954-75* (Manchester:
Manchester University Press, 2012).

28 Politics, *WL*, 26 November 1955; factories, 29 October 1955; designers, 14 May
1955; police, 30 April 1956; Geneva, 14 April 1956; banks, 28 April 1956; peace
comm, 21 January 1956; pay and conditions, 26 May 1956. Makins, *Evelyn Home*,
p. 174. Lesley Johnson and Justine Lloyd, *Sentenced to Everyday Life: Feminism
and the Housewife* (Oxford: Berg, 2004), pp. 23–45.

29 E.g. Korinek's study of the Canadian *Chatelaine*, almost half the readership of
which was rural–agricultural in the 1950s and 1960s. *Roughing It*, pp. 182–4,
363–5.

30 NPC, *WL*, 29 October 1955 and see n. 15 for a sample of Macra entries.

31 *WL*, 29 September 1956.

32 ICA membership, *WL*, 21 June 1958; for histories of these two organizations, see
Aileen Heverin, *ICA*; Alan Hayes (ed.), *Hilda Tweedy and the Irish Housewives
Association: Links in the Chain* (Dublin: Arlen House, 2011).

33 *WL*, 19 April 1952.

34 E.g. Norah Lofts, *WL*, 7 April 1951; Monica Dickens's *The Happy Prisoner*
was serialized from 13 January 1951; Barbara Cartland, 14 July 1951; Pamela

Hinkson, 4 April 1953 and 2 April 1955; A. A. Milne, 7 August 1954; Marghanita Laski, 22 September 1956; Faith Baldwin, 17 September 1955; and Maura Laverty, 12 January 1952, 4 April 1953, 6 February 1954, 22 January 1955, 20 May 1955, 25 May 1957. Laverty will be explained in greater detail in the next chapter.

35 'Are you one of these', *WL*, 2 May 1953, 16 May 1953, 13 June 1953 and so on for about a year. A Man Looks at You, 4 February 1956 ('Do you have a hobby?'); girls' education and emigration, 3 March 1956; women in public life, 17 March 1956; cigarette, 31 March 1956.

36 *WL*, 13 January 1951; 28 August 1955.

37 Aunts Unlimited, *WL*, 21 February 1953; for information on Universal Aunts, see Lucy Lethbridge, *Servants: A Downstairs View of Twentieth-century Britain* (London: Bloomsbury, 2013), pp. 175–9.

38 Makins, *Evelyn Home*, 'the Irish lived in a world of their own', p. 142.

39 *WL*, 31 October 1953. Information on 'M. E. Francis' comes from Mary Blundell, *Margaret Blundell, An Irish Novelist's Own Story by Her Daughter* (Dublin: Catholic Truth Society of Ireland, n.d.c.1955); Margaret Blundell nee Sweetman was born in 1859 and died in 1930.

40 *WL*, 20 March 1954 for those with a specific Marian year theme; also 25 October 1958.

41 Finola Kennedy, *Frank Duff: A Life Story* (London: Continuum, 2011).

42 Stage, *WL*, 10 March 1951; Film office, 9 July 1955; PPU e.g. Ursuline Thurles, 23 August 1952.

43 Louise Fuller, *Irish Catholicism Since 1950: The Undoing of a Culture* (Dublin: Gill & Macmillan, 2002), pp.19–51.

44 *WL*, 13 December 1952, 22 November 1958.

45 *WL*, 28 April 1956.

46 The new look was in, *WL*, 16 August 1958; see Topical Teen Page, 25 October 1958.

47 *WL*, 25 October 1958. The provincial breakdown was as follows: Leinster 12 (36 per cent); Munster 9 (17 per cent), Connacht 3 (9 per cent), Ulster 1 (3 per cent). Britain supplied 7 (21 per cent).

48 *WL*, 21 July 1956; 19 July 1958; 27 September 1958; 6 December 1958. The Christmas number always appeared in early December, for advertising purposes.

49 *WL*, 14 February 1959.

50 *Woman's Realm* April 1958–December 1960.

51 On the popularity of *Woman's Realm* see White, *Women's Magazines*, pp. 170–1 and D. Kynaston, *Modernity Britain, Volume 1: Opening the Box 1957-9* (London: Bloomsbury, 2013), pp. 113–14.

Chapter 2

1	Makins, *Evelyn Home*, pp. 53–4. Claire Rayner, *How Did I Get There From Here?*,
	pp. 333–5 and *passim*; Angela Willans (a.k.a. Mary Grant on *Woman's Own*),
	'Not Being Able To Help Was Agony', [British] *Independent*, 20 January 1993;
	www.independent.co.uk/news/media/media-not-being-able-to-help-was-agony;
	Linda James (Valerie McGrath), *Dear Linda: A Selection of Problems Sent in to*
	the Sunday World 1970-74 (Cork: Mercier Press, 1974), p. 6; Angela Macnamara,
	Yours Sincerely (Dublin: Veritas, 2003). For a discussion of Macnamara's responses
	in the *Sunday Press*, especially on homosexuality, see Paul Ryan, *Asking Angela*,
	and more specifically his article, 'Asking Angela: discourses about sexuality in
	an Irish problem page 1963–1980', *Journal of the History of Sexuality* 19, no. 2
	(May 2010), pp. 317–39. I am indebted to Darragh D'arcy for the Willans/Grant
	reference.

2	Who was Mrs Wyse? The late artist Barry Castle told me that her mother, the
	journalist, novelist, cookery writer, broadcaster and playwright Maura Laverty
	(1907–66) was Mrs Wyse (and also Dr Garry Myers and Delia Dixon the beauty
	expert) in *WL* in the 1930s and 1940s, but whether she continued in this role into
	the 1950s, I do not know. (Dr Myers and Delia Dixon were dropped at this stage,
	but Laverty regularly wrote stories for the magazine; see Chapter 1.) Certainly the
	tone of Mrs Wyse in the 1950s is similar to that of the 1930s and 1940s, and the
	agony aunt's attitudes and style are very like those of Maura Laverty, evident from
	her journalism and other writing. Laverty, a journalist for nearly four decades
	and the author of four critically acclaimed, banned novels in the 1940s, was best
	known to Irish people in the 1960s as a cookery writer, a broadcaster and the
	originator of Ireland's first television soap opera, *Tolka Row*. For discussion of
	Maura Laverty's life and work, see C. Clear, 'The Red Ink of Emotion: the social
	vision of Maura Laverty (1907–1966)', *Saothar 28: Journal of the Irish Labour*
	History Society (2003), pp. 90–9.

3	A small number of men and boys wrote in problems to *WL* too, but as the
	emphasis in this book is on girls and women, they will not be referred to directly
	or discussed.

4	*WL*, 16 May 1953.

5	Am I in Love, *WL*, 9 August 1952, similar problem 3 November 1951, 8 January
	1955, 17 March 1956; 2 lovers, 24 March 1951; too young, 20 October 1951,
	15 December 1951, 8 September 1951, 1 September 1956; office, 31 August 1957;
	married man, 26 December 1953.

6	No mention marriage/lazy lover, *WL*, 9 January 1954, 12 January 1952, 13
	November 1954, 12 April 1958, 13 September 1958; 15 years, 5 May 1951;
	doormat, 28 April 1956; boyfriend neglecting, *Woman's Realm* (hereafter *WR*),

12 July 1958; then jealousy, *WL*, 31 March 1956; drunkenness, 24 January 1953, 21 June 1958; bossiness, 26 May 1956; nastiness in company, 6 March 1954; dancer, 13 October 1956; for granted, 1 November 1952.

7   *WR* problems: won't let her out without him, *WR* 15 October 1960; saw him violent, 24 September 1960; jealous, 21 March 1959, 9 April 1960; moody, 21 March 1959; lukewarm, 22 October 1960.

8   Man 10 years older, *WL*, 5 April 1952; 36-year-old man, 5 May 1951; man 35, 12 January 1952, man 17 years older, 10 July 1954; teacher, 24 March 1951.

9   Four years' seniority on woman's side no problem, *WL*, 5 December 1951, 6 March 1954; worried parents, 1 March 1958; woman 35, 15 February 1958; woman 47, 5 September 1952; man 9 years younger, 22 September 1951.

10   Religious difference *WL*, 4 April 1953; 'not of our class', 7 July 1957; local family, 9 July 1955; boy higher social status, 15 October 1955.

11   Telephonist, *WR*, 6 June 1959; solicitor, 26 September 1959; better educated, 14 March 1959.

12   City girl and farmer, *WL*, 25 July 1953; similar problem, *WR*, 31 January 1959; 'servant boy', *WL*, 16 October 1954; nurse, 5 March 1955.

13   Three bold boys, *WL*, 24 March 1951, and similar problem, 30 August 1958; only child boarding school, 2 June 1951.

14   Factory worker, *WL*, 28 November 1953; 15-year old, 8 March 1952. There was only one troublesome teenager from parents' point of view, 19 January 1951.

15   Problem today, *WL*, 7 April 1951; poor salary, 2 June 1951; hysterical, 13 January 1951.

16   Family rude to fiancé, *WL*, 7 July 1956; future mother-in-law nasty, 7 January 1956; join the household, 27 September 1958; sister-in-law, 14 June 1952.

17   Nasty co-resident mother-in-law, *WR*, 6 September 1958, and 23 April 1960; over-critical mother, 3 January 1959; incompetent opposite mother-in-law, 10 December 1960; fraught daughter-in-law, 19 November 1960; zero tolerance for critical and demanding sisters-in-law, 24 January 1959, 26 November 1960. On Irish extended family, see C. Clear, *Women of the House*, pp. 171–201.

18   *WL*, 12 June 1954.

19   Name only, *WL*, 23 July 1955,; train housekeeper, 16 August 1958; home of own, 22 November 1958.

20   *WR*, 9 January 1960.

21   Two wrongs, *WL*, 30 August 1958; working mother, 14 May 1955; victimized, 26 November 1955; adult brothers, Christmas number 1952.

22   Ugly duckling, *WL*, 6 February 1954; lonely soul, 20 October 1951; 27-year-old son, 13 June 1953.

23   'Orphan', 27 January 1951: similar problem, 26 December 1953.

24 Wartime baby, *WR* 13 February 1960; wanting to find mother, *WR*, 3 September 1960.

25 Sweet 16, *WL*, 3 November 1951; drapery apprentice, 29 January 1951; jangling, 18 October 1952; cheeky colleague, 19 February 1955.

26 Growing older, *WL*, 31 March 1953, 18 April 1953.

27 Married a year and scared of future, *WL*, 28 November 1953; bored already, 20 February 1954; overwhelmed, 16 June 1951.

28 Tables and chairs, *WL*, 7 March 1953 and another undemonstrative husband, 6 March 1954; domestic slant, 21 February 1953; 5 children no help, 31 March 1953; prefers men friends, 29 September 1956; possibly unfaithful, 24 March 1951.

29 *WR*, 11 April 1959. David Kynaston, *Modernity Britain Vol 2: A Shake of the Dice* (London: Bloomsbury, 2014), pp. 229–31 has also drawn attention to magazine problem pages' lack of sympathy for wives.

30 Seething with rage, *WL*, 22 August 1953; best of bargain, 14 July 1951.

31 *WR*, 2 April 1960.

32 Social events, *WL*, 29 November 1953; nanny, 22 January 1955; overburdened granny, 5 July 1958.

33 *WL*, 24 December 1954; 2 April 1955; hasn't ruined you yet, 22 November 1958.

34 *WL*, 2 April 1955; 14 November 1953; 10 January 1953.

35 In six out of eight marriages (seven of them non-farming) begun between 1947 and 1961 in the previous generation of this writer's extended family, the wife had a higher standard of completed education and/or professional training than the husband. It should be added that this did not cause any apparent tensions in these marriages and that the husbands and wives were culturally on a level with one another, but perhaps women who wrote in problems to magazines had higher expectations and lower thresholds of discontent.

36 No interest in marriage, *WL*, 10 May 1958; daughter, 16 August 1958; 40 and depressed, 11 October 1958; 48-year-old 'girl', 15 January 1951.

37 *WR*, 'loner' 15 November 1958; scaring off men, 11 October 1958.

38 Twenty-seven is young, *WL*, 14 April 1956; long grey trail, 13 December 1952; Trying too hard, 28 November 1953, 18 February 1956.

39 Widows and widowers worried about remarrying, *WL*, 3 November 1953; 17 October 1953; 4 September 1954; 29 May 1954; 24 December 1955; 19 January 1957; 13 April 1957; 9 November 1957.

40 Restaurant etiquette, *WL*, 3 November 1953; weddings, 16 May 1953; parties, 20 August 1955. Facts of life (requests for books on) 21 April 1951, 18 October 1952, 23 August 1953; 2 May 1953; 15 April 1954 and many more.

41 *Cri de Coeur*, *WL*, 21 August 1954.

42 E.g. *WR*, 30 August 1958, 19 July 1958; 27 September 1958; 27 December 1958; 6 February 1960; 1 October 1960.

43 Canada, *WR*, 16 August 1958; Germany, 20 September 1958; Malta, 24 December 1960; unspecified, 29 November 1958.

44 Editor comment re: Tanganyika, *WR*, 19 July 1958; Brisbane, 25 October 1958; Bechuanaland, 29 November 1958; Cape Town, 19 July 1958; Rhodesia, 9 August 1958; New Zealand, 11 October 1958; Pakistan, 13 December 1958; Natal, 16 August 1958; Delhi, 27 December 1958; Nyasaland, 24 September 1960.

45 Rolling stone, *WL*, 29 November 1952 and again 29 May 1954.

Chapter 3

1 Marjorie Ferguson, *Forever Feminine*, pp. 30–3; T. F. O'Higgins advertisement, *WW*, 1 May 1966, and apology/explanation that this was an advertisement and not a feature, 15 May 1966.

2 Mrs Kitty Barrett, Clonmel, *WW*, 26 April 1963.

3 Mary Leland on women in the Dáil & Seanad, *WW*, 15 October 1965, on a wife's legal rights, 15 March 1966, on the Mormons in Ireland, 27 January 1967 and on women in unpensionable jobs, 1 February 1966. Veronica Kelly on prostitution, 15 April 1966; Heather Lukes on bedsitter life, 10 February 1967; the same author on wives who go out to work, 21 October 1966. Veronica Kelly on children in institutions, 15 April 1966 and at least three articles on education, by Veronica Kelly, 1 March 1966, Sheelagh Lewis, 21 October 1966 and Maeve Binchy 7 July 1967. Veronica Kelly on interracial marriage, 14 October 1966; Monica McEnroy on the female religious life, 13 January 1967. One of the first publications of the new Irish women's history appeared in *WW*, Máire Comerford's 'Carve Their Name in Pride: women of 1916', *WW*, 1 April 1966. Mentions of Dolly MacMahon, 30 August 1963; Maureen Potter, 25 November 1966; Imogen Stuart, 30 September 1966; Katherine Walsh, 20 January 1967.

4 O'Sullivan, 'By The Way', *WW*, 15 May 1963; 31 January 1964; Caroline Mitchell editorial letter, 15 April 1965.

5 One-fiftieth comment, *WW*, 1 September 1964; Collins, *WW*, 14 June 1964, 15 July 1964, 1 October 1964, 30 September 1965; O' Donoghue, 23 June 1967, 14 July 1967, 8 December 1967, 15 March 1968, 12 July 1968, 24 January 1969; Sheila O'Farrell, 14 October 1963, 1 March 1966, 27 January 1967, 17 February 1967, 4 August 1967, 8 September 1967, 22 December 1967, 19 July 1968, 21 February 1969, 5 September 1969, 19 September 1969; Bunyan, 10 February 1967, 14 July 1967, 17 November 1967, 21 June 1968, 31 October 1969; P. D., 7 April 1967, 30 June 1967, 14 July 1967, 24 November 1967, 5 April 1968, 24 May 1968, 26 July 1968; Hutton, 21 October 1966, 23 February 1968, 21 June 1968, 15 November 1968; Quinn, 17 February 1967, 3 November 1967, 27 September

1968, 11 July 1969, 3 October 1969, and *Young Woman,* 1 September 1967, 24 November 1968; Burke, *WW*, 15 April 1966 and *Miss*, September 1965.

6 Ballaster and Beetham, *Women's Worlds*, pp. 146–7.

7 Clancy Brother, *WW* Christmas issue 1965; Kennedy 31 July 1963; pineapple jelly, 15 February 66; 'guaranteed Irish', 30 June 1967.

8 Mrs Stakem, *WW*, 15 August 1966; 14 October 1966; 11 November 1966; 1 December 1967; and so on up to, 20 December 1968. Mrs Landers began a little later, 24 February 1967, 7 April 1967, 7 July 1967, and kept going till 19 September 1969.

9 One of the many letters written by Jean Bunyan from Listowel praised the mother-in-law who had helped her to rear seven children, but letters like this were very rare. *WW*, 10 February 1967.

10 'Fair-minded', *WW*, 14 March 1964; Crotty, 1 March 1966; and on 27 January 1967, Mrs O. J. Deegan, 'Itinerants' Friend', Sheila O'Farrell, M. F. Mallow. Mrs B. N., Nenagh, 16 June 1967; J. K., Tullamore and M. M., Limerick, 7 February 1969; B.C., Tipperary, 18 April 1969.

11 Overpaid politicians, *WW*, 14 June 1968; rich throwing away food, 9 August 1968; Biafran war and other matters, 29 November 1968; no council house, 29 November 1968.

12 Papist persuasion, *WW*, 14 February 1964; 'The Cloistered Life', 13 January 1967; qualities needed for religious life, 24 February 1967. Figures on vocations taken from Louise Fuller, *Irish Catholicism Since 1950*.

13 Sermons, *WW*, 9 August 1968; female ordination, 23 August 1968; head-covering Fermanagh and Miss C. L., 1 August 1969; dissenter Galway origin, 19 September 1969; mixed religion unable to adopt, 10 May 1968; praise of Fr Cleary, 29 March 1968; populism deplored, 17 May 1968; Cardinal Heenan, 28 February 1969.

14 Bean Uí Chochláin, *WW*, 1 April 1965; Ní Mhuineacháin, 29 March 1968; letters from Blackrock and Dublin 8, 18 November 1966; M. O. Roscommon, 6 January 1967; 'A Parent' Tuam, less Irish more hygiene, 13 January 1967; M. K. 21 March 1969; Ní Néill, 3 October 1969.

15 Mrs M. J. L., *WW*, 15 March 1968; dissenting letters Sligo and Castlebar, 26 April 1968; T. M. R., Dublin, 5 May 1968; M. H. D. 'friendly hand', 31 May 1968; MacDonald, 8 June 1969; A. O'R. 19 September 1969.

16 M. L., Waterford, *WW*, 15 November 1968; 'gentlest of creatures', 13 December 1968; inequalities of wealth, 20 December 1968; do as she likes, 3 January 1969.

17 No regrets, *WW*, 30 November 1963; old kitchen in new house, 7 April 1967; lamenting the thatch, 22 March 1968.

18 Unexpected callers, Thurles (pro), Sligo (con), *WW*, 19 May 1967; men and body hair, 3 October 1969; endearments, 1 June 1966; Strokestown wisdom, 15 September 1964; half-a-lifetime, 13 December 1968.

19 Sweet 16, Clonmel, *WW*, 1 July 1965; John Healy, *No-One Shouted Stop: The Death of an Irish Town* (Cork: Mercier Press, 1966, 68); Offaly student, 16 June 1967; Ballina, 29 September 1967; Tipperary, 19 January 1968; praise for Fr Cleary, 29 March 1968; falling by wayside, 25 April 1969; M. G. 27 September 1968; exploited hotel worker, 24 May 1968; Jean Bunyan story, 31 October 1969.

20 Lowered standards, *WW*, 7 December 1967; Jacobs, 9 February 1968; labourers despised, 5 July 1968; worried about continued equality, Abbeyfeale, 28 April 1968, Flynn, 30 August 1968; Mayo breaking bond, 14 March 1969; feed and clothe Wexford, 2 May 1969; without transport, 27 October 1967; sick parent, 7 March 1969; cherished equally, 19 July 1968.

21 Beatlemania, *WW*, 15 July 1964; 'broad-mindedness' Christmas issue 1965; not all long-haired, 15 August 1966; parents complaining, 15 August 1966; rioting students, 26 July 1968; weary of cudgels, 18 April 1969; Cassian Sweeney, 24 January 1969; grants taken away, 9 May 1969; adults not teens ruining country, 11 April 1969; defending student idealism, 23 May 1969; drainage and ancient monuments, 23 May 1969.

22 Hard-working teen couple, *WW*, 11 November 1966; supporting young marriage, 22 March 1968; against it Mrs M. H., 5 July 1968; tied down, 23 May 1969.

23 The campaign of Frank Crummy against corporal punishment was covered extensively by an equivocal Tanis O'Callaghan in 'Torture of Our Children: do you agree with corporal punishment?', *Young Woman*, 15 September 1967, and I can remember Dr Cyril Daly being held up to ridicule when he appeared on *The Late Late Show* in the early 1970s. Against corporal punishment, *WW*, 15 February 1966; three letters, two against, one for, 22 August 1969, and National teacher against, 14 October 1969.

24 Joy and amusement, *WW*, 1 March 1965; 'Jacqueline', Charles Mitchel column, 10 March 1967.

25 'Mod Mad', *WW*, 30 September 1966; housekeeping and nursing, 16 February 1968; girls' education never wasted, 15 March 1968, even university education, 12 May 1967 and Mrs E. Lucey, Macroom, Co Cork, 30 August 1968; 25 per cent never married, and good match likelihood, 10 May 1968; typing skills, 31 May 1968; badly paid office work, 19 May 1967; compulsory home economics, 1 September 1968, for boys as well as girls, 20 June 1969; kick for what they want, 17 March 1967.

26 Early-to-bed advocates, *WW*, 20 October 1968 and 13 December 1968; mother of 10 loving school holidays, 17 January 1969; children's allowances, nest egg, 3 March 1967; Laois, Tipperary, Kildare and Wicklow suggestions, 21 April 1967; not for young ladies and gentlemen, 20 January 1967. For Children's Allowance information, see Appendix 1.

Chapter 4

1 'Girls' in office, *WW*, 31 August 1963; National teacher, 31 August 1963; hairdresser, 2 December 1966; stay-at-home simple joys, 16 October 1965; Leitrim granny, 30 April 1964 and the same two salaries fear addressed, 3 May 1968; not when children small, 20 January 1967; some activity outside home all the same, 3 November 1967; Cobh, 2 December 1966; Galway, 2 December 1966; stay-at-home father, 21 October 1966; wasting highly trained secretary, 5 July 1968; so long as they don't neglect household responsibilities, 7 November 1969; home knitters, Cavan, 19 January 1968 and Dublin and Kilkenny, 1 March 1968.

2 Sean O'Sullivan's opinions: By the Way' *WW*, 30 November 1963, 14 March 1964; Angela Macnamara, 'Can I Help You' *passim*, but for example, 1 May 1966, 1 September 1967, 16 June 1967. All the letters quoted here were on a page called 'The Pill: what readers think', *WW*, 14 October 1966. Monica McEnroy's original article which sparked debate, 'On The Pill', had appeared in *WW*, 23 September 1966.

3 Mother of 4, *WW*, 11 November 1966; mother of 7, 31 March 1967; a shame to hear Catholic mothers, 24 November 1967; neighbours admire us, 22 September 1969; left family planning to God, 21 June 1968. Evidence from England and Scotland of people not necessarily Catholic and family planning: Kate Fisher, *Birth Control, Sex and Marriage in Britain 1918-1960* (Oxford: Oxford University Press, 2006), pp. 76–108 and 109–88; Helen Clark and Elizabeth Carnegie, *She Was Aye Workin': Memories of Tenement Women in Edinburgh and Glasgow* (Edinburgh: White Cockade, 2003), pp. 78 *passim*; Maureen Sutton, *We Didn't Know Owt: A Study of Sexuality, Superstition and Death in Women's Lives in Lincolnshire in the 1930s, 40s and 50s* (Donington: Shaun Tyas, 2012), pp. 185–99.

4 Loaf under arm, *WW*, 2 June 1967; 25 child bearing years, 29 September 1967; hardship and squalor, 26 January 1968; mental anguish, and heartbreak, both 28 July 1967.

5 Wouldn't mind another five, and knowledge to plan, both *WW*, 26 January 1968; all reactions to Humanae Vitae down to selfish people make bad parents, 6 September 1968.

6 Holy Father should be obeyed, *WW*, 27 September 1968; pleasure without responsibility, 4 October 1968 (and finalist in competition 11 October 1968); Pill not a panacea, 9 May 1969; anti-Biezanek, 8 August 1969. Anne Biezanek wrote a book about her experiences, *All Things New* (London: Peter Smith, 1964). Learned theologians, *WW*, 26 April 1968 and similar point, 16 May 1969.

7 Three Hail Marys, *WW*, 7 April 1967; *An Triail*, 3 March 1967; jail unmarried fathers, 24 March 1967; lack of sex education directly responsible for unmarried mothers, 12 May 1967; city convent, 6 October 1967; and disagreements from

Laois, 10 November 1967, Kilkenny, 17 November 1967; Tullamore, 24 November 1967; Birr, 1 December 1967 and Wicklow, 1 December 1967; boat to Fishguard, 6 October 1967. Mairéad Ní Ghráda's play *An Trial* (Baile Atha Cliath: Rialtas na hEireann, 1978) dealt with an unmarried mother's plight and was first put on stage on 22 September 1964 as part of Dublin Theatre Festival.

8 Plenty of unmarried mothers long ago, *WW*, 12 December 1969; heartbreak to some joy to others, 5 May 1967; comparable letters in *Woman's Own* from adopting parents, 1 January 1966, 15 January 1966, 19 February 1966, 17 September 1966, 22 October 1966, 12 November 1966, and from mother who gave up baby, reassured by earlier letters, 16 April 1966. On the cultural acceptance of anonymous adoption, see Deborah Cohen, *Family Secrets: Living with Shame from the Victorians to the Present Day* (London: Penguin, 2013), pp. 77–142.

9 Reference to Mrs Condell, *WW* Christmas issue, 1965; 'Party Worker, 1 June 1966; more female TDs, 15 August 1966; apathy, 17 November 1967; younger men, 28 April 1967 and the sons who will rule our lives, 5 April 1968, but the same writer on equality, 13 June 1969; supporting men on strike, 26 April 1968; women suffer, 8 November 1968; Minister for Housekeeping, 16 May 1969 and similar letter in *Woman's Own*, 22 October 1966.

10 Berenice Russell article, *Young Woman*, 27 October 1967; Female assisting relative Athy, *WW*, 1 May 1965; farmer's wife, 15 May 1966, and sour responses to, both, 1 March 1966; impertinent young Cork farmer, 7 April 1967; demands of farmer boyfriend at home, 19 May 1967; teenage farmer questions, 26 May 1967; 'wonderful mother', health and happiness and farmer has to be careful, all, 21 July 1967; nine bachelors, 27 August 1967; dame not game, 30 September 1966; angry at farm women complaining, 16 September 1966; reference to Knock Marriage Bureau, 15 August 1969; ICA faulted for not training women, 7 June 1968. For additional information on this very active protofeminist organization, see Linda Connolly, *Irish Feminist Movement*.

11 Information on place of birth, see C. Clear, *Women of the House*, pp. 109 and 96–125, and decline of breastfeeding, pp. 126–43. More rest at home, *WW*, 14 October 1966; left alone in labour, 11 November 1966; 28 hours 18 December 1966; husbands staying; maternity home help, 2 May 1969; people who could only talk about children boring, 13 October 1967.

12 'Spinster' corny, *WW*, 14 August 1963, unclaimed treasure, 30 September 1963, single because too fussy, 14 October 1963; Katharine Holden, *The Shadow of Marriage, passim*; not freaks, *WW*, 19 September 1969; criticizing women for faulting undemonstrative husbands, 30 June 1967; act the dumb cluck, 16 February 1968.

13 No dancehall, *WW*, 23 February 1968; and the four indignant responses, 5 April 1968.

14 Wake up widows, *WW*, 15 March 1968; reared seven children to Leaving Certificate, 7 February 1969; go places and is happy, 11 November 1966.

15 Peeling vegetables, *WW*, 26 April 1963; buttons, 1 June 1963; wonderful mother, 15 April 1965; no loneliness, 15 June 1966; riches, 14 May 1964; grandchildren, 30 June 1964; little surprises, 9 June 1966; polishing shoes, 13 January 1967; always breakfast in bed, 10 February 1967; wives shouldn't get tea in bed, 28 April 1967; never got tea in bed, 10 March 1967; change out of housekeeping money, 14 April 1967; *Quicksilver*, 8 November 1968; marriage ceremony, 12 December 1969.

16 Dismay at divorce, *WW*, 16 February 1968; 'Divorce' article, 24 November 1967; Britain's Bloody Mistake', 22 August 1969.

17 Letter praising Sean Ross Abbey, *WW*, 1 November 1968; Martin Sixsmith, *The Lost Child of Philomena Lee* (London: Pan, 2010); on Cabra, Eileen Murphy, 'The Heartbreak Stories of Two Unmarried Mothers', *YW*, 15 July 1967; and Tanis O'Callaghan, 'A Plea for Compassion', *YW*, 1 September 1967; county home reference, Monica McEnroy, 'Born Out of Wedlock', *WW*, 10 February 1967.

18 Man's world, *WW*, 10 March 1967; women not baking bread letter, 3 February 1967 and indignant response to it 24 March 1967; woman's place in home, 14 June 1964 and 15 August 1966.

19 Ferguson, *Forever Feminine*, pp. 54–6.

Chapter 5

1 For discussion on Laverty and Macnamara, see notes 1 and 2, Chapter 2. I have been unable to find any information on the short-lived (in print) Sylvia Grace.

2 Cousin marriage, *WW* 'Your Health', 1 May 1966 and Angela Macnamara's page, 9 August 1968.

3 VD TV, *WW*, 12 May 1967; pregnant in car, 26 April 1968; no girl over 13, 19 May 1967; 'scandalous' ignorance, 3 April 1967; 4 girls, 14 July 1967; 16-year-old daughter, 4 August 1968; innocence versus ignorance, 23 September 1966; Helga, 18 July 1969; hymen, 10 November 1967; embryo, 30 September 1965; miscarriage, 28 July 1967; French letter 6 October 1967, and 'should not be used', 25 April 1968; French kissing, 30 April 1964, 10 November 1967; abortion, 28 April 1967; breast feeding, 12 July 1968; pregnant without having sex, 4 August 1967, 10 January 1969; first time one has sex, 3 November 1967 and again, 10 November 1967; sex without knowing it, 4 October 1968; tampons, 15 February 1966, 9 June 1967; immodest touching, 4 July 1968; passionate kissing, 28 April 1967, 6 September 1968; books, 18 August 1967, 24 April 1968, 12 July 1968, 9 May 1969.

4 'Bikini set', *WW*, 15 November 1965; Is kissing always wrong, 31 October 1963, no longer completely happy, 14 July 1964, arouse his own passions, 16 October 1965, motorbike accident, 19 April 1968. Girls setting pace all other agony aunts, see Marjorie Ferguson, *Forever Feminine*, pp. 54–5; guinea pigs, *WW*, 14 June 1964, girls' heads on shoulder, Christmas issue 1964; mini-miniskirts, 15 March 1968, 'hard to tempt', 4 October 1968, boys just want to shift, 14 April 1967.

5 This assurance that boys/men who respected girls/women would not pressurize them into intimacy came up so often that just one example is given here, *WW*, 1 February 1965; other girl into trouble, 16 March 1969; medical student boyfriend, Inter Cert girlfriend, 9 August 1968; 30-year-old doctor boyfriend, 12 April 1968; the car as site of danger, 24 March 1967; the bedsitter likewise, 19 July 1968; vulnerable far-from-home worker, 8 December 1967; lonely in a city uninstructed, 1 November 1965; far from kind 33-year-old, 31 May 1968; 19-year-old pregnant by married man, 5 April 1968; 16-year-old pregnant by 40-year-old, 11 April 1969; 18-year-old pregnant by 30-year-old, 18 April 1969; rear child in family, 30 June 1964; parents shocked at pregnant engaged daughter, 14 March 1964.

6 Fifteen-year-old law of God, *WW*, 7 October 1966; bad experience aged 11, 26 May 1967; kissed by 27-year-old, 23 June 1967; wife put out rumours, 14 February 1969; used so cruelly, 15 March 1968; tell parents or police, 12 July 1968; waitress in café, 10 October 1969; 16-year-old offered 'roll of notes' by married man in hotel, 12 July 1967; predatory landlord, 24 October 1969.

7 Incest, *WW*, 5 January 1968 and 'near-relation', 16 February 1968.

8 Don't have to tell boyfriend about past sexual experiences, *WW*, 30 September 1966, 13 October 1967, 27 October 1967, 22 August 1969; religious life virginity not mandatory, 12 April 1968, 24 January 1969. Pal's fiancée with a past, 24 February 1967.

9 Doesn't have to tell boyfriend about baby, *WW*, 17 January 1969; assaulted 2 years previously, 16 August 1968; boyfriend no good if dropped her for this reason, 7 November 1969 and 17 January 1969; daughter in England had baby with 'coloured' man, 30 August 1968; 'babies not husbands', 7 July 1967, 11 July 1969; and pregnant/non-virgin brides can wear white if they like, 1 March 1965, 24 November 1967, 8 March 1968, (the holier than thou response) 21 February 1969.

10 Not interested in 'physical side', *WW*, 1 August 1964; not the slightest physical emotion, 7 April 1967; attracted to own sex, 2 August 1968, didn't like men kissing her, 5 July 1968.

11 Primary purpose children *WW*, 1 May 1966; surround yourselves with comfort, 16 June 1967; 'do have a baby soon', 1 September 1967; book on natural family planning, 24 November 1967, and uncritical provision of natural spacing information, 26 June 1969.

12 Husband has to 'have intimacy', *WW*, 17 November 1967; can only afford 4, 3 November 1967; haven't implemented it properly, 8 June 1969; instructions and book, 28 November 1969; too late for the Pill, 10 January 1969. On girls' sexual maturity, Carol Dyhouse, *Girl Trouble: Panic and Progress in the History of Young Women* (London: Zed Books, 2013), pp. 105–36.

13 Angela Macnamara, *Yours Sincerely*, pp. 81–5; need for sex education queried, *WW*, 15 September 1964; three motherless girls, 16 March 1967; leaving the car, 23 August 1968. Resist pressure to have sex *Woman's Own* (hereafter *WO*), 5 March 1966; no need to divulge details of past, 19 March 1966 and 16 July 1966; is petting wrong, 8 January 1966; avoid getting carried away, 22 January 1966. British National Marriage Guidance Council leaflet recommending 'heavy petting', Claire Langhamer, *The English in Love: The Intimate Story of an Emotional Revolution* (Oxford: Oxford University Press, 2013), p. 159.

14 Advice and information, *WO*, 25 June 1966, 30 July 1966; safe period comment, 5 February 1966.

15 Paul Ryan, *Asking Angela, passim*; 13-year-old's guilt, *WW*, 5 April 1968 and see comment at end of this note; mother would 'kill' her, 27 September 1968; close dancing, 20 December 1968; you don't allow much, 2 August 1968; engaged couples, 17 February 1967, 4 August 1967 and 29 March 1968; voice our opinions, 27 September 1968; 'grave sin', 1 October 1964. Irish Catholic female readers over the age of 50 might remember that strong feeling of shame and guilt for knowing 'the facts of life' when they were not 'supposed to' and then, once they had been 'told', the strict instructions not to impart this knowledge to anybody else; this probably stemmed from enlightened mothers' fears that other mothers would blame them for destroying their daughters' 'innocence'.

Chapter 6

1 There were so many of all of these kinds of problems that only a sample of references to specific ones mentioned is given here. How to 'go with' a boy, *WW*, 27 August 1967; what to do/how to act on a date, 15 October 1965, Christmas issue 1965, 21 July 1967, 29 August 1969. 'Two girls' looking for boys in general, 10 March 1967, 21 November 1969; wanting particular boys to notice them, 17 August 1968; in unrequited love, 28 July 1967, 6 September 1968; wanting to break off gently, 27 June 1969; not knowing what to do on a date, 9 February 1968; and never get asked to dance, 16 February 1968. Youngsters advised not to 'go steady', 30 June 1964, 15 January 1966, 15 April 1966, 15 July 1964. He doesn't know I exist/crying my heart out for him, 1 February 1965, 24 November 1967, 21 March 1968, 1 August 1968. Sending anonymous cards, 30 June 1967; comment

on telephoning, 15 August 1964. Romeo and Juliet, 3 October 1969. Torn between two lovers, 30 September 1963; man in city and man 'at home'. On the historical background, see Robin Kent, *Aunt Agony Advises: Problem Pages Through the Ages* (London: W. H. Allen, 1979), pp. 1–121.

2 Boyfriend never asks girlfriend to meet family, *WW*, 31 July 1963; sulks, 15 June 1963; free to meet other girls but doesn't want her to meet other boys, 15 September 1965, 15 January 1966; boyfriends who drank, 15 July 1966, 17 November 1967, 10 May 1968; violent drunken 39-year-old, 8 September 1967; very demanding 'mean and selfish' boyfriend, 31 January 1964; 'immature' selfish boyfriend life miserable, 15 February 1965; women rearing children outside marriage, 1 November 1968, 15 November 1968. (The fact that these two quite unusual letters appeared so close together could indicate that one encouraged the other or could signal a new openness on the part of the magazine to problems like this.) Nineteen-year-old, fiancé 23 years older, 15 July 1964; 20-year-old with 45-year-old boss, 4 July 1969, 20-year-old with 44-year old, 4 October 1968; older woman, 29 March 1968, 6 September 1968; different religion 25 and 47, 23 February 1968; different religion teenagers, 1 September 1964; Protestant with car, 21 June 1968; don't convert Protestant boyfriend, 1 July 1966.

3 'Negro', *WW*, 30 November 1963, and 'coloured boyfriend', 13 January 1967; fearful of boyfriend's higher-status family, 13 January 1967, 13 June 1969. Labourer versus tradesman prospect, 28 June 1968; 'desperately in love', 1 June 1969; man whose manners weren't up to par, 28 November 1969; man who wasn't 'all action', 5 September 1969; aunt forcing neighbour's attentions, 14 April 1967.

4 Overtired mother of 5, *WW*, 26 April 1963; over-controlling husband, 1 June 1963; can't expect husband to help with housework after day's work 31 August 1963; people more to be pitied than the *bean a'tighe*, 30 September 1963. A full reference to Betty Friedan's book, which appeared in this year, can be found in the notes to the introduction to this volume. Young wife appalled at prospect of housework, 5 May 1967; persuade husbands to help, 31 March 1964; working wife let him see how tired you are, 27 January 1967; spoilt sons make spoilt husbands, 28 October 1966; go out without husbands, 1 March 1965, 11 November 1966; six children no friends, 5 May 1967. Lack of friends was a real problem – as a child in the 1960s and 1970s I can remember the parent generation of my family being somewhat contemptuous of married women (never single women) who went out with or were close to 'friends' as opposed to family and extended family.

5 Bride's blues, *WW*, 27 January 1967; charmer no more, 15 September 1964; wanting more romance, 13 January 1967; husband calling her Mammy, 15 March 1968; husband only getting sex once a week, 28 June 1968, every three months, 5 December 1969; women not liking sex, husband 'undemonstrative',

14 April 1964; husband doesn't 'satisfy' her, 9 December 1966; not since the baby, 1 December 1967, and a similar problem in the same issue; hadn't adapted to 'intimate' side of marriage, 10 November 1967; wonderful husband and two doctors not helping, 19 September 1969; whether pregnant or not, 14 June 1968; man worried about pregnant wife, 26 April 1968; liberties and nothing else, 23 September 1966.

6 Ten stormy years, *WW*, 10 October 1969; very violent situation, 12 December 1969; cruel husband gone to England, 1 August 1966; comment on 'unfaithfulness problems', 1 February 1966; brother-in-law, 14 April 1964; 'gone cold', 14 October 1963, neglect, 21 October 1966; reserves of patience and love, 8 March 1968; heavy drinking the only problem, 14 February 1969.

7 Affair with best friend's husband, *WW*, 12 May 1967; 27-years-married woman having affair, 31 January 1969; young married woman having affair, 14 March 1969; possible workplace affair, 25 July 1969. Technically unmarried married man relationship, 13 December 1968; second union, 11 April 1969. Mary Grant's advice to those in similar situations is exemplified in her comment to one such problem, where the man's original marriage had broken up through mutual consent, *WO*, 26 February 1966: 'There are many happy, loving families who have not had the blessing of legal status.' Peter Hennessy, *Having It So Good: Britain in the Fifties* (London: Penguin, 2007), pp. 129–31, discusses marriage breakdown in the 1950s.

8 Unfaithful while wife expecting second baby, *WO*, 30 July 1966; snap out of it and take him back, 30 April 1966 and more or less the same message, 16 July 1966, 27 August 1966; husband wanting to go, 9 April 1966; after reasonably happy 20 years, 22 October 1966; lower standard of living, 26 November 1966; married 34 years, 12 March 1966. Brutal husbands, one about to be divorced, one just divorced, both, 24 September 1966. Husband hits her, 2 years feels like 52, 1 January 1966; another violent husband, 26 February 1966; fiercely jealous husband, 20 August 1966; humiliates her in company, 3 September 1966; mean with money, 5 March 1966, 2 July 1966; no loving words during sex, 27 August 1966; will this prevent conception? 2 July 1966; 55 and still going strong, 15 October 1966 (and a similar 'problem' and response, *WW*, 15 December 1967), and husband's disinclination for sex a problem, *WO*, 10 September 1966.

9 Violent boyfriend, *WO*, 22 October 1966; bad-tempered, 28 October 1966; petty offenders, 19 February 1966, 25 June 1966, 27 August 1966; boyfriend chance to work abroad, 19 March 1966; student dilemma, 15 October 1966; trying to catch boyfriend with pregnancy, 4 June 1966 and test him with fake pregnancy, 10 September 1966; breach of promise married man, 14 May 1966; and other married men problems 6/2, 25/6, 30/7, 6/8 and 13/8, plus a 17-year-old who was meeting in secret a 40-year-old married friend of her parents, 30 April 1966.

10 Irish girl pregnant, *WO*, 13 August 1966; engaged and wanting to end pregnancy, 9 April 1966; bitter about unmarried mothers, 16 July 1966; the student's advice about girls as friends, 21 May 1966; assurances to single women that way of life valid, 28 May 1966, 16 July 1966, 5 November 1966, sister who calls her a 'cabbage', 9 July 1966; Irish girls – life is an awful strain, *WW*, 29 September 1967.

Chapter 7

1 Bathroom, *WW*, 14 March 1964; telephone, 14 April 1964; trying hard to be patient, 8 November 1968; mother won't allow them to marry before 21, 2 February 1968; obliged to obey parents, 30 April 1964; fuddy-duddy parents, 28 October 66; 16-year-old burdened with housework, 7 February 1967; money from part-time jobs, Christmas issue 1964; 17-year-old sneaking out on dates, 14 June 1964; 21-year-old student small town, 29 November 1968; junior clerk curfew, 15 February 1964.

2 Not all teenagers the same, *WW*, 17 March 1967; 18-year-old likewise engaged, 14 March 1964, and 19-year-old in similar predicament, 17 April 1967; 20-year-old friend top of class rearing motherless siblings, 7 July 1967; Canada, 18 August 1967; mother with arthritis, 16 September 1966.

3 Seventeen-year-old looking after house while mother at work, *WW*, 1 June 1963; helping in parents' shop, 11 August 1967; 40-year-old carer would like to marry, 13 December 1968; different from everybody else, 8 August 1969; arthritic/alcoholic uncle (1) 2 September 1967, and arthritic/alcoholic uncle (2) 28 February 1969.

4 Over protective parents of heart-complaint woman, *WW*, 26 January 1968, and partial invalid, 24 October 1969. Four teenage boys, 30 June 1964; boys being punished for lies, 1 August 1965; excessive severity, 15 September 1965 and books including Spock, 15 February 1965. Dr Benjamin Spock's *The Common Sense Book of Baby and Child Care* (New York: Duell, Sloan and Pierce, 1946) was a byword for permissive, unacceptably soft parenting among my parents and their peers (all married c. 1948–54 – I was born in 1960). I was amazed, when babysitting once, to read in the Dr Spock volume belonging to the young couple (married a generation later, significantly) a child-rearing philosophy and practice quite similar to that of my parents.

5 Features and articles about adoption, *WW*, 15 July 1964, 12 May 1967, 27 July 1967, 13 June 1969, 20 June 1969. Married 5 years considering adoption, 31 December 19; adopted person advised not to contact birth mother, 20 January 1967; wiser to have child adopted, 31 December 1963; telling the child, 24 October 1969.

6 Mother-in-law buzzing, *WW*, 31 January 1964; other mother/mother-in-law
   problems, 15 May 1963, 15 June 1963, 14 November 1963. Roscommon sister-in-
   law, 14 October 1963; middle-aged sibling tangle of obligation 31 July 1963.

7 Nursing *WW*, 26 March 1963, 14 August 1963, 30 September 1963 and
   Christmas issue, 1964. Drama school 31 December 1963, dressmaking, 15 June
   1963. What to wear to an interview, 14 April 1964, 3 September 1965. Lay
   missionary, 16 September 1965. Religious life, 14-year-old, 15 October 1964;
   28 too old? 27 June 1969; daughter wanting to be nun, 18 December 1966;
   broken-hearted wanting to enter convent, 31 January 1969 and 14 February
   1969. On the female religious life in twentieth-century Ireland, Yvonne
   McKenna, *Made Holy: Women Religious in Twentieth-century Ireland* (Dublin:
   Irish Academic Press, 2005).

8 Husband's unhealthy eating, *WW*, 15 May 1963; two girls at work, 1 August 1964;
   husband reluctant to pray, 14 December 1963 and response, 30 December 1963;
   'scruples', 5 May 1967 (see note at end). Confession, 17 February 1967; sex while
   pregnant, 6 January 1967; confessor doesn't understand difficulty, 1 August 1966;
   sinned already, 31 October 1969; fear of immodestly touching while washing,
   7 April 1967. Protestant girl dissuaded from converting, 28 February 1969; is
   single life a vocation? 5 September 1969; daily communicant, 1 May 1965; single
   life other girls pity me, 3 September 1965; and single and 40, 13 September 1968.
   'Scruples' is the fault of believing you have committed sin without actually having
   done so. A Catholic Truth Society of Ireland pamphlet, Rev W. P. O'Keeffe, CM,
   Scruples: How to Avoid Them (Dublin: CTSI, 1944, 1960) was reprinted several
   times and was found in many devout Catholic homes up to the 1970s, including
   the one in which I grew up.

9 All these are taken from *WW* 'Social Know-how' in 1969: cancel wedding, pay for
   flowers, can widow wear white, funeral etiquette, 24 January; and christening, how
   to organize a dance and Christian names, 21 February.

10 Storing cheese, and omelette, *WW*, 'Check-pot', 14 April 1967; croutons,
   barmbrack and sheep's heart, 1 March 1969; mock cream and iced coffee,
   19 September 1969.

11 Fifteen years on the family farm, *WW*, 'Counsel's Opinion', 26 September 1969;
   engagement ring, 14 February 1969.

12 The first issue of every month during 1965–6, and occasionally thereafter, offered
   advice on different careers; e.g. medicine, *WW*, 'Careers Advice', 1 August 1966;
   advertising and PR 1, March 1966; and the writer who just wanted to get married,
   10 March 1967.

13 'Your Health', *WW*, 15 September 1964; Varicose veins and the other problems,
   25 July 1969; and the Pill as contraceptive, 23 August 1968. The belief that it
   was dangerous to wash hair and feet while menstruating was also common in

Lincolnshire in the 1940s and 1950s, and I also heard it in Limerick city in the early 1970s. Maureen Sutton, *We Didn't Know Owt*, pp. 19–36.

14 Breastfeeding dismissed, 'Mother and Child Feeding Problems by a Child Specialist', *WW*, 30 September 1963; and bottle-feeding presented as norm 'Your Baby Comes Home', 1 September 1964. Promoted in Young Motherhood Bureau, 1 February 1965, 15 May 1966 and several times thereafter. Home birth, 19 December 1969; mothers working outside home, 11 July 1969; smoking in pregnancy, 15 May 1966.

15 Twelve to fourteen too young, *Woman's Own* problem page (hereafter *WO*), 5 February 1966, 19 February 1966; 16 pushing it, 8 January 1966, 19 March 1966, 8 October 66, 5 January 1966. Seventeen-year-old's worried mother, 19 November 1966; parents forbidding 20-year-old to go out with man, 3 November 1966.

16 Peter Hennessy, *Having It So Good*, pp. 492–6; Dominic Sandbrook, *Never Had It So Good: A History of Britain from Suez to the Beatles* (London: Abacus, 2005), pp. 103–7, 124–5. *Cathy Come Home*, directed by Ken Loach and written by Jeremy Sandford and Ken Loach, was first broadcast on 16 November 1966 and concerned a young couple's ultimately doomed attempts to find emergency accommodation.

17 Two worried grandmothers, *WO*, 30 April 1966 and 12 November 1966; amused letter about modern grandmother 'racing around on her scooter', Mrs M. Jones, Bucks, 14 May 1966. On continuity in family patterns in Britain, David Kynaston, *Modernity Britain Volume 2*, pp. 161–6.

18 Harlow, from Mrs M. Stevenson, *WO*, letters page, 12 November 1966; leaving the farm, M. M., Limerick city, *WW*, letters page, 11 July 1969.

Conclusion

1 *WW*, 31 July 1963, letters to the editor.

2 Odhams and Amalgamated Press were at the forefront of the consolidation movement in periodical publications in the UK at this time, according to Howard Cox and Simon Mowatt, *Revolution from Grub Street: A History of Magazine Publishing in Britain* (Oxford: Oxford University Press, 2014), p. 83.

3 Mrs Oishi, Cheshire, *WO* letters page, 26 November 1966; Mr A. R. Kimmings, Middlesex, 19 February 1956; Mrs M. L., Cork, *Woman's Way* letters page, 7 March 1969.

4 *WR* problem page, 12 July 1958.

5 Letters on emigration, *WW*, (one letter) 10 June 1967; 29 September 1967; 19 January 1968; 29 March 1968; 27 September 1968 (two letters); 25 April 1969; 24 October 1969.

6   Nurse in Surrey, *WW*, letters page, 10 February 1967; Mrs V. Burriss children
    learning language and legends, 9 June 1967 and north south friendship,
    18 December 1966; Irish emigrants to England 'ne'er-do-wells', 31 October 1969;
    not all smug suburbia, 15 August 1969. In fairness, Mrs J. O'Driscoll, Cork, 8 June
    1969, to whom Peck was reacting, was not so much attacking British suburbs as
    lamenting Irish imitations of them.

7   Irish magazine beautiful balance *WW*, 14 October 1966; married hospital nurse
    working in England, 1 November 1966; Englishmen the best husbands *WR* letters
    page, 2 May 1959.

8   Foolishly spending money on education rather than house improvement, *WW*,
    8 March 1968; Judith Flanders, *The Making of Home* (London: Atlantic, 2014),
    pp. 1–6. (Oddly, Flanders includes Ireland in a sort of pan-British culture of
    'home' and does not appear to notice the language difference); making-do in
    Kerry, *WR*, 12 July 1958; cottage coming up in the world, WW, 4 November
    1966.

9   Cannot rule her life, *WR* problem page, 14 February 1959; cut me out of her life,
    14 March 1959; pressure on newly married daughter, 24 December 1960.

10 Deborah Cameron, 'A Self Off The Shelf? Consuming women's empowerment',
    in Maggie Andrews and Mary M. Talbot (eds), *All the World and Her Husband:
    Women in Twentieth-century Consumer Culture* (London: Cassell, 2000),
    pp. 210–23.

11 Kissing no longer happy, *WW* problem page, 14 July 1964; over-scrupulous non-
    kisser, 19 October 1968.

12 Ferguson, *Forever Feminine*, pp. 39–77; better educated, *WW*, problem page,
    22 September 1967.

13 E.g. *Miss,* June 1965, vol. 1, no. 2, Thelma Mansfield chaired a discussion on 'Teen
    Topics' including going steady, sex, corporal punishment and whether or not
    girls should pay their way on dates. *Miss,* October 1965, Clare Boylan, 'How Not
    to Catch a Man'; and January 1966, 'A Girl's Guide to Office Men', and October
    1966, 'Sex, Religion and the Younger Set', *YW*, 15 July 1967, no. 3, carried articles
    on the film *The Group* (the film of the Mary McCarthy book), on 15 September
    on 'Torture of Our Children in School: Corporal Punishment' and 27 October
    1967 on country girls in Dublin. Problems advising against heavy petting, *Miss,*
    September 1965 and October 1966; and *YW*, 15 September 1967; stay with
    violent husband, *YW*, 24 November 1967. These are tremendously interesting and
    attractive magazines with a high level of reader engagement – justice cannot be
    done to them here. But, sadly and tellingly, they did not last.

14 *WR*, letters 24 September 1960; *WW*, letters, 1 March 1966.

15 J. Scanlan, *Inarticulate Longings*, p. 5.

16 *WL*, 22 June 1957; husband calling wife Mammy, *WW*, 15 March 1968.

Appendix 1

1   Most of the information about developments in these decades is taken from
    J. J. Lee, *Ireland* (whose chapter on the period 1945–58 is entitled 'Malaise',
    pp. 271–328; the following chapter, on the 1960s, is entitled 'Expansion',
    pp. 329–410) and from Dermot Keogh, *Twentieth-century Ireland: Nation and
    State* (Dublin: Gill & Macmillan, 1994), whose chapter on the 1950s is entitled
    'The Politics of Drift', pp. 214–42 and on the 1960s, 'Seán Lemass and the Rising
    Tide of the 1960s', pp. 243–94.

2   *Report of the Commission on Emigration and Other Population Problems 1948–54*
    (Dublin: Stationery Office, 1956), R. 84. On female National teachers, Eoin
    O'Leary, 'The INTO and the marriage bar for women national teachers 1922–58',
    Saothar: Journal of the Irish Labour History Society 12 (1987), pp. 47–52. On
    business women, Therese Moylan, 'Women entrepreneurs and self-employed
    business-owners in Ireland 1922–1972', PhD diss., NUI, Galway, 2015.

3   Enda Delaney, *Demography*, pp. 112–287. The stereotype of the Irish nurse has
    some basis in reality: in the 1950s, Delaney notes, 11 per cent of Irish-born
    women in Britain were nurses or midwives, p. 207. On male emigrants, see
    Ultan Cowley, *The Men Who Built Britain: A History of the Irish Navvy* (Dublin:
    Wolfhound, 2001), pp. 109–256.

4   On children's allowances and their introduction, see Clear, *Women of the House*,
    pp. 27–67 and *passim*. On health developments, Ruth Barrington, *Health,
    Medicine and Politics*, pp. 137–278.

5   On women's legal status, Yvonne Scannell, 'The Constitution and the Role of
    Women', in Brian Farrell (ed.), *De Valera's Constitution and Ours* (Dublin: Gill &
    Macmillan, 1988), pp. 123–36.

Appendix 2

1   John Horgan, *Irish Media: A Critical History Since 1922* (London: Routledge, 2001)
    only has newspaper circulation figures from the 1990s onwards. Norah Casey, in
    conversation with me (15 August 2013, in Harmonia's offices, Dundrum, Dublin),
    averred that it is nearly impossible to find magazine circulation figures before the
    1980s.

2   *Dáil Eireann Debates*, 24 March 1955, vol. 149; response of Mr Sweetman,
    Minister for Finance, to a question from Mr J. Larkin on circulation figures for
    newspapers and periodicals in which government advertisements appear,
    http://historical-debates.oireachtas.ie/D/0149/(D.)0149.1955032400024.html.

Woman's Life did not furnish any figures, nor did *Irish Tatler and Sketch* or *Woman's Mirror*, and such an inquiry/response did not feature again in the Dáil debates in this decade.

3   Nancy Dingle, Gene Tierney, *Woman's Mirror* (hereafter *WM*) April 1953; Rosemary Timperley/Tyrone Power, April 1951; Barbara Bel Geddes (later Miss Ellie in *Dallas*), October 1951; Rosemary Clooney, June 1954; 'Baby on Holiday'/ Bogart family and Audrey Hepburn, July 1955; and several pictures of Joan Crawford and family, 'What Do Your Children Read?', August 1955, and 'Habits ...', October 1953. Glynis Johns typifies the modern beauty, March 1955, but appeared also, June 1954. Doris Day, September 1951 and October 1952.

4   Household hint competition winners, *WM* November 1952; 'Memo for Any Husband' by June Carson, January 1954, was one of the very few relationship articles in this magazine.

5   Bríd Mahon, *WM* February 1951; Paddy Dunlea, March 1951 and April 1952; Dublin Marionette Group, April 1951; Pepita Keating and Maureen Cusack, February 1951; playwright Louise Murphy, November 1951; Dublin Esperanto Club, May 1951; Fr Mathew Players, January 1951; Royalettes, April 1952; Old Belvedere Society, November 1951; Mollie Brazil, October 1951; League of Health, April 1951.

6   I am indebted to Dr Therese Moylan, Institute of Art, Technology and Design, Dun Laoghaire, for this information on the O'Kellys.

7   Maureen O'Hara, *WM* August 1951; no interest in politics, November 1953.

8   I looked at *Model Housekeeping* from November 1955 to October 1963 and from November 1961 to October 1964. The story set in Ireland that I came across was 'Sufficient for the Day', by Mary E. M. O'Donovan, in January 1957 – a very subtle, unresolved story about a child being reared in a public house with neglectful parents, a loving 'maid' and good neighbours. Books reviewed in April 1956 included Nora Burke, *Jungle Child*; Edward Grierson, *The Second Man*; William Sansom, *Contest of Ladies*; John Wiles, *Scene of the Meeting*; James Hanley, *Leave*; Phyllis Harker, *The Beginner Housewife*; Hilda Hewett, *Week at the Seaside*; and plays included James Cheasty, *A Stranger Came* and Seamus Byrne, *Design for a Headstone*. Choice of the month was Marvine Howe, *One Woman's Morocco*. Plays by Beckett and Sartre at the Pike Theatre were reviewed in September 1962 alongside *The Student Prince* in the Olympia. A holiday article in August 1957, 'In Pursuit of the Sun', dealt with Zanzibar, Sicily and Malta; in June 1963, the destination was Portofino. Spring cleaning illustrated with Sacre Coeur, March 1964, 'Preparing for the Great Clean-up' by Patricia; article by the same journalist in September 1964 complaining about deportment not being taught in schools and flower shows not being judged by horticulturists (and wondering where 'loofahs' have gone) illustrated by the Canaries and Dalmatia.

9   I am thankful to Norah Casey, CEO of Harmonia Publishing, for giving me an interview and a lot of background information on this publication.

10 Cover advertisements, any issue of *Irish Tatler and Sketch*, 1951–65. Dudley–Childers forthcoming wedding, *Irish Tatler and Sketch*, October 1952; Little–Macnamara engagement, January 1953 (this was Angela Macnamara who has been discussed extensively in this book); Bonar Law–Neill wedding, November 1959; Lenihan–Devine wedding, December 1958.

Appendix 3

1   Information on Irish population taken from *Census of Ireland* 1946, vol. II, Table 1C and *Census of Ireland* 1971, vol. III, Table 7a and 8 and vol. V, p. xiii and Table 1B. Information on British married women working taken from Deborah Simonton, *A History of European Women's Work 1700 to the Present* (London: Routledge, 1998), pp. 191–3.

Bibliography

Official publications

Report of the Commission on Emigration and Other Population Problems 1948–54
(Dublin: Stationery Office, 1956), R. 84.
Censuses of Ireland, 1946, 1961, 1971.

Newspapers and periodicals, including women's magazines

Irish Tatler and Sketch, October 1952 to May 1966.
Miss, June 1965 to December 1966.
Model Housekeeping, November 1955 to May 1963.
Rural Ireland: Muintir na Tire Official Publication (annual), (Tipperary: Muintir na Tire
    Publications, 1950–64).
Woman's Life, 8 January 1951 to 14 February 1959.
Woman's Mirror, January 1951 to February 1956.
Woman's Own, January to December 1966.
Woman's Realm, July to December 1958; January to June 1959.
Woman's Way, April 1963 to December 1969.
Young Woman, 31 May 1967 to 22 December 1967.

Unpublished dissertation

Therese Moylan, 'Women entrepreneurs and self-employed business-owners in Ireland
    1922–1972', PhD diss., NUI, Galway, 2015.

Secondary sources: Books and articles

Ballaster, R., Beetham M., Frazer, E. and Hebron, S., *Women's Worlds: Ideology,*
    Femininity and the Woman's Magazine (London: Macmillan, 1991).
Barrington, Ruth, *Health, Medicine and Politics in Ireland 1900–1970* (Dublin: Institute
    of Public Administration, 1987).

Biezanek, Anne, *All Things New* (London: Peter Smith, 1964).

Blundell, Mary, *Margaret Blundell: An Irish Novelist's Story by Her Own Daughter* (Dublin: Catholic Truth Society of Ireland, 1955).

Braithwaite, Brian, *Women's Magazines: The First 300 Years* (London: Peter Owen, 1995).

Cameron, Deborah, 'A Self Off The Shelf? Consuming women's empowerment', in Maggie Andrews and Mary M. Talbot (eds), *All the World and Her Husband: Women in Twentieth-century Consumer Culture* (London: Cassell, 2000), pp. 210–23.

Clark, Helen and Carnegie, Elizabeth, *She Was Aye Workin': Memories of Tenement Women in Edinburgh and Glasgow* (Edinburgh: White Cockade, 2003).

Clear, Caitriona, 'Hardship, Help and Happiness in Oral History Narratives of Women's Lives in Ireland' *Oral History* 31, no. 2 (Autumn 2003), pp. 33–42.

Clear, Caitriona, 'The Red Ink of Emotion: the social vision of Maura Laverty (1907–1966)', *Saothar 28: Journal of the Irish Labour History Society* 28 (2003), pp. 90–99.

Clear, Caitriona, *Social Change and Everyday Life in Ireland 1850–1922* (Manchester: Manchester University Press, 2007).

Clear, Caitriona, *Women of the House: Women's Household Work in Ireland 1922–1961* (Dublin: Irish Academic Press, 2000).

Cohen, Deborah, *Family Secrets: Living with Shame from the Victorians to the Present Day* (London: Penguin, 2013).

Connolly, Linda, *The Irish Women's Movement: From Revolution to Devolution* (Dublin: Lilliput, 2003).

Cowan, Ruth Schwarz, *More Work For Mother: The Ironies of Household Technology from the Open Hearth to the Microwave* (New York: Basic, 1982).

Cowley, Ultan, *The Men Who Built Britain: A History of the Irish Navvy* (Dublin: Wolfhound, 2001).

Cox, Howard and Mowatt, Simon, *Revolution from Grub Street: A History of Magazine Publishing in Britain* (Oxford: Oxford University Press, 2014).

Curtin, C. and Varley, A., 'Marginal Men? Bachelor farmers in a west of Ireland community', in C. Curtin, P. Jackson and B. O'Connor (eds), *Gender in Irish Society* (Galway: Officina Typographica, 1987), pp. 287–308.

Dancyger, Irene, *A World of Women: An Illustrated History of Women's Magazines* (Dublin: Gill & Macmillan, 1978).

Delaney, Enda, *Demography, State and Society: Irish Migration to Britain 1921–1971* (Liverpool: Liverpool University Press, 2000).

Dyhouse, Carol, *Girl Trouble: Panic and Progress in the History of Young Women* (London: Zed Books, 2013).

Ferguson, Marjorie, *Forever Feminine: Women's Magazines and the Cult of Femininity* (London: Heinemann, 1983).

Finn, Tomás, *Tuairim: Intellectual Debate and Policy Formation: Rethinking Ireland 1954–75* (Manchester: Manchester University Press, 2012).

Fisher, Kate, *Birth Control, Sex and Marriage in Britain 1918–1960* (Oxford: Oxford University Press, 2006).

Flanders, Judith, *The Making of Home* (London: Atlantic, 2014).

Friedan, Betty, *The Feminine Mystique* (New York: W.W. Norton, 1963).

Fuller, Louise, *Irish Catholicism Since 1950: The Undoing of a Culture* (Dublin: Gill & Macmillan, 2002).

Hayes, Alan (ed.), *Hilda Tweedy and the Irish Housewives Association: Links in the Chain* (Galway: Arlen House, 2011).

Healy, John, *No-One Shouted Stop: The Death of an Irish Town* (Cork: Mercier Press, 1966, 1968).

Hennessy, Peter, *Having It So Good: Britain in the Fifties* (London: Penguin, 2007).

Hermes, Joke, *Reading Women's Magazines: An Analysis of Everyday Media Use* (Oxford: Polity, 1995).

Heron, Marianne, *Sheila Conroy: Fighting Spirit* (Dublin: Attic, 1993).

Heverin, Aileen, *ICA: The Irish Countrywomen's Association: A History* (Dublin: Wolfhound, 2000).

Holden, Katherine, *The Shadow of Marriage: Singleness in England 1914–1960* (Manchester: Manchester University Press, 2007).

Horgan, John, *Irish Media: A Critical History Since 1922* (London: Routledge, 2001).

Horgan, J., O'Connor, B. and Sheehan, H. (eds.), *Mapping Irish Media: Critical Explorations* (Dublin: UCD Press, 2007).

James, Linda (Valerie McGrath), *Dear Linda: A Selection of Letters to the Problem Page of the Sunday World 1970–74* (Cork: Mercier Press, 1974).

Johnson, Lesley and Lloyd, Justine, *Sentenced to Everyday Life: Feminism and the Housewife* (Oxford: Berg, 2003).

Kelly, Mary J. and O'Connor, Barbara (eds.), *Media Audiences in Ireland* (Dublin: UCD Press, 1997).

Kennedy, Finola, *Frank Duff: A Life Story* (London: Continuum, 2011).

Kent, Robin, *Aunt Agony Advises: Problem Pages Through the Ages* (London: W. H. Allen, 1979).

Keogh, Dermot, *Twentieth-century Ireland: Nation and State* (Dublin: Gill & Macmillan, 1994).

Kiberd, Damien (ed.), *Media in Ireland: The Search for Diversity* (Dublin: Four Courts/ Open Air, 1997).

Korinek, Linda, *Roughing It in the Suburbs: Reading* Chatelaine *Magazine in the 50s and 60s* (Toronto, ON: University of Toronto 2000).

Kynaston, David, *Modernity Britain Volume 1: Opening the Box 1957–9* (London: Bloomsbury, 2013).

Kynaston, David, *Modernity Britain Volume 2: A Shake of the Dice* (London: Bloomsbury, 2014).

Langhamer, Claire, *The English in Love: The Intimate Story of an Emotional Revolution* (Oxford: Oxford University Press, 2013).

Lee, J. J., *Ireland 1912–1980* (Cambridge: Cambridge University Press, 1989).

Lethbridge, Lucy, *Servants: A Downstairs View of Twentieth-century Britain* (London: Bloomsbury, 2013).

Lindsay, Paul (ed.), *The Media and Modern Society in Ireland* (Celbridge: Social Study Conference, 1993).

Macnamara, Angela, *Yours Sincerely* (Dublin: Veritas, 2003).

MacNamara, Medb and Mooney, Pascal, *Women in Parliament 1919–2000* (Dublin: Wolfhound, 2000).

McKenna, Yvonne, *Made Holy: Irish Women Religious at Home and Abroad* (Dublin: Irish Academic Press, 2006).

Makins, Peggy, *The Evelyn Home Story* (London: Fontana, 1976).

Morash, Chris, *A History of the Media in Ireland* (Cambridge: Cambridge University Press, 2010).

Ní Ghráda, Mairéad, *An Triail* (Baile Atha Cliath: Rialtas na hEireann 1978: An Gúm, 1997).

O'Brien, John A. (ed.), *The Vanishing Irish* (London: W. H. Allen, 1954).

Oram, Hugh, *The Advertising Book: The History of Advertising in Ireland* (Dublin: MO Books, 1986).

O'Keeffe, C. M., Rev W. P C. M., *Scruples: How to Avoid Them* (Dublin: CTSI, 1944, 1960).

O'Leary, Eoin, 'The INTO and the marriage bar for women national teachers 1922–58', *Saothar: Journal of the Irish Labour History Society* 12 (1987), pp. 47–52.

Rayner, Claire, *How Did I Get Here From There?* (London: Virago, 2003).

Richards, M. and Elliott, B. Jane, 'Sex and Marriage in the 1960s and 70s', in D. Clark (ed.), *Marriage, Domestic Life and Social Change: Writings for Jacqueline Burgoyne* (London: Routledge, 1991).

Rooks, Noliwe, *Ladies Pages: African-American Women's Magazines and the Culture That Made Them* (Newark, NJ: Rutgers, 2005).

Ryan, Paul, 'Asking Angela: Discourses about sexuality in an Irish problem page 1963–1980', *Journal of the History of Sexuality* 19, no. 2 (May 2010), pp. 317–39.

Ryan, Paul, *Asking Angela Macnamara: An Intimate History of Irish Lives* (Dublin: Irish Academic Press, 2011).

Sandbrook, Dominic, *Never Had It So Good: A History of Britain from Suez to the Beatles* (London: Abacus, 2005).

Savage, Robert, *A Loss of Innocence? Television and Irish Society 1960–72* (Manchester: Manchester University Press, 2010).

Scanlan, Jennifer, *Inarticulate Longings: The Ladies' Home Journal, Gender and the Promises of Consumer Culture* (London: Routledge, 1995).

Scannell, Yvonne, 'The Constitution and the Role of Women', in Brian Farrell (ed.), *De Valera's Constitution and Ours* (Dublin: Gill & Macmillan, 1988).

Scheper-Hughes, Nancy, *Saints, Scholars and Schizophrenics: Mental Illness in Rural Ireland* (Berkeley: University of California, 2001).

Sheils, Michael, *The Quiet Revolution: The Electrification of Rural Ireland* (Dublin: Institute of Public Administration, 1974).

Simonton, Deborah, *A History of European Women's Work 1700 to the Present* (London: Routledge, 1998).

Sixsmith, Martin, *The Lost Child of Philomena Lee* (London: Pan, 2010).

Spock, Benjamin, *The Common Sense Book of Baby and Child Care* (New York: Duell, Sloane and Pearce, 1946).

Sutton, Maureen, *We Didn't Know Owt: A Study of Sexuality, Superstition and Death in Women's Lives in Lincolnshire in the 1930s, 40s and 50s* (Donington: Shaun Tyas, 2012).

Tinkler, Penny, *Constructing Girlhood: Popular Magazines for Girls Growing Up in England 1920–1950* (London: Taylor & Francis, 1995).

Walker, Linda, *Shaping our Mothers' World: American Women's Magazines* (Jackson: University of Mississippi, 2000).

White, Cynthia, *Women's Magazines 1693–1968* (London: Michael Joseph, 1970).

William Trevor, *Collected Stories* (London: Penguin, 1983).

Winship, Janice, *Inside Women's Magazines* (London: Pandora, 1987).

Index

Lightning Source UK Ltd.
Milton Keynes UK
UKOW05f0925230617

303864UK00001B/43/P